Money and Macroeconomic Policy

Money and Macroeconomic Policy

Essays in Honour of Bernard Corry and Maurice Peston, Volume One

Edited by
Sami Daniel

Associate Dean, Faculty of Human Sciences, Kingston University, UK

Philip Arestis

Professor of Economics, University of East London, UK

John Grahl

Professor of International Business, University of North London, UK

Edward Elgar

Cheltenham, UK • Northampton, MA, USA

Published by
Edward Elgar Publishing Limited
Glensanda House
Montpellier Parade
Cheltenham
Glos GL50 1UA
UK

Edward Elgar Publishing, Inc.
6 Market Street
Northampton
Massachusetts 01060
USA

A catalogue record for this book is available from the British Library

Library of Congress Cataloguing in Publication Data
Money and macroeconomic policy / edited by Philip Arestis, Sami Daniel, John Grahl.
— (Essays in honour of Bernard Corry and Maurice Peston : v. 1)
Includes index.
1. Macroeconomics. 2. Economic policy. 3. Money. 4. London School of Economics and Political Science—Faculty. I. Corry, Bernard. II. Peston, Maurice Harry. III. Arestis, Philip, 1941– IV. Sami, Daniel, 1939– . V. Grahl, John. VI. Series.
HB172.5.M647 1998
339—DC21 98–22389
CIP

ISBN 1 85898 578 1

Printed and bound in Great Britain by
Biddles Ltd, Guildford and King's Lynn

Contents

Figures

Tables

Notes on the contributors

Michael Anyadike-Danes was born in Australia in 1951. He obtained his BEc and MEc degrees at the University of Sydney and his doctorate at Queen Mary College in 1979. He has worked at the Reserve Bank of Australia, the London School of Economics, the Department of Applied Economics at the University of Cambridge and the Observatoire Française des Conjonctures Economiques. Since 1997 he has been a senior researcher at the Northern Ireland Economic Research Centre, and University of the West Indies. Amongst his recent publications are *A Manual of Macroeconomic Principles for the Eastern Caribbean,* and 'Run into the sand? The limits of growth in Barbados', which appeared in the *Cambridge Journal of Economics.*

Philip Arestis is Professor of Economics at the University of East London. He has also taught at the universities of Surrey and Cambridge (Department of Extra-Mural Studies) and Greenwich University (where he was Head of the Economics Division). He is joint editor of *International Papers in Political Economy,* has edited or served on the editorial boards of a number of journals and was a member of the Council of the Royal Economic Society. He has edited a number of books and is the author of several others, including *The Post-Keynesian Approach to Economics: an alternative analysis of economic theory and policy* (1992) and *Money, Pricing, Distribution and Economic Integration* (1996). He has published widely in journals and books on post Keynesian economics, macroeconomics, monetary policy and applied econometrics.

Keith Bain studied at the University of Queensland and is Principal Lecturer in the Department of Economics at the University of East London. He is the author of chapters in several books on international trade, stabilization policies and various aspects of monetary economics, and has published journal articles in *British Review of Economic Issues, Cyprus Journal of Economics, Economies et Sociétés, Journal of Economic Issues* and *Review of Social Economy.* He is joint author (with Peter Howells) of *An Introduction to Monetary Economics* (1985), *Government and the Economy* (1987), *Understanding Markets* (1988) and *Financial Markets and Institutions* (2nd edn 1994).

David Currie (Lord Currie) is Professor of Economics at the London Business School, and was formerly Deputy Principal (1992–5) and Director of the Centre for Economic Forecasting (1988–95). Before joining LBS in 1988, he was

Professor and Head of Economics at Queen Mary College, University of London. He has published extensively in the fields of forecasting and macroeconomic policy. His research interests have now extended to the field of government regulation and he now heads the Regulation Initiative at LBS. His books include *The Operation and Regulation of Financial Markets* (1987), *Policy Rules, Credibility and International Macroeconomic Policy* (1994) *North–South Linkages and International Macroeconomic Policy* (1995), *The Pros and Cons of EMU* (1977) and *Making the Euro Work* (1998).

Sami Daniel was born in Basrah, Iraq and obtained his BSc (Econ) and MSc (Econ) at the London School of Economics where he also worked as a research assistant. He is Associate Dean of the Faculty of Human Sciences at Kingston University, having been Head of the School of Economics and Politics there from 1971 to 1987. He has taught at Middlesex University and (as visiting fellow) Queen Mary College and the University of Konstanz. He was the first national secretary of the Association of Polytechnic Teachers in Economics (1971–9) and the first economist from the former polytechnic sector to serve on the Council of the Royal Economic Society. He also served with Maurice Peston and Bernard Corry on the CNAA Economics Board. His major area of research interest is the economics of organizations.

Joe A. Ganley did his PhD at Queen Mary College. His thesis on public sector applications of Data Envelopment Analysis (subsequently published in book form by North-Holland, 1992) was supervised by Maurice Peston. He joined Oxford Economic Forecasting in 1988 before moving in 1990 to the Bank of England to work in Economics Division. He moved in 1994 to Monetary Assessment and Strategy Division to work on monetary policy. He is now senior manager in Markets and Trading Division where he runs a team of economists doing research into market risks to financial stability. Joe has published on various aspects of public sector finance, monetary policy and financial markets.

Murray Glickman, born in 1947, is (like Bernard Corry and Maurice Peston) an East Londoner. Educated at Oxford, Sussex and City universities, he has worked at the University of East London (and its predecessor institutions) since 1975, initially in the Department of Accounting and Finance and more recently in the Economics Department. His published work is in the area of alternative and, in particular, post Keynesian perspectives on Finance theory – his major area of research interest.

Charles A.E. Goodhart CBE, FBA is the Norman Sosnow Professor of Banking and Finance at the London School of Economics. Before joining the LSE in 1985, he worked at the Bank of England for seventeen years as a monetary adviser, becoming Chief Adviser in 1980. In 1997 he was appointed one of the outside independent members of the Bank of England's Monetary Policy Committee. Earlier he had taught at Cambridge and LSE. Besides numerous articles, he has written a couple of books on monetary history, and a graduate monetary textbook, *Money, Information and Uncertainty* (2nd edn, 1989); and has published two collections of papers on monetary policy, *Monetary Theory and Practice* (1984) and *The Central Bank and the Financial System* (1995); and an institutional study of *The Evolution of Central Banks*, revised and republished (MIT Press) in 1988.

John Grahl is Professor of International Business at the University of North London. Until September 1998, he was Reader in European Economic Integration at Queen Mary and Westfield College, University of London. He is the author of many books and articles on the European Union and other aspects of European political economy. His most recent book, *After Maastricht: a guide to European monetary union*, was published by Lawrence & Wishart in 1997.

Brian Henry is Director of the Centre for Economic Forecasting, London Business School. Previously he has been senior economic adviser at the Bank of England and an economic adviser at the International Monetary Fund, and held teaching posts at the London School of Economics, University College London and Cambridge. His research interests are in macro and monetary economics and in economic modelling – areas in which he has published widely.

Peter Howells is Professor of Economics at the University of East London. He studied at the University of Kent and the London School of Economics. He has published extensively on endogenous money in *Journal of Post Keynesian Economics*, *Cyprus Journal of Economics* and *Review of Social Economy*. Other papers on aspects of monetary economics have appeared in *Cambridge Journal of Economics*, *Eastern Economic Journal*, *Journal of Economic Issues* and *Weltwirtschaftliches Archiv*. He is joint author (with Keith Bain) of *An Introduction to Monetary Economics* (1985), *Government and the Economy* (1987), *Understanding Markets* (1988) and *Financial Markets and Institutions* (2nd edn 1994).

Haizhou Huang, who recently joined the International Monetary Fund in Washington, has lectured at Queen Mary and Westfield College and at the Chinese University of Hong Kong. He studied electrical and systems engineering in China, and obtained his PhD in Business from Indiana University in Bloomington USA in 1994. He was Research Fellow with the Financial Markets Group at the London School of Economics from 1995 till 1997. He has published on the soft budget constraint and optimal choices of R&D projects financing, innovation and competition, and new growth theory.

David Laidler has been Professor of Economics at the University of Western Ontario since 1975. Born in North Shields in 1938, he was educated at the London School of Economics (BSc Econ 1959), the University of Syracuse (MA 1960) and the University of Chicago (PhD 1964). Prior to taking up his present position, he held appointments at the University of California, Berkeley (Assistant Professor, 1963–6), the University of Essex (Lecturer 1966–9) and the University of Manchester (1969–75). He was a founding committee member of the Money Study Group, is a past-president of the Canadian Economics Association and is a Fellow of the Royal Society of Canada. He has published numerous works on monetary economics and its history.

Gerard Lyons is Chief Economist and Executive Director of DKB International, the wholly owned London subsidiary of Japan's Dai-Ichi Kangyo Bank. He studied at Liverpool University, Warwick University and at Queen Mary College where he prepared his doctoral thesis on 'Testing Efficiency of Financial Futures Markets'. He established DKB International's Economic Research Department, having previously been Chief UK economist of Swiss Bank Corporation and UK stockbroker Savory Milln. He has also worked as an economist at the Chase Manhattan Bank and conducted research at the Henley Centre for Forecasting.

James Nixon is a research fellow at the Centre for Economic Forecasting (London Business School). His interests include macroeconomic model building and the analysis of macroeconomic policy. Prior to joining the LBS, he was an Economic Adviser at HM Treasury, where he spent several years working on the UK forecasting team.

David A. Peel was born in Leeds, England in 1950. He obtained a BA in economics with first class honours from the University of Warwick in 1971. After a short period as research assistant to Keith Cowling, he commenced postgraduate studies at the University of Leeds. These were not completed as he left to take up a lectureship at the University of Liverpool in 1972. He was promoted to Senior Lecturer in 1978 and Reader in 1982. He became Professor and Head of Department at the University of Wales, Aberystwyth in 1984. He left Aberystwyth in 1994 to take up a chair at the University of Liverpool. He is now Professor of Economics at Cardiff. He is the author of a number of books and has published numerous journal articles.

Frank Skuse is Head of Economics at the University of East London. He studied economics at the University of Melbourne and Monash University in Australia. He has taught economics at Monash University, University of East London and IUT Dijon, France. He has published in *Economie Appliquée*, *Economies et Sociétés* and *International Review of Applied Economics*, as well as contributing to two books.

Alan E.H. Speight was born in Gloucester, England in 1960. He obtained his BA in economics at the University of Essex in 1981, and MSc and PhD at Queen Mary College in 1983 and 1988 respectively. He has held lectureships in Economics at the University of Aberdeen and University of Wales, Aberystwyth, and is currently Senior Lecturer in Economics at the University of Wales, Swansea. He is the author of *Consumption, Rational Expectations and Liquidity: theory and evidence* (1990) and has published numerous journal papers on the empirics of consumption, the term structure of interest rates, non-linear business cycle dynamics and related issues.

Introduction

Sami Daniel, Philip Arestis and John Grahl

This is the first of three volumes published to celebrate Bernard Corry's and Maurice Peston's contributions to British academia in general, and to economics in particular. Bernard and Maurice have had a major influence on the development of economics as a discipline in the UK: not just economics as an academic discipline, but the way it is taught. In the 1960s, both moved from the London School of Economics (LSE), where they had been readers, to what was then Queen Mary College (QMC), University of London, now Queen Mary and Westfield College (QMW). They set up, and subsequently developed and expanded, a successful Economics Department; they both stayed at QMW until their retirement. Over the years they have acquired enormous respect and admiration from colleagues throughout the world.

Maurice and Bernard have much in common in addition to being the famous QMC and QMW Economics Department double act. They were both East End boys, both were briefly evacuated in the Second World War, both were students at the LSE (Bernard saw the last year of the Higher School Certificate, Maurice the first of the A level). They both did National Service after graduating. They both taught at the LSE and (as visiting professors) at the University of California at Berkeley. At the LSE they formed part of the famous M^2T (Methodology, Measurement and Testing) Seminar for the Young Turks of the time.[1] Their academic interests coincide in two very important areas: they have both maintained a longstanding interest in macroeconomics and in economic policy. They have both served as economic advisers (Bernard on a part-time basis, Maurice on full time as well as part-time stints). Both are Labour Party members of long standing. They both played an important role in the development of economics in the new university sector through their work for the Council for National Academic Awards (CNAA): they both served as chairmen of its Economics Board (see Daniel, 1998) and gave their support to the fledgling Association of Polytechnic Teachers in Economics (APTE). They took 'early retirement' at the same time, becoming very active emeritus professors (Bernard was Dean of the Faculty when theoretically on a half-time contract). They officially retired within a year of each other. They jointly edited the volume of essays in honour of Lord Robbins (Peston and Corry, 1972). When it came to organizing a Festschrift for Bernard and Maurice, it was clear that most potential contributors would wish to contribute to a joint Festschrift: so now they share something else. They are the only academics to our knowledge to have a joint three-volume Festschrift.

BERNARD CORRY

Bernard Corry was born in East London in 1930 and, apart from a brief period of evacuation during the Second World War, went to school there at Leyton County High School. He read for the BSc (Econ.) on a state scholarship, graduating in 1951, and worked on his doctorate at the LSE, supported by a University of London scholarship. His PhD, awarded in 1958 (see Corry, 1962) was on the macroeconomic thought of the classical political economy, which signalled two life-long interests he pursued with enormous fervour. He was a tutor at the LSE in 1954–6, before being offered a temporary assistant lectureship at the University of Durham in 1957–8. After a year, he was given tenure as a lecturer. His return to the LSE in 1958 as assistant lecturer thus represented, initially, a demotion. One reason for the return was that he had been teaching more or less everything at Durham.[2] Soon, however, he was promoted to lecturer (1961) and reader (1964). At the LSE, he was now able to specialize in the history of thought and macroeconomics. His seminar (with Kurt Klappholz) on Smith, Ricardo and Marshall, and his lecture course on Swedish monetary theory, were very popular with undergraduates. In 1968, he moved to QMC as Professor of Economics. There he helped Maurice to shape the Department of Economics and, in particular, to establish the MSc programme and the graduate school. The graduate school won wide recognition for its quality and its thorough preparation in contemporary economics. Bernard was the driving force – both as a teacher and as overall organizer. One early signal of his success was gaining substantial support from the Social Sciences Research Council (SSRC) in scholarship funds. He was Head of the Department of Economics at QMC (1974–85) and Dean of the Faculty of Social Sciences in the years 1974–7 and 1988–91.

His two specialisms, history of thought and macroeconomics, were enriched by a third major interest, labour economics, initially sparked by his interest in income distribution[3] and work on regional mobility.[4] It was not surprising, therefore, that between 1968 and 1972 he was Senior Economic Adviser at the Department of Employment and Productivity, advising Barbara Castle on regional labour markets and (now again fashionable) minimum wages. Over the years, Bernard published extensively in all these three areas.

He was an important member of the CNAA Economics Board right from its inception, chaired it for a number of years (he was chairman between 1974 and

1982), and the success story of economics in the ex-polytechnic sector is due to a very large extent to his efforts to give academic respectability to the then new sector. More significantly, though, he has been an extremely close friend of the departments of economics throughout the university sector, acting as external examiner, chairman of visiting CNAA parties to validate new degrees, reading papers to staff seminars and merely visiting departments to advise and see his many friends. Economics departments in the new universities owe Bernard a great deal for his contributions to their work. They benefited enormously from Bernard's encouragement, kindness and constructive criticism (particularly on the importance of research and its tight link to teaching). Whether they listened to him as much as they should is, of course, another story! As chairman of visiting CNAA panels and of the Economics Board of the CNAA, his influence was substantial, both at the formal sessions and in the after-dinner visits to bars and pubs! That involvement helped the CNAA institutions at that early and critical stage of their development. His humane and flexible approach was extremely helpful.

Those of us lucky enough to have been taught by Bernard are grateful for his teaching. His ability to teach skilfully is, of course, well known. His colleagues report that Bernard scored consistently top marks on the internal teaching assessment by the students of the Department of Economics. His friendly concern with students, both undergraduate and postgraduate, his encouragement of discussion, particularly 'after hours', not only made for excellent staff–student relations but left deep intellectual marks and helped shape many a burgeoning economist.[5]

For many years Bernard was the main force at the Association of University Teachers of Economics (AUTE) annual conference, now the Royal Economic Society (RES) conference. He was secretary of the AUTE from 1960 to 1978, and later its chairman, from 1980 to 1985. Bernard's work for the AUTE conference, with the smallest amount of secretarial assistance, was Herculean. He occupied himself with every aspect of the event: the venue and accommodation, attracting papers and inviting special lecturers, timetabling, publicity – even catering arrangements. The AUTE conference rapidly became what, in its new form, it remains, the largest UK symposium of the economics profession. Bernard was also the key figure in publishing the output as AUTE Conference volumes, which have now been replaced by the special conference volume of the *Economic Journal.* His interest in the polytechnics was also reflected in this work: he encouraged large numbers of polytechnic economists to contribute to the annual AUTE conferences, thus getting many of them started on active research and publication. And, of course, he encouraged and helped the Association of Polytechnic Teachers in Economics (APTE) which made him Honorary Vice-President and then Honorary President. Another professional development in which Bernard played a pioneering role was the establishment of specialist research groups. He established, with SSRC financial backing, the labour economics research group. That innovation developed into, and remains, a key platform for communication and debate among economists in Britain. Both in his specialist work in labour economics and macroeconomics, and in his design of the masters programme at QMC, Bernard was keen to strengthen the empirical basis of research in economics and to promote a closer and more continuous interaction between theory and evidence.

MAURICE PESTON

Maurice Peston was born in 1931 in London. In fact he is almost a local in relation to QMW. He was educated at Hackney Downs School before graduating in economics at the London School of Economics, and doing graduate work at Princeton University. He had been a reader before he left the School in the mid-1960s to start up the Department of Economics at QMC, becoming Professor of Economics and the first head of that department in 1965. Under his and Bernard's guidance, the department grew and achieved its balance of high-quality research and good teaching for which it is internationally famous.

Maurice started his academic career as a microeconomist (he enjoyed the problem-solving nature of the subject, and was particularly interested in public finance), although three of his early publications were the famous papers on balanced budget multipliers, one of which he wrote with his friend William Baumol[6] (see Peston, 1954; Baumol and Peston, 1955; Peston, 1958). But his deep interest in macroeconomics is reflected in his *Review of Economic Studies* paper on the aggregation problem (Peston, 1959a), a paper of which he is justly proud. Here he argued that the aggregation problem was not a problem of indices or of measurement: 'economic theory at any level of aggregation exists on a par with economic theory at any other level, and if an aggregation problem exists, it is because economic theory at some level is unsatisfactory' (Peston, 1959a, p. 59). The conclusion of the article reads almost like a manifesto:

> Instead of being concerned with rules which allow macro-variables to be derived from (or at least related to) micro-variables, the analysis of aggregates ought to be concerned with the invention and improvement of macrotheory. Thus if a macroeconomic equation ... is found to be invalid, it is not because its variables are incorrect aggregates of micro-variables, but because it includes some irrelevant variables, excludes some relevant ones, and incorrectly postulates how these variables behave. The aggregation problem as understood at present is no help towards this end. Indeed, it acts as a strait-jacket on economic theory at all levels. (Ibid., p. 63)

Maurice was among the first to make use of sophisticated computer models. In the early 1970s, he initiated an extremely successful project in the application of optimal control techniques in economics. Some of us know the project well enough for, in the late 1970s, we benefited substantially from it. This work was of paramount importance in terms of its policy implications. It recognizes that, while policy can have powerful effects on the level and pace of economic activity, there are constraints on both its implementation and impact. The policy maker is thought to have a number of objectives and instruments, but there are penalties when the objectives are not achieved. This work had an early influence on British economic policy and also on subsequent developments in the area of economic policy. It was pioneering both in the application of dynamic control theory to questions of economic policy and in its use of advanced techniques of time series analysis.

Amongst his many contributions, Maurice was Economic Adviser to the Treasury[7] from 1962 to 1964, to the Ministry of Defence between 1964 and 1966, and to the House of Commons Select Committee on Nationalised Industries from 1966 to 1970. In the 1970s he became economic adviser to Labour in government and opposition:[8] he was variously Special Adviser to the Secretary of State for Education and Science from 1974 until 1975, and Adviser on Prices between 1976 and 1979. He was awarded a peerage in 1987 and became Lord Peston of Mile End and thus directly active in politics: Opposition Spokesman on Energy and on Education and Science in 1987, and concerning Treasury matters from 1990 to 1992. He was also spokesman on industry for the Opposition in the House of Lords.[9]

Maurice's wide range of activities includes being a member of the Social Sciences Research Council (SSRC) and chairman of its Economics Board from 1976 until 1979, a Council Member of the Royal Pharmaceutical Society of Great Britain since 1986 and chairman of the Office of Health Economics since 1991. Since 1972, he has been editing the highly successful journal *Applied Economics* and, more recently, *Applied Financial Economics* and a third one under the title *Applied Economics Letters.* But he always found time to indulge his passionate support for Arsenal Football Club. This keen interest in football resulted in a long stint (initially as member, and later chairman) on the football Pools Panel.

As chairman of the Economics Board of the CNAA between 1967 and 1973, Maurice contributed substantially to the development of economics degrees in the then polytechnic sector, bringing a helpful and constructive approach. With the late Tom Evans, he organized the CNAA conference on 'Recent Developments in Economics', in 1971, which had a great impact on the teaching and development of economics in the polytechnic sector. He chaired the final session of the five-day conference which created the Association of Polytechnic Teachers in Economics (which elected him, a year later, as its first Honorary President). Those of us who were on the receiving end will never forget

Maurice's firm chairing of CNAA visits to departments of economics. As a chairman he commanded respect, admiration, not to mention some trepidation! The continuing quality of economics education in the new universities is in no small measure the consequence of Maurice's sterling work in this regard.

CONTRIBUTORS TO THE FESTSCHRIFT

The contributors to these volumes include people who first knew Bernard and Maurice as colleagues (David Currie, Meghnad Desai, Pat Dillon, Charles Goodhart, Hugh Gravelle, Brian Henry, Haizhou Huang, Eli Katz, Morris Perlman, Ray Rees, Max Steuer and Adrian Ziderman), as their students or research assistants (Philip Arestis, Mike Anyadike-Danes, Nick Barr, David (Danny) Blanchflower, Ken Burdett, Rod Cross, Sami Daniel, Miriam David, Ciaran Driver, Joe Ganley, John Grahl, Peter Groenewegen, Sam Hollander, David Laidler, Gerry Lyons, Rob Matthews, Barry Moore, Eric Pentecost, Alan Speight and David Wall), or through professional contact (Keith Bain, Peter Howells, Murray Glickman, Steve Nickell, Mike Marshall, Patrick Minford, Bob Nobay, Paul Ormerod, David Peel and Frank Skuse). Many of these people have also got to know them in many other ways. And we all regard them as dear friends. We offer these essays in their honour, and in recognition of their many achievements and contributions.

VOLUME ONE

The contributions to this first volume focus on macroeconomic policy, which has been a central concern of Bernard Corry and Maurice Peston throughout their careers. They begin with three chapters which deal in different ways with broad trends in the formulation of macro policy in advanced countries. David Laidler considers the trend towards inflation targeting in the design of monetary policy; he regards this assignment of policy as essentially correct, but argues that the monetary regime can still be so calibrated as to avoid damage to employment, while fiscal and structural measures are still available to promote higher levels of employment. The other two chapters take a more critical view of recent policy trends. Frank Skuse, referring to Kalecki's seminal paper on 'Political Aspects of Full Employment', argues that a change in the political balance of interests between capital and labour helps to account for the abandonment of full employment as the key macro policy objective. Philip Arestis and Murray Glickman argue that recent global experience of market-oriented macro policies confirms the post Keynesian view that capitalist economies are essentially unstable. For them the reinstatement of government intervention focused on the management of aggregate demand is therefore a precondition for any significant improvement in international macroeconomic performance.

In Part II, four chapters consider different aspects of central bank independence, which has become a key theme in contemporary monetary policy. In Chapter 4, Keith Bain and Peter Howells consider the role of the central bank in historical perspective. They argue that it is misleading simply to see the 'privatization' of monetary policy as a return to the long-run norm: the previous independence of central banks was largely dictated by the imperatives of the gold standard and frequently led to tensions with national governments. Today, on the other hand, governments have been as enthusiastic to surrender power as central banks themselves have been to grasp it. These modern developments, and the weakness of opposition to them, should be explained in terms of the theory of macroeconomic policy. John Grahl's contribution, drawing on discussions of central banks as lenders of last resort, suggests that central bank independence focused exclusively on price stability may lead to financial instability. In Chapter 6, Gerard Lyons also takes a critical view of central bank independence and stresses four main arguments against it: other factors besides monetary institutions are needed to explain low inflation; possible conflicts may arise between monetary and fiscal policy; the danger of political interference in interest rates is replaced by the risk of monetary overkill; and central bank independence may involve a loss of democratic accountability. Charles Goodhart and Haizhou Huang consider in detail one aspect of the discussion leading to arguments for central bank independence: the inflationary bias which has been detected in monetary policy. They argue that this bias arises not because the authorities want to fool the people but because the general public wants a boom and the politicians do not have the strength to resist it. In this framework, which can be used to explore several important issues in monetary policy formation, central bank independence is interpreted as a counterbalance to political pressures.

Next come three papers which consider the prospects for macroeconomic policy in the near future. In Chapter 8, David Currie examines the impact of forthcoming European monetary union on policy in Britain and elsewhere. There is a general need to enhance labour and product market flexibility to make EMU work well, while Britain has to deal with the key issue of the timing of entry into the EMU. Currie considers the interaction of these issues. Also in the framework of EMU, Joe Ganley examines the recent convergence in European bond markets. Some of this convergence has been cyclical, but the creation of the Euro might be enough in itself to drive together the bond yields of likely member countries. But bond market convergence in these circumstances need not be a signal that a broader economic convergence has also been achieved. In Chapter 10, Brian Henry and James Nixon examine future interactions between monetary and fiscal policy: in a world of inflation targeting, fiscal tightening will necessarily be offset by a loosening in monetary policy if the economy is not to be run permanently below trend. Such loosening can have a positive effect on consumption in the short run, especially in a country such as the UK which has a high preponderance of mortgage debt. Nevertheless, this effect is not sufficient to offset the reductions in overall aggregate demand – it is found that, contrary to the so-called 'German' argument, cuts in government spending are associated with falls in output and increases in unemployment.

The last two chapters consider problems of macroeconomic policy outside the established industrial countries. David Peel and Alan Speight examine the dynamics of the zloty–dollar exchange rate between 1988 and 1990. Using non-linear models, they are able to explain around one-quarter of the variation in the data, largely as the result of successfully modelling the recovery of the Polish zloty after its collapse in September 1989. However, their models are unable to account fully for the market turbulence during August and September 1989, which might therefore be attributed to the political events of the period rather than to a hyperinflationary regime. Michael Anyadike-Danes examines the Eastern Caribbean Central Bank, which manages the common currency of eight 'micro-states' in that region and, as its principal policy instrument, requires that currency issue be backed by holdings of foreign assets. Member governments retain some control over fiscal policy within this regime, but the constraints they face are tight since access to international capital markets is limited and domestic sources of funds are confined to the commercial banks. In this context the pace and direction of adjustment depends critically upon domestic currency holdings while the impact of policy turns on the size of the commercial banks' credit multiplier. Anyadike-Danes also asks whether there can be anything essentially macroeconomic about an island economy with a population of less than 100 000.

ACKNOWLEDGEMENTS

Special thanks must go to the contributors for their willingness to respond to our comments and suggestions with forbearance and good humour. Thanks are also extended to Shirin Yassin of the Faculty of Human Sciences at Kingston University, and to June Daniels and Christine Nisbet of the Department of Economics, University of East London, for their secretarial assistance. We are also grateful to Joan McSweeney, Secretary to the Economics Department of QMW for her help, and to Eilis Rafferty of QMW Library for bibliographic information. Finally, Edward Elgar and his staff, particularly Jane Croft and Ian Garbutt, provided excellent support in the preparation of the three volumes.

NOTES

1. The late Chris Archibald, Kurt Klappholz, Kelvin Lancaster, Richard Lipsey, Max Steuer and Jim Thomas spring to mind. The late Bill Phillips was the only 'established' member of the department who was invited to attend the seminar.
2. For a very interesting and entertaining account of his early years as an economist, see the interview he had with Keith Tribe, published as Chapter 12 in K. Tribe (ed.), *Economic Careers: economics and economists in Britain 1930–70*, London: Routledge, 1997.
3. See Corry (1966), This article developed from teaching interests.
4. His work with Jennifer Roberts on unemployment and regional mobility was 'pipped at the post' by Oliver (1964). Although their contribution was significantly different from Oliver's, and although they continued work on it and extended the time period covered (see Corry and Roberts, 1967), the two authors decided not to submit their paper for publication: those were the days when there was no pressure to publish! But their work led to interest in activity rates (see Corry and Roberts, 1970; Corry and Roberts, 1974; and their report, Roberts and Corry, 1973).
5. He inspired many satirical student sketches performed in the 1960s at the LSE by a group called the Red Robbins Ensemble. Its repertoire included a song about him to the tune of 'The Drunken Sailor', which had the lines: 'Hey up and up he rises ... give the man a Chair here'. He was also 'featured' in one of its sketches, a spoof of him talking about his list of the world's top ten economists.
6. Maurice has great affection for William Baumol whom he met at Princeton, and follows his work very closely. He felt strongly about it to write in the same area: see for example, Peston (1957), following up Baumol (1956); Peston (1959b) and (1967), following Baumol's work on revenue maximization; and Peston (1980) which clarified the distinction between cost and volume terms, and the relative price effect, a class of problem he first encountered at the Treasury in 1962 as Clarke's Law, but which became associated with William Baumol, as in, for example, Baumol and Bowen (1965).
7. Amongst the many papers he wrote at the time, one recently received the attention it deserves. It advocated the introduction of student loans (but *not* student payment of fees).
8. His work as Economic Adviser was lauded by Roy Hattersley at the recent conference at QMW in celebration of Maurice's work. One story in particular is worth repeating here:

> I was appointed Shadow Education Minister in what I can only describe as desperate circumstances. Ted Short gave up the job at 3 o'clock on a Thursday afternoon. I was appointed an hour later. At 6 o'clock, at a meeting of the Parliamentary Labour Party, I learnt, to my surprise, that I was to lead for the Opposition on the Monday afternoon in a debate entitled 'Framework For Expansion'. That, though I did not know it at the time, was the name of a new Education White Paper. With forty-eight hours to prepare, I naturally turned to Maurice Peston. He was – somewhat to my annoyance – transfixed by the statistical note with which it ended.
>
> I recall now him explaining with a combination of incredulity and glee that the government had got its figures wrong. Far from the Education budget expanding, in real terms there would be contraction over the next two financial years. He tried to explain the position to me, at one point exclaiming, 'But you did Part I Statistics.' I told him that I had been referred and that I had to take Part I Statistics a second time at the end of my final year. In despair, he wrote me a passage which explained the accounting errors and urged me to read it to the House of Commons.
>
> It was a sign of my confidence in Maurice Peston's judgement that I did just that. The result was consternation all round. Norman St John Stevas – winding up the debate for the government – spoke for, I fear, both sides of the House when he expressed astonishment that I should, 'Take on the Secretary of State in an area where she is so strong and he is obviously so weak'. It was generally agreed that I had made an ass of myself.
>
> After the debate I asked Maurice Peston how I might retrieve the situation. 'Say it again,' he told me. 'For we are right and she is wrong.' I recall rather resenting the plural pronoun.

But it seemed too late to start telling people it was Peston who miscalculated, not me. So I wrote letters to newspapers. I included the paragraph in handouts and I went on radio programmes and read out the statement again. On the following Friday morning, Stuart McLure – editor of the *Times Educational Supplement* and doyen of education journalists – phoned to express his interest in my persistence. He had no doubt that I was wrong. But the nature of the error, which I persisted in repeating, intrigued him. He was, he said, going to ask for a ruling from the one man who really understood these things – Maurice Peston.

I can quote almost verbatim the leader which appeared on the following week in the *TES*. It concluded 'Seven days ago we accused Roy Hattersley of miscuing. Today we have to concede that he potted black. It was Margaret Thatcher who got her sums wrong.' My statistical experience having at last been acknowledged, I phoned round all the newspapers to demand that they made up for their earlier, and totally unjustifiable, lack of faith. Some of them actually made amends. So I wrote to Margaret Thatcher asking her to concede that she was wrong. I still await the reply.

9. Roy Hattersley gives an interesting account of the effect of Maurice's direct manner on the prospects of his political career:

> He is an essentially serious man. But he has always chosen to hide the strength of his feelings under the pretence of flippancy and sometimes even cynicism. I regard that as an admirable quality – much to be prized in an age of conspicuous piety. It may be, however, that Maurice's slightly cavalier attitude towards objects of veneration – ideas, institutions and individuals – has in the recent past worked to his disadvantage. I recall, back in 1970, going with him to see a football match at Stamford Bridge. One of the directors, now a Labour peer, but then no more than a world famous actor, told Maurice Peston, in suitable lovey fashion, that he had longed for years to meet him. Maurice replied that the man had never heard of him until they met that afternoon. I have no doubt that his manner has offended a large number of other peers. I can think of no other reason why he has not become a member of the government.

REFERENCES

Baumol, W.J. (1956) 'Acceleration without magnification', *American Economic Review*, **46**.

Baumol, W.J. and Bowen, W.G. (1965) 'On the performing arts: the history of their economic problem', *American Economic Review*.

Baumol, W.J. and Peston, M.H. (1955) 'More on the multiplier effects of a balanced budget', *American Economic Review*, **45**, 140–48.

Corry, B.A. (1962) *Money, Saving and Investment in English Economics, 1800–1850*, London: Macmillan.

Corry, B.A. (1966) 'The role of technical innovation in the theories of income distribution', *American Economic Review*, **LVI** (2) (Proceedings).

Corry, B.A. and Roberts, J.A. (1967) 'Inter-regional migration and unemployment: 1950–63', LSE Economics Department, mimeo.

Corry, B.A. and Roberts, J.A. (1970) 'Activity rates and unemployment: the experience of the United Kingdom 1951–66', *Applied Economics*, **2**.

Corry, L.A. and Roberts, J.A. (1974) 'Activity rates and unemployment – some further results', *Applied Economics*, **6**.

Daniel, S. (1998) 'CNAA Economics: the development of economics in the new universities', in S. Daniel, P. Arestis and J. Grahl (eds), *The History and Practice of*

Economics: Essays in honour of Bernard Corry and Maurice Peston, volume 2, Cheltenham, UK/Lyme, USA: Edward Elgar.

Oliver, F.R. (1964) 'Inter-regional migration and unemployment: 1951–61', *Journal of the Royal Statistical Society, Series A*, 42–69.

Peston, M.H. (1954) 'A note on the balanced budget multiplier', *American Economic Review*, **44**, 129–30.

Peston, M.H. (1957) 'Acceleration and magnification', *American Economic Review*, **47**.

Peston, M.H. (1958) 'Generalising the balanced budget multiplier', *Review of Economics and Statistics*, **40**, 288–91.

Peston, M.H. (1959a) 'A view of the aggregation problem', *Review of Economic Studies*, 58–64.

Peston, M.H. (1959b) 'On the sales maximisation hypothesis', *Economica*, **26**, 128–36.

Peston, M.H. (1967) 'Changing utility functions', in M. Shubik (ed.), *Essays in Mathematical Economics in Honour of Oscar Morgenstern*, Princeton: Princeton University Press.

Peston, M.H. (1980) 'The ratio of public to private expenditure and the relative price effect', *British Review of Economic Issues*, 46–51.

Peston, M.H. and Corry, B.A. (eds) (1972) *Essays in Honour of Lord Robbins*, London: Weidenfeld & Nicolson.

Roberts, J.A. and Corry, Bernard (1973) 'Changing composition of the labour force: 1950–72', *SSRC Archives*.

Selected publications of Bernard Corry and Maurice Peston

BERNARD CORRY

Corry, B.A. (1958) 'The theory of government expenditure in classical economic policy', *Economica.*

Corry, B.A. (1959a) 'Malthus and Keynes', *Economic Journal.*

Corry, B.A. (1959b) 'A testimonial from Ricardo', *Economica.*

Corry, B.A. (1962) *Money, Saving and Investment in English Economics, 1800–1850*, London: Macmillan.

Corry, B.A. (1966) 'The role of technical innovation in the theories of income distribution', *American Economic Review*, **66** (2) (Proceedings).

Corry, B.A. (1972) 'Lauderdale and public debt', in M.H. Peston and B.A. Corry (eds), *Essays in Honour of Lord Robbins*, London: Macmillan.

Corry, B.A. (1975) 'Should economists abandon hope?', *History of Political Economy.*

Corry, B.A. (1978) 'Keynes in the history of economic thought', in A.P. Thirlwall (ed.), *Keynes and Laissez-faire*, London: Macmillan.

Corry, B.A. (1986) 'Keynes's economics: a revolution in economic theory or economic policy?', in R.C.D. Black (ed.), *Ideas in Economics*, London: Macmillan.

Corry, B.A. (1996) 'The politics of the natural rate of unemployment', in R. Cross (ed.), *The Natural Rate after Twenty-five Years*, Cambridge: Cambridge University Press.

Corry, B.A. (1997a) 'Unemployment in the history of economic thought', in B.A. Corry (ed.), *Unemployment and the economist*, Cheltenham, UK/Lyme, US: Edward Elgar.

Corry, B.A. (1997b) 'Keynes's use of the term "involuntary employment": a historical perspective', in P. Arestis, G. Palma and M. Sawyer (eds), *Capital Controversy, Post-Keynesian Economics and the History of Economic Thought*, London: Routledge.

Corry, B.A. and Laidler, D. (1967) 'The Phillips relation: a theoretical explanation', *Economica.*

Corry, B.A. and Roberts, J.A. (1970) 'Activity rates and unemployment: the experience of the United Kingdom 1951–66', *Applied Economics*, **2**.

Corry, B.A. and Roberts, J.A. (1974) 'Activity rates and unemployment – some further results', *Applied Economics*, **6**.

Corry, B.A., Nugent, J. and Saunders, D. (1982) 'Female unemployment in the UK', in C. Ungerson (ed.), *Sexual Divisions*, London: Tavistock Publications.

Corry, B.A., Ormerod, P. and Rigg, J. (1990) *The Economic Impact of the Arrival in the UK from Hong Kong of 50,000 Heads of Households and their Dependants,* Henley Centre.

MAURICE PESTON

Baumol, W.J. and Peston, M.H. (1955) 'More on the multiplier effects of a balanced budget', *American Economic Review*, **45**, 140–48.

Blaug, M., Peston, M.H. and Ziderman, A. (1967) *Utilization of Educated Manpower: preliminary report*, Edinburgh: Oliver and Boyd.

Peston, M.H. (1954) 'A note on the balanced budget multiplier', *American Economic Review*, **44**, 129–30.

Peston, M.H. (1957) 'Acceleration and magnification', *American Economic Review*, **47**.

Peston, M.H. (1958) 'Generalising the balanced budget multiplier', *Review of Economics and Statistics*, **40**, 288–91.

Peston, M.H. (1959a) 'A view of the aggregation problem', *Review of Economic Studies*, 58–64.

Peston, M.H. (1959b) 'On the sales maximisation hypothesis', *Economica*, **26**, 128–36.

Peston, M.H. (1960) 'Returns to scale', *Oxford Economic Papers*, (NS) **12**, 133–40.

Peston, M.H. (1967) 'Changing utility functions', in M. Shubik (ed.), *Essays in Mathematical Economics in Honour of Oscar Morgenstern*, Princeton: Princeton University Press.

Peston, M.H. (1969) 'Aspects of the pricing policy of nationalised industries', in J. Margolis and H. Guiton (eds), *Public Economics: an analysis of public production and consumption and their relations to the private sector*, New York: St Martin's Press.

Peston, M.H. (1971) 'Tax mix and effective demand', *Public Finance*, **26**, 493–6.

Peston, M.H. (1972) 'Correlation between targets and instruments', *Economica*, **39**, 427–31.

Peston, M.H. (1973) 'Note on tax changes and fluctuations in national income', *Journal of Political Economy*, **81**, 1467–70.

Peston, M.H. (1974) *Theory of Macroeconomic Policy*, Oxford: Philip Allan (2nd edn 1982).

Peston, M.H. (1979) 'When is a problem of economic policy solvable?', *Thames Papers in Political Economy*, Autumn.

Peston, M.H. (1980a) 'The ratio of public to private expenditure and the relative price effect', *British Review of Economic Issues*, 46–51.

Peston, M.H. (1980b) *Whatever Happened to Macroeconomics*, Manchester: Manchester University Press.

Peston, M.H. (1981) 'An aspect of the crowding out problem', *Oxford Economic Papers*, **31**, 19–27.

Peston, M.H. (1982) *The British Economy: an elementary macroeconomic perspective*, Oxford: Philip Allan (2nd edn 1984).

Peston, M.H. and Quandt, R.E. (1986) *Prices, Competition and Equilibrium*, Oxford: Philip Allan.

Peston, M.H. and Whitin, T.M. (1954) 'Random variations, risk and returns to scale', *Quarterly Journal of Economics*, **68**, 603–12.

Peston, M.H. and Yamey, B.S. (1960) 'Intertemporal price relationships with forward markets: a method of analysis', *Economica*, **27**, 355–67.

Peston, M.H., Katz, E. and Gravelle, H.S.E. (1976) 'Public sector pricing with foreign demand', *Applied Economics*, **8**, 1–10.

PART I

The Trend of Macroeconomic Policy

1. Notes on inflation targeting*

David Laidler

INTRODUCTION

I have known Bernard Corry and Maurice Peston from the very beginning of my career. Bernard was my tutor during my third year at the LSE in 1958–9, and though I do not recall meeting Maurice in the classroom at that time, he was one of those 'younger members of the staff' who set the intellectual tone of economics at the School. Serious teaching based on relevant research was very much the order of the day then. Later, I served with both of them on the CNAA Economics Committee in the early 1970s – serious teaching and relevant research again. I have maintained contact with Bernard over the years as a result of our shared commitment to the history of economic thought, and with Maurice through our association with Philip Allan.

When I began my studies, the Bretton Woods system was firmly in place, monetary policy was a matter of maintaining the exchange rate, and inflation, though much discussed among academics, was close to negligible in the advanced economies of the world. The years since then have been, to put it mildly, interesting for a monetary economist with a concern for policy, and good for his career too, whatever they may have done to the smooth working of the economy! But suddenly, in the mid-1990s, the inflation environment looks a little like that of 30 or 40 years ago. At the end of 1996, *The Economist*'s 'league table' of inflation rates in major industrial countries had the United States at the very top, with prices having risen at a rate of only 3.3 per cent over the previous year.[1]

That remarkable statistic gives a clear indication of the extent to which a macroeconomic problem which dominated policy debates for most of my career has, for the time being at least, been dealt with in the western world. Moreover, there are very few who would deny that the trick has been worked with monetary policy. The revival of some very old fashioned monetary

* Much of this chapter is written as a response to a recent conference on these issues as they arise in Canada which I organized on behalf of the C.D. Howe Institute of Toronto, and whose proceedings appear in Laidler (1997). I owe a special debt to my colleague at the Institute, Bill Robson, with whom I have discussed the issues involved here over a number of years, and who has had a considerable influence on my approach to them, particularly on the relationships among liberal political principles, central bank accountability and autonomy, and the institution of inflation targets.

economics – already out of style, but still taught when I began my studies – which emphasizes the dependence of the value of money on the interaction of the supply and demand for it, was a necessary precondition to the re-establishment of something close to price level stability.[2] A number of countries have made use of formal inflation rate targets as they have brought down and then stabilized that variable; not all, to be sure, for there have been some notable exceptions, not least the United States, Japan and, indeed, Germany, along with those members of the European Monetary System whose currencies have been pegged to the mark, but the United Kingdom, Canada and New Zealand, among others, have all adopted formal inflation targets in one way or another in the 1990s. Thus monetary policy regimes of a type advocated by Henry Simons (1936) and before him by Irving Fisher and his colleagues in the Stable Money Association have at long last begun to be put to the practical test.[3]

This chapter discusses the reasons for inflation targets having had such a wide appeal in the 1990s, the forms that they do, and might, take, and the extent to which they impinge on the capacity of macroeconomic policy to achieve other goals, not least those associated with the level of real income and employment.

WHY INFLATION TARGETS?

Inflation targets amount to more than general statements of an intent to aim for low, negligible, zero (readers are invited to add their own choice of 'feel-good' adjectives to this list) inflation. They involve commitments to bring the percentage rate of change of a particular price index within certain precisely quantified bounds, measured over a precisely specified time period, by a precisely specified date. The first question to be asked about them is, then, what is to be gained from adding quantitative precision to statements about virtuous intentions: what does a promise to attain, say, inflation in the range of 1 to 3 per cent, as measured by year over year changes in the consumer price index, by the end of next year, add to a pledge to attain negligible inflation as soon as it is feasible to do so?

The first and most obvious answer here is that a clearly formulated quantitative target for the outcome of monetary policy makes an excellent starting point for ensuring that it is conducted in a coherent and consistent fashion. To be sure, a general mandate to ensure price stability does represent a large step in the right direction here, recognizing as it does that monetary policy's long-term influence is exerted only on the purchasing power of money, but it is nevertheless the case that the day-to-day actions of policy makers involve quantitative choices about the values of variables under their direct control. It is not enough, for example, in the face of incipient inflationary pressures, to conclude that a higher discount rate and a slower rate of growth of central bank liabilities might be desirable. Decisions need to be made about how much higher, and how much slower. A well specified quantitative target for the outcome of policy must inevitably give a strong impetus to attempt to quantify the linkages between that outcome and policy's instruments, and hence to the creation of a coherent operating framework, which will not mechanically dictate policy actions, but which will provide a common frame of reference relative to which those responsible for policy can exercise their judgement in any particular set of circumstances.

It would, of course, be sufficient for a central bank to have its own private targets to generate this outcome. But inflation targeting regimes are anything but private affairs, and for good reason. It is uncontroversial that a monetary policy which is widely understood and predictable is more likely to achieve its price level goals than one which is not, and that it is conducive to stability of real variables into the bargain. Inflation targets are capable, not only of bringing extra discipline to the conduct of policy, but also of providing an anchor for the private sector inflation expectations upon which the actual outcome of policy to a degree depends. The 'credibility' of policy may (not must) thus be enhanced by explicitly quantified and publicly announced inflation targets.

The fact is that, throughout the great inflation of the 1970s and 1980s, politicians and central bankers routinely extolled the advantages of low inflation and the desirability of restoring it. No policy maker ever made an explicit commitment to maintain high or moderate inflation for the next few years, whatever his or her intentions might actually have been.[4] It is safe generalization, however, that in that period general statements of good intentions were heavily discounted by the public. Thus, when there really was a change of policy makers' understanding and intentions, and there does seem to have been one over the last six or seven years, there had to be a change in the rhetoric of policy if there was to be the slightest chance of communicating that fact to the general public. It is no accident that countries where inflation had been relatively high were more likely to adopt explicit targets than countries where a further reduction of inflation has involved a relatively small departure from recent experience.

This is not to say that the adoption of targets anywhere represented nothing more than a naive attempt to bring about and exploit a downward revision of private sector inflation expectations by way of an announcement effect, thereby rendering contractionary policy painless on the unemployment front. In the 1970s, some advocates of the rational expectations hypothesis may have believed, on the basis of taking too literally the analysis of Sargent and Wallace (1976), that economic policy worked like that, but the experience of the early 1980s in, for example, the United Kingdom, but in North America too, soon laid such ideas to rest. Inflation reduction policies were widely publicized in advance then, albeit not by means of explicitly set targets for the time path of that variable, but their implementation brought about large increases in unemployment that would hardly have occurred had expectations adjusted to policy announcements independently of experience. Announcement effects, that is to say, to the extent that anyone ever believed in their effectiveness, were discredited by experience long before inflation targeting became fashionable.

In the early 1990s, policy makers must have already been painfully aware that they were dealing with agents whose past behaviour suggested that they would believe only what they saw, and it is hard to accept that they believed that the new device of pre-announced quantitative targets for inflation would speed up the learning processes of wage and price setters by any significant amount. To judge from the recessions that have accompanied them, the transitions to low inflation which the implementation of targets heralded probably benefited from announcement effects no more than did earlier slowdowns. This, however, should not be taken to imply that the capacity of inflation targets to generate credibility is unimportant, for it implies only that they do not matter much for the transition from one policy regime to another. When it comes to the actual performance of a new ongoing low inflation regime, things may well be altogether different. The evidence here is currently being generated in a number of countries, and is by no means all in as yet.

If recession accompanied inflation reduction even after the adoption of explicit targets, that is probably because expectations, and price and wage setting behaviour driven by them, which were appropriate to the earlier regime persisted for a while into the later one. Once expectations had caught up with experience, however, there was much to be said for re-enforcing them. After all, shocks of one sort or another hit markets all the time, and how price and wage setters respond to them must depend in part upon how they expect the monetary authorities to react. A well established belief that those authorities are serious about keeping inflation low is a deterrent to aggressive price and wage setting, makes the authorities' task easier and perhaps reduces the costs associated with its accomplishment into the bargain.[5]

That is to say, the very inertia of inflation expectations which makes inflation hard to reduce can also, if managed properly, help to make inflation easier to keep down, because what might be involved here is inertia in the manner whereby experience impinges upon experience. It is well known that extrapolative models of expectations formation which cope with data from the early 1960s onwards rather well seem to fail when confronted with pre-First World War experience, or that of the early years of the Bretton Woods system. In the latter cases, regressive expectations systems do much better. To create credibility for a low inflation regime by way of inflation targets might be expected to restore a similar, desirably stabilizing, pattern to expectations formation. If this does come about, the benefits here will go far beyond price and wage setting behaviour. The more credible is a low inflation regime, the less of a premium will capital markets demand against the risk of a recurrence of inflation in the future, and the lower are the *real* costs of debt service. For countries with large debt hangovers from the 1970s and 1980s, this is a bonus well worth having. If well specified quantitative targets for the maintenance of low inflation impinge upon private sector behaviour in this way, they are worth maintaining as a permanent feature of the policy environment.

It is nevertheless doubtful that any of the foregoing reasons were at the front of the minds of politicians and central bankers when they devised inflation targeting programmes of one sort or another at the turn of the last decade. The countries which have adopted targets are among those which had relatively poor inflation performances in the 1970s and 1980s, but they are also, perhaps not uncoincidentally, among those whose traditions of central bank independence are rather weak – or, to put a more positive slant on the matter, whose traditions of subjecting macroeconomic policy decisions to democratic control are rather strong. It is a well known implication of public choice theory that such traditions impart an inflationary bias to policy.

Here it is important to be clear that public choice theory does not say that inflation is what the public wants and that democratic institutions deliver it. Rather the proposition is that inflation is *not* what the public wants, *but* that democratic institutions deliver it nevertheless. For example, time inconsistency in policy arises not because the electorate like inflation, but because they like high employment and will vote for it, because they do not fully understand that its aggressive pursuit carries the danger of future inflation with it and, critically, because the timing of elections can lead policy makers who know better to discount the risks of future inflation too heavily. To give another example, interest groups, each seeking rents through the political process, ignore the negligible effect that their individual preferred policies will have on the economy-wide inflation rate, and politicians therefore have no incentive to take account of those effects either in accommodating their clients; this despite the fact that the aggregate outcome of so doing is to deliver an inflation rate higher than those clients would, in their capacity as citizens at large, support.

There are at least two possible ways out of this dilemma. One is to take the choice of the inflation rate, if not out of politics altogether, then at least away from the immediate line of fire, by vesting it in a central bank that is not answerable to the electorate. That is what countries like Germany, Switzerland and, to a lesser extent, the United States have done. In each case, it would take an act of the relevant legislature to change this state of affairs, rather than a simple decree on the part of the current executive. The other is to make that choice a conspicuous political issue in its own right, and then to make the central bank responsible to the electorate for implementing whatever choice is made. That is, in effect, what used to be done when politicians, with the support of the electorate, opted for the gold standard, or a fixed exchange rate on some stable key currency, and then mandated the central bank to maintain that exchange rate.

Whatever may be their other virtues, it is also appropriate to look at inflation targets as an alternative means of implementing this type of political solution.

It used to be argued that a fixed exchange rate imposed 'discipline' on politicians. So it did under the Bretton Woods system, though the discipline was, of course self-imposed; and when in the late 1960s self-discipline broke down, for reasons far too complex to go into here, inflation, which no politician explicitly advocated – quite the contrary – was one of the results.[6] Inflation targets, adopted by elected politicians, should be regarded as a means of re-instituting that self-discipline. They should also be thought of as a means of re-asserting democratic control over central banks; for a central bank which does not get clear instructions from its political masters cannot be held accountable by them for its activities.

SOME DESIRABLE CHARACTERISTICS OF A TARGETING REGIME

If inflation targets are politically desirable, then, questions about ways to formulate them arise. Which price index is to be used to measure inflation? How long a time period is inflation to be measured over for targeting purposes? How large a margin of error is the central bank to be permitted? How binding is that margin of error supposed to be? And if it is violated, should bygones be bygones as far as future policy is concerned, or should past errors be offset in the immediate future? The answer to none of these questions is straightforward, and they interact with one another into the bargain.[7]

Consider the choice of price index. Monetary policy affects the price level because it affects nominal aggregate demand and because, in the long run, the level of real output is (or is thought to be) determined by supply-side factors. The price level that corresponds to this economic argument is surely a gross domestic product (GDP) deflator of some sort. If the main raison d'être of inflation targeting is its effect on wage and price setting behaviour, and on the confidence that capital markets are willing to invest in a given regime, then there is much to be said for adopting such an index as the focus of policy. The agents involved here are relatively sophisticated and can be expected to understand the nature of such an index, the reasons why it is published at rather long intervals, and often with a considerable time lag, too, in many countries, and also the reasons why first estimates of its value are so open to revision. But if the raison d'être of targeting is, as I have argued, to an important extent a matter of honouring democratic political principles, this is not a good choice. The absence of timeliness and immediate accuracy make such a deflator a poor basis for holding a central bank accountable for its activities. Moreover, crucially, the public at large, as opposed to the business and financial community, does not understand it.

This last consideration provides an overwhelming argument for casting inflation targets in terms of whatever consumer price index is customarily widely reported in the media, and for setting targets in terms of what has come to be called the 'headline' rate of inflation. If that headline rate is subject to shocks whose effects monetary policy is powerless to combat (effects such as variations in food and energy prices produced by the weather, to give one common example) then that is something that simply has to be lived with. There is no technical harm in stripping a price index of such components in order to produce an estimate of some 'core inflation rate', nor is there any political harm in publicizing its behaviour along with that of the headline rate. To make such an adjusted series the main focus of policy, particularly if the adjustment in question is carried out by the monetary authorities themselves rather than an independent statistical agency, is, however, to open an inflation targeting regime to the suspicion that its published outcome is the result of data tampering as well as of the economy's actual performance, and it would be hard to think of a quicker way of eroding its public acceptance than that.

In addition to being widely understood and published with a rather short time lag, the headline inflation rate also has the great advantage of being seldom, if ever, revised. Information on policy failures, when they occur, can thus be made rapidly available. Here, however, there is a trade-off to be considered. The longer the time period over which inflation is averaged for targeting purposes, the smoother is the resulting series, and the easier are targets to attain; but at the same time, the longer the period of averaging, the more slowly does information about failures become available. The performance of a targeting regime based on a year-to-year inflation measure, a particularly desirable time interval because in many countries it is already that over which headline inflation is measured, and because it dispenses with the need for seasonal adjustment of data, can be monitored with, at best, a six-month time lag. Attempts to smooth the data by further averaging over time can only increase that lag.

Now the temptation to smooth the price index being targeted stems from the obvious fact that monetary policy is an extremely imprecise art, so that, the longer the time period over which an inflation measure is averaged, the less far is actual performance likely to stray from that intended. An alternative, or supplementary, device for dealing with this problem, extremely widely adopted, is to set a target range for inflation, rather than a specific value, typically with a span of two percentage points. Simply to do this, however, without further clarification, introduces an element of ambiguity into the policy regime. To take a concrete example, does a target range of 1 to 3 per cent per annum for consumer price index (CPI) inflation represent what Pierre Siklos (1997) has called a 'zone of indifference', with the authorities being equally satisfied with any outcome within that range; or is there something especially desirable about the centre of that range, with its limits defining 'zones of intolerance' and their violation being regarded as a policy failure?

Here a little attention to the relationship between inflation targets and the econometric techniques that must inevitably underlie the monetary authority's operating framework helps to clarify matters somewhat. The underlying issue is surely that any inflation forecast conditional upon a particular setting of policy instruments comes in the form of a central estimate that is subject to confidence intervals. Thus the further from the centre of a given target range is the inflation rate actually being aimed at, the greater, other things equal, will be the probability of violating one boundary or another. Hence it is hard to think of those boundaries as defining a 'zone of indifference'. At the same time, statistics knows no such thing as a 100 per cent confidence interval, so those boundaries can hardly be thought of as defining a zone of absolute intolerance either. Better by far, then, to treat them as what they must be in the ongoing econometric exercises that underlie the design of policy, namely the upper and lower bounds of a confidence interval around a central target.

If the object of the exercise is to communicate the monetary authorities' intentions to a relatively sophisticated audience consisting of financial markets and those agents involved in wage and price setting, there would surely be no harm, and probably considerable benefit, in stating inflation targets in just such a way: that is, as a central value and a range within which it is intended to maintain the inflation rate a certain percentage of the time. And such a general statement could be supplemented at regular intervals by commentary on the specific risks to which their achievement is subject in the near future. To take this latter step would involve putting a time-varying probability on violating the boundaries over a given horizon, or set of horizons, but it is hard to see how public information about the authorities' estimate of this probability could be of anything but benefit to private sector agents, many of whom would, in the nature of things, be making their own estimates of just this parameter on a regular basis. And provided that, over the longer run, the authorities' estimate of the frequency of violations of the target range was confirmed by events, it is hard to see how this exercise could do anything but enhance their credibility.

Even so, the creation and maintenance of credibility is only one aim of an inflation targeting regime. As was stressed above, an inflation targeting regime increases the capacity of the public, or at least its elected representatives, to hold the central bank accountable for its performance. It seems to be widely believed that well defined boundaries for inflation targets enhance accountability, because sanctions, up to and including the dismissal of their senior officials, can then be imposed upon central banks when those boundaries are violated. In this way of looking at things, the boundaries in question clearly define the thresholds of zones of intolerance. For several years the contract between the government of New Zealand and the Reserve Bank was held up as a model of the way in which well defined targets and accountability went together in just this way. But as both Siklos (1997) and Michael Parkin (1997) have noted, the experience of 1995, when the contracted target range of inflation was breached in New Zealand, suggests that there is a serious flaw in this arrangement. It turned out that the only agency capable of providing the data upon which a judgement of culpability could be made was the Bank itself and, not surprisingly, the governor was accorded the benefit of the doubt.

This experience suggests that an accountability mechanism that only comes into play when a given boundary is crossed, and which then carries with it the threat of severe penalties, is too clumsy to function effectively, and this, as Parkin (1997) has argued, does seem to have implications for the way in which inflation targets are designed and the way in which errors are punished. As has already been noted, monetary policy cannot control inflation precisely and it has already been suggested that, as far as the credibility of a policy regime is concerned, to treat a target range for inflation as defining a confidence interval is the natural way to recognize this fact. This approach also has a natural application in the context of accountability, as Parkin has suggested. Instead of treating any inflation rate within prestated boundaries as equally desirable, and any violation of them as intolerable, he would treat any deviation of inflation from its central target range as being subject to sanctions, whose severity would, however, increase at an increasing rate with the size of the deviation. Under such an arrangement, the monetary authorities would always find themselves under some pressure, which would increase gradually but inexorably as their performance deteriorated.

Whether, under such a regime, punishment should be imposed on the authorities in terms of deductions from the salaries of key officials, reductions in operating budgets or in some milder form is not a matter that I have any strong feelings about. But a considerable degree of accountability under such a set-up could be ensured by the simple device of requiring regular and public reporting on the part of the central bank to the public at large by way of an *inflation report* along British lines, and/or to a legislative committee. One can be reasonably sure that the degree of discomfort that such a reporting requirement would impose on the officials involved would increase rather rapidly with the distance of realized inflation from its central target value, and would become particularly intense if preset confidence intervals were violated too often or for too long.[8] The possibility of dismissal for poor performance could still exist under such arrangements and, being a sanction of last, rather than first, resort, its credibility as a threat, and hence its capacity to induce diligent behaviour on the part of central bankers, would surely be enhanced.

Even with the most competent and diligent of central bankers in charge, targets are going to be missed and boundaries are going to be violated sometimes. One cannot avoid the question of what policy should do in the wake of such events, and the most illuminating way of formulating that question is in terms of a choice between a regime which targets the inflation rate per se, on the one hand, and on the other, one which targets a time path – which may have a positive trend – for the price level. Under the former set-up, after a deviation from target, policy would simply seek to return inflation to its desired path, but under the second inflation would have to be lower (or higher) than its chosen long-run average value for a while.

At first sight, a policy of letting bygones be bygones seems preferable. Even though that involves turning the price level into a random walk, hence rendering the climate for very long-term decisions less certain, it also removes an element of short-term variability from inflation. Here, however, first sight might be overlooking something. If it is indeed the case that one role for inflation targeting is to anchor the expectations that underlie wage and price setting, a regime whose commitment was to a target path for the price level would be a larger deterrent to aggressively inflationary pricing responses to short-term shocks than one which would validate them after the event. Furthermore, a central bank which was committed to reversing the inflationary consequences of its own policy errors, rather than to validating them, might be less error-prone in the first place.[9] In short, it is not clear after all that letting bygones be bygones will actually produce less short-term inflation volatility.

INFLATION TARGETS AND UNEMPLOYMENT

The argument so far is easily summarized. The inflation rate is an important economic variable, and it is uniquely susceptible to control by monetary policy. Though there is no logical necessity to exercise that control within a regime of formal inflation targets, there is much to be said for doing so. Not only can such a regime help to anchor private sector expectations a little more firmly, but, crucially, it permits that aspect of monetary policy which ought to be subject to electoral control, namely the choice of its goal, to be so subjected, while at the same time enhancing the accountability of the central bank for the efficiency with which it carries out its appointed tasks. The kind of inflation targeting regime which best promotes these ends is one which sets its goals in terms of the most widely understood and publicized consumer price index; focuses on a year over year measure of the inflation rate; specifies a central target time path for prices, and a confidence interval around it; makes provision for a regular public accounting on the part of the central bank of its successes and failures in hitting its targets; and makes some provision for the correction of failures as and when they arise.

All of this is well and good, but there is something missing: the focus of the argument is entirely on inflation. What about the effects of monetary policy on unemployment? It is not a sufficient answer here to invoke long and variable time lags, and to argue that, because of them, monetary policy should not be geared to achieving real, as opposed to nominal, goals. That is a valid argument against a central bank attempting to 'fine-tune' real variables, but it is not a valid argument for ignoring the patently obvious fact that monetary policy does have consequences for unemployment which need to be taken into account in the design of an inflation targeting regime.[10] To begin with, there is the question of whether there might, after all, exist a long-run trade-off between inflation and unemployment.

There are two ways in which such a trade-off might arise. First, the labour market might work so as to produce complete dependency of the natural unemployment rate on the actual rate: full hysteresis, as the jargon of macroeconomics would have it. Here the evidence is mixed. There seems to be no evidence for this phenomenon in the United States and, less flexible though that country's labour markets are, it seems to be possible to reject it for Canada too, as Nott (1996) has shown. These considerations suggest that those factors which might bring hysteresis about in any economy – the loss of labour force skills through unemployment, or the absence of capital which might have been accumulated in the absence of a recession – are not in themselves strong enough to create it. If the capacity of certain characteristics of highly organized labour markets, which are often summarized in Assar Lindbeck's phrase 'insider–outsider effects', to generate full hysteresis is a serious possibility, then this might have implications for the level at which a target range for inflation is set, but it does not seem to me to undermine the case for setting such targets at some level. More importantly, however, the real implication of hysteresis in labour markets is surely that the institutional arrangements which generate it need reforming, rather than that the monetary policy regime should simply accommodate itself to them.

There is a second set of reasons as to why a long-run inflation–unemployment trade-off might exist which, in the current state of knowledge, cannot be quite so easily dismissed. James Tobin (1972) long ago conjectured that there might exist downward stickiness in the level of money wages that is independent of the state of inflation expectations and that, therefore, a modestly positive long-run inflation rate might 'lubricate' the labour market and generate a lower unemployment rate than would accompany price level stability. This argument has recently been revived by Akerlof *et al.* (1996) and Fortin (1996) and given an empirical basis, for both studies claim to find evidence of just such absolute wage stickiness.

This is not the place to enter into debate about the robustness of the evidence in question, other than to note, following Howitt (1997), that data collected during and in the immediate wake of two decades of significant inflation may not provide a reliable guide to what will happen if and when price level stability has become the norm. The key point here is rather that these arguments, like those concerning full labour market hysteresis, do not bear on the case for or against inflation targeting per se, but on the choice of the average inflation rate to aim for within such a regime. The more seriously one takes them, the more attractive does a long-run average inflation target of, say, 3 per cent per annum come to look relative to something lower.[11] 'There is not much more that can be said in general about this matter at present: we need a good deal more evidence than we now have to decide the issue and, in any event, there is no particular reason to believe that the evidence will tell the same story in all economies.

Questions about shorter-run phenomena also arise. If one believes, as for example Irving Fisher did in the 1920s, or as Milton Friedman (for example, 1960), not to mention Karl Brunner and Allan Meltzer (for example, 1978) did in the 1960s and 1970s, that monetary policy is itself the source of most cyclical fluctuations, then stabilizing the inflation rate will also do much to eliminate short-run variations in unemployment. But, if one takes a more eclectic view of the causes of the cycle, one must consider the danger that, in concentrating on keeping inflation within bounds to the exclusion of all else, monetary policy might contribute to the severity of cyclical unemployment problems.

Here again we have an argument that does not bear so much on the institution of inflation targeting per se as it does on the design of the particular regime. It has been argued above that inflation targets are most appropriately set in terms of a mean inflation rate combined with a confidence interval around it. The more concern there is about non-monetary shocks inducing cyclical responses, the wider must that confidence interval be set. The adoption of inflation targets implies, not that monetary policy should be designed without regard to its influence on cyclical unemployment, but rather that, because we do not have the knowledge that might enable us to use that influence to fine-tune unemployment, the best we can do is create the background of macroeconomic stability that is implicit in a low and relatively unvarying inflation rate. There is no point in designing a regime that significantly enhances instability of real variables, nor is there any point in failing to do what we can to improve the behaviour of the price level because such real instability exists. These are issues to be taken into account in the precise design of an inflation targeting regime, not reasons for abandoning the concept.

One other aspect of the interaction of inflation and unemployment is worth discussing here, namely the special problems that arise in the period immediately following a successful and noticeable reduction in inflation as a consequence of adopting and achieving targets. There is good reason to believe that the short-run Phillips curve is non-linear, that marginal gains in lowering inflation relative to expectations diminish as the unemployment rate increases. There are also good reasons to believe that labour markets are characterized, not by full but by partial hysteresis, so that, in the wake of a recession, the unemployment rate below which inflation begins to rise relative to expectations is temporarily higher than the long-run natural rate.[12] This combination of facts implies that, if an upper bound on inflation becomes a strongly binding constraint upon policy, the speed with which a reasonable level of employment can be restored will also be constrained.

This is not a permanent problem, to be sure. Rather it is a feature of the transition from a relatively high to a relatively low inflation regime, but it is potentially important, nonetheless. If it does not amount to an argument against inflation targets, it is undoubtedly a caveat to be taken into account in their design. It makes upper limits on the inflation rate that are regarded as firmly binding over short time periods look less attractive than they otherwise would. To the extent that a demonstration of monetary policy's ability to achieve and maintain low inflation is important to establishing the credibility of an inflation targeting regime, there is an important trade-off to be considered here. But given that the setting of inflation targets ought to be a matter of political choice, and given that credibility earned at the expense of a prolonged period of high unemployment is unlikely to engender popular support for them, there is a lot to be said for slowing down the pace at which credibility is earned in order to ensure that it has a little more durability. The implications of these considerations for treating an inflation target range as defining a confidence interval, rather than as a partition of inflation behaviour between the acceptable and the unacceptable, is surely obvious.

To sum up, then: the adoption of an inflation targeting regime for monetary policy does not imply that unemployment problems should be ignored. The regime can be designed to ensure that, if monetary policy is not to be deployed to the active pursuit of employment goals, its conduct is at least so calibrated as not to do damage on this front. And, of course, there still remain fiscal tools, not to mention structural measures, which can be brought to bear here.

CONCLUDING COMMENT

The foregoing paragraph has an old fashioned ring to it. If one were to substitute the phrase 'pegged exchange rate regime' for 'inflation targeting regime', it could have been written, and perhaps was written by someone, at the time when I first encountered Bernard Corry and Maurice Peston at the LSE. There has been some change in the way in which we think about macroeconomic policy in the intervening years; but not perhaps as much as we thought while it was going on.

NOTES

1. It should be noted that the US inflation rate is measured with a bias that may be as high as one percentage point per annum, so that the true inflation rate there is almost certainly well under 3 per cent.
2. Though such ideas were more likely to be encountered in lectures and classes on the history of economic thought than on monetary economics. I learned more useful monetary economics as an undergraduate from Henry Thornton's *Paper Credit* (1802) than I did from contemporary textbooks on monetary theory, which had better remain nameless.
3. For an account of US policy debates in the 1920s and 1930s that puts contemporary debates about such proposals in their historical context, see William Barber (1986).
4. My own inclination is to lay far more blame for the inflation of the 1970s and 1980s on bad economic analysis that underestimated the influence of monetary policy on the price level, and overestimated the influence of much else, than on the deliberate machinations of politicians and central bankers intent on hoodwinking the electorate.
5. John Grant (1997) discusses this matter in a recent and fascinating paper, arguing that the 'rhetoric' of monetary policy extends far beyond the setting of clear policy goals and into the design and implementation of a well publicized and stable operating framework designed to achieve them.
6. That is to say, politicians had lost sight of what it was that fixed exchange rates were preventing. They thought that balance of payments problems inhibited the achievement of real economic growth. (See note 4 above.)
7. Though it does not follow them in detail, this section has been greatly stimulated by recent papers by Pierre Siklos (1997) and Michael Parkin (1997).
8. Parkin (1997) analyses a regime under which a central target for the inflation rate is set, and deductions from the central bank's budget are made as a quadratic function of inflation's deviation from that target. He does not, of course, advocate anything quite so mechanical in practice, but argues persuasively that the rising marginal cost attached to errors that such a regime embodies is a better way to discipline a bank and its executives than one in which all-or-nothing costs are imposed upon them depending upon whether a particular threshold of error is violated.
9. I owe this argument to Bill Robson.
10. Stanley Fischer (1994) makes this valid point with great persuasiveness.
11. The precise number, 3 per cent, is Fortin's estimate of the inflation rate above which downward money-wage stickiness would cease to be a problem in Canada.
12. There is no reason to suppose that either non-linearities or partial hysteresis effects are equally important, or unimportant for that matter, in every economy. Much must depend upon the nature of labour market and related institutions. But both seem to be present in Canadian data. See Loretta Nott (1996).

REFERENCES

Akerlof, G.A., Dickens, W.T. and Perry, G.L. (1996) 'The Macroeconomics of Low Inflation', *Brookings Papers on Economic Activity*, **1**, 1–59.

Barber, W. (1986) *From New Era to New Deal, Herbert Hoover, The Economists and American Economic Policy 1921–1933*, Cambridge: Cambridge University Press.

Brunner, K. and Meltzer, A.H. (1978) 'Introduction', *The Problem of Inflation, Carnegie Rochester Conference Series*, Vol. 8, Amsterdam: North-Holland.

Fischer, S. (1994) 'Modern Central Banking', in F. Capie *et al.* (eds), *The Future of Central Banking*, Cambridge, Cambridge University Press.

Fortin, P. (1996) 'The Great Canadian Slump', *Canadian Journal of Economics*, **29** (November) 761–87.

Friedman, M. (1960) *A Program for Monetary Stability*, New York: Fordham University Press.

Grant, J. (1997) 'The Bank of Canada's Operating Framework', in Laidler (ed.), *Where We Go From Here*.

Howitt, P.W. (1997) 'Costs and Benefits of Negligible Inflation', in Laidler (ed.), *Where We Go From Here*.

Laidler, D. (ed.) (1997) *Where We Go From Here – Monetary Policy and the Future of Inflation Control in Canada*, Toronto: C.D. Howe Institute.

Nott, L. (1996) 'Hysteresis in the Canadian Labour Market: Evidence from the 1990s Research Report', #9605, Dept. of Economics, University of Western Ontario.

Parkin, J.M. (1997) 'Monetary Policy and the Future of Inflation Control in Canada – an Overview', in Laidler (ed.), *Where We Go From Here*.

Sargent, T.J. and Wallace, N. (1976) 'Rational Expectations and the Theory of Economic Policy', *Journal of Monetary Economics*, **2** (May) 169–83.

Siklos, P. (1997) 'Charting a Future for the Bank of Canada', in Laidler (ed.), *Where We Go From Here*.

Simons, H. (1936) 'Rules Versus Authorities in Monetary Policy', *Journal of Political Economy*; reprinted in F.A. Lutz and L.W. Mints (eds), *Readings in Monetary Theory*, London: George Allen & Unwin, for the AEA, 1952.

Thornton, H. (1802) *An Enquiry into the Nature and Effects of the Paper Credit of Great Britain*; reprinted with an Introduction by F.A. von Hayek, London: George Allen & Unwin, 1939.

Tobin, J. (1972) 'Inflation and Unemployment', *American Economic Review*, **62** (March) 1–18.

2. Kalecki's 'Political Aspects of Full Employment' revisited[1]

Frank Skuse

Bernard Corry has long had an interest in labour economics and questions of unemployment: indeed, at a seminar given at the University of East London (UEL) not long before his retirement, he bemoaned the fact that unemployment had fallen off the agenda and that much of macroeconomics had been subsumed into labour economics. Maurice Peston has published widely in the field of economic policy and aggregate demand management and has also shown an interest in the question of employment levels. It therefore seemed appropriate, in honouring them for their contribution to economics, to go back to an important paper on employment from an earlier age and reappraise its relevance today.

In 1943, Kalecki published a path-breaking paper (Kalecki, 1943a) entitled 'Political Aspects of Full Employment', a paper which took a somewhat pessimistic view of the prospects for a return to full employment in the capitalist democracies in the period following the cessation of hostilities. It was followed by other papers (Kalecki, 1944, 1945) in which he gave more detailed consideration to the types of policy initiative that would be needed to steer such economies towards the full employment goal.

The purpose of the present chapter is to consider the arguments presented by Kalecki and evaluate their relevance, with particular regard to the UK economy, some 50 years after their original publication. This revisiting occurs in a context in which the problem of unemployment has become a less important priority of governments, replaced by the demands of controlling inflation and pursuing 'sound' public finances. One indicator of this can be found in the Maastricht Treaty and its imposition of convergence criteria in terms of interest rates, inflation rates and public finance ratios, but not unemployment. This chapter has four sections: a summary of Kalecki's position on the problems of achieving full employment; the relevance to the 1990s of Kalecki's political barriers; aspects of the experience of the UK economy since the late 1970s in the light of Kalecki's arguments; and a concluding section.

KALECKI'S ARGUMENT

The central tenet of Kalecki's argument in the 1943 paper was simple: technically, the means to achieving full employment existed. The impact of Keynes's *General Theory* (Keynes, 1936) and the work undertaken by Kalecki himself in connection with the business cycle (see, for example, Kalecki, 1943b) had given a key role to aggregate demand, and particularly fluctuations in investment spending, as the key factor in determining levels of aggregate activity. Thus in order to engineer full employment it was, Kalecki argued, sufficient to create the appropriate level of aggregate demand. With the wisdom of hindsight, such faith in manipulating this variable to such good effect may seem optimistic, but it was a view in keeping with its time. Kalecki argued that it was possible by this means not only to *create* full employment but also to *maintain* it over time. It could thus be argued that he was incorporating long-run dynamics more explicitly than Keynes (see Sawyer, 1985, p. 194).

The real problem militating against full employment in either time scale is a political and institutional one. Kalecki argued that the interests of the capitalist class are such that they will object to government involvement in creating and maintaining higher levels of employment. This opposition has three aspects:

1. An objection to government involvement in the manipulation of aggregate demand per se: it deprives capitalists of power in the sense that government no longer has to have regard in policy decisions to maintaining private sector confidence. Capitalists consequently lose a constraining influence on government.
2. An objection to the impact of government expenditure aimed at expanding aggregate demand: if the state undertakes investment spending it is in competition with private interests and crowds out private investment by taking over what capitalists regard as their legitimate sphere of activity. If, however, expenditure takes the form of a subsidy of consumption, this breaks the ethic of the market capitalist system according to which reward, at least of labour and employment, should be related to effort expended.
3. An objection to the commitment to the *maintenance* of full employment: establishing this over the long run is argued to alter the balance of power between employer and employee in favour of the latter. Capitalists, Kalecki argued, see some level of unemployment as a normal and desirable feature of a market capitalist system.

In subsequent publications, 'Three Ways to Full Employment' (Kalecki, 1944) and 'Full Employment by Stimulating Private Investment?' (Kalecki, 1945), he elaborated on the ways in which governments might endeavour to move an economy towards full employment and considered the likely impact of these measures. He argued that governments in capitalist democracies have three basic methods available to stimulate demand: direct creation of demand through state investment and/or forms of subsidy of consumption; stimulating private investment; and redistribution from high to low income, that is towards that section of society with higher propensity to consume.

Kalecki was generally pessimistic about the ability of investment, either in the government or in the private sector, to act as the motor for the move to full employment and as sustainer of it. There would always be a finite volume of feasible projects available for state investment, possibly inadequate to the required expansion of demand. It is important to note here Kalecki's insistence that only investment projects which are economically viable should be undertaken. There is a clear rejection of the use of socially unjustified projects as means simply of creating jobs. In the private sector, difficulties would be likely to emerge in encouraging private investment. Kalecki's argument is that it would require cumulative support if full employment was to be maintained over the longer run. There is clearly a floor to interest rate reductions designed to stimulate investment and the result would be the impossibility of generating adequate investment over the longer run. This led him to the conclusion that using investment demand as the stimulus to full employment could only be achieved through greater direct state involvement in production, which is precisely what is resisted by the capitalist class. Kalecki is thus led to the conclusion that the most effective policies to bring about full employment will have to involve some form of state subsidy of consumption in order to raise demand or the even more politically sensitive redistribution of income from high-income to low-income sectors of the population.

MODERN RELEVANCE OF KALECKI'S ARGUMENT

This section considers the relevance of Kalecki's ideas, as summarized above, 50 years after they were published. In doing this, emphasis is on the experience of the United Kingdom since the coming to power of a New Right-influenced government in 1979. Inevitably, such a starting point is arbitrary and there was evidence that, even prior to 1979, governments were showing increasing reluctance to follow policies directed at securing full employment. Nevertheless, 1979 marks a watershed in UK economic policy and a significant break with the previous period.

We start with a consideration of the relevance of Kalecki's political constraints on full employment. There can be little doubt that the question of unemployment has been relegated in importance as a key objective of economic policy and replaced by the need to control inflation (see, for example, Arestis and Skuse, 1989; Skuse, 1995; Britton, 1996). Indeed, it can be suggested that, in addition to the constraints identified by Kalecki, the experience of the 1970s led to the emergence of a fourth constraint, the fear of inflation, and that this has proved as powerful a brake on pursuit of full employment as Kalecki's original trio. Related to this has been a questioning of the ability of governments to bring about full employment by manipulation of demand and a greater emphasis on the labour market as the explanation for higher levels of unemployment, with the associated resort to supply-side policies and attempts to make labour markets more flexible. Thus a fundamental question mark appears over Kalecki's starting point that a government does in fact have the means to create full employment in the way that he envisaged. Governments in many democratic capitalist societies have abandoned this approach. This applies even to apparently left-leaning governments such as the Keating government in Australia and, in all likelihood, that of Blair in the United Kingdom, let alone to the Thatcher/Major administration. The argument advanced is that greater flexibility in labour markets is the essential prerequisite to removing unemployment and that the government cannot achieve this objective through reflationary expansion of demand.

Central to the New Right agenda has been greater reliance on market mechanisms and a concerted attempt to reduce the extent of government involvement and provision. This has manifested itself in an unwillingness to consider active fiscal policy designed to engineer changes in aggregate demand for fear of increasing inflationary pressures, and a greater reliance on monetary policy in various forms as the measure to control macroeconomic variables. It is not clear, however, that this is entirely captured by Kalecki's argument that government must do nothing to undermine business confidence, at least in the real economy. It would appear to be more related to the desire to avoid at all costs following a policy that risked threatening the new policy priority of controlling inflation. Indeed, it has been argued that it is in the interests of capital for governments to use aggregate demand management in a way that is contradictory to Kalecki's argument. As Dow (1964) argues, the low levels of unemployment experienced in the 1950s in particular are in part due to government willingness to use discretionary fiscal policy appropriately to create an environment of stability in which private investment could occur. More importantly for the argument here, this high level of demand and employment would not have occurred 'if the world of business had not acquired some confidence that governments could and would so intervene when necessary' (Dow, 1964, p. 364). What changed between the 1950s and the late 1970s was the breakdown of the immediate postwar consensus between labour and capital (Britton, 1996 pp. 7–8) and the replacement of the presumption in favour of the 'right to work' by the 'right to manage'. Capital saw its interests best served by the operation of more flexible labour markets and a change in the balance of power between labour and capital which is entirely consistent with Kalecki's arguments.

On the other hand, the increasing globalization of capital and importance of multinational and transnational firms does place pressures on the government to pursue policies which help to maintain business confidence. The UK government throughout the 1980s and 1990s was concerned to attract inward investment, most notably from Japanese car manufacturers anxious to establish capacity within the European Union (EU). This became of particular importance owing to the decline in manufacturing industry experienced by Britain in the first half of the 1980s. Unwillingness on the part of the Conservative government to sign the EU Social Chapter is another example of the change in balance of power between capital and labour.

What has clearly changed since Kalecki wrote is the power of market ideology, and this helps give 'business/industrial leaders' more leverage over the state. It is not an argument based on government intervention operating indirectly by affecting negatively the state of business confidence, but a more ideologically based and direct assertion that the market will provide the best solution and that the state should dismantle as much government intervention as possible.

Where Kalecki's confidence-based argument may have greater relevance in a UK context is with respect to financial markets where the power of an internationally open market makes it important that the government be seen to adopt policies that will be well regarded in the City, and not cause destabilizing liquidity flows in the age of deregulated markets. While it is difficult to disentangle all of the factors causing price movements in financial markets, casual observation throughout the first half of the 1990s indicates that it was not uncommon for markets to react adversely in response to falls in unemployment level, even when the absolute level remained high. A desire to avoid destabilizing such markets may well act as a significant lever on government policy and reinforce the priority of an inflation target over concern at employment levels. It is not so clear that the UK government has felt so constrained in policy with respect to the real economy, for example with a willingness to use interest rate policy in a way that is counterproductive to confidence, investment and employment and to limit expansion at the first sign of possible upward pressure on inflation. The Labour government's decision to delegate interest rate determination to the Bank of England is likely to strengthen this.

The second aspect of Kalecki's argument concerns the objection to the *direction* of spending undertaken by government. This would appear to be as relevant in the 1990s as when Kalecki first wrote. The United Kingdom has seen changes which have significantly altered the balance between public and private sector provision in a wide range of activities as a result of the massive programme of privatization. The private sector and private shareholders have taken over what had previously been regarded as public provision. Such changes have taken place in a range of areas, from public transport to health provision. In addition, the Conservative government has increasingly looked to involve private sector capital in what previously would have been public projects and to shift the public/private balance in favour of the latter. Such initiatives look set to continue under the Labour government.

The consequence of these changes is that large areas of investment spending have been returned to private hands and in addition the monopoly position previously enjoyed by public utilities has in many cases been eroded as competition has been allowed. British Telecommunications is perhaps the most obvious example but competition is also evident in both rail and gas industries. Investment decisions are now taken by (albeit regulated) private companies based largely on straight commercial criteria and government has effectively ceded most of the influence it previously exercised over investment levels in these industries. In addition many of these newly privatized businesses have seen reductions in employment levels as significant numbers of staff have been made redundant (for example, in British Gas and British Telecommunications) in the interests of efficiency and shareholder dividends.

The final element of Kalecki s argument concerns capitalist anxiety at losing the disciplinary effect of unemployment if the state succeeds not only in achieving full employment but also in maintaining it. This argument seems to be of continuing relevance 50 years on, as evidenced by government's willingness to accept higher levels of unemployment at all stages of the cycle. It is also part of the shift that has seen the discussion of unemployment shift away from aggregate demand management problems to questions of labour market flexibility and adjustment and reassertion of the argument that wage control is the key factor in raising levels of employment. Such a view is entirely consistent with the general notion of an excess supply of labour acting as a brake on real wage growth. Indeed, it may be that the nature of unemployment and the existence of long-term core and structural unemployment mean that higher levels may be necessary to exercise this disciplinary effect. Britton (1996) indicates that growing unemployment through the 1960s was not obviously the consequence of deficient aggregate demand but more due to an upward trend in the non-accelerating inflation rate of unemployment (NAIRU). This becomes, in the sense of Kalecki's argument, 'acceptable' to both capital and that part of the workforce which remains in employment. There is further evidence from the 1980s that, even at the peak of booms, the level of unemployment was rising; for instance, the lowest level of *long-term* unemployment between 1979 and the early 1990s (occurring in the third quarter of 1990) was 40 per cent above the corresponding figure in 1979 (see Skuse, 1995).

Kalecki appears to have had in mind what may now appear a rather simplistic version of the impact of unemployment on 'discipline', namely that any increase in its level would have the required effect. From a modern perspective, we would wish to add that the history of the level of unemployment and its structure are as important as its absolute level. Hysteresis effects become relevant. Related to this, we should distinguish between the 'insiders' and 'outsiders' (Lindbeck and Snower, 1987) and their differential impact. Changes in unemployment amongst outsiders may not have the disciplinary impact that Kalecki envisaged, meaning that insiders may retain influence and wage bargaining power despite rising unemployment. The consequence of this is that very savage increases in unemployment may be needed to maintain the disciplinary threat of dismissal, and consequently it may be in the interests of capital to oversee even higher levels of unemployment on a periodic basis to maintain the credibility of the disciplinary threat.

Associated with the relocation of the causes of unemployment within the labour market itself has been a systematic attempt to limit the rights of organized labour in the United Kingdom. This too is at least consistent with Kalecki's argument as to the desire of capitalists not to be party to a shift in the balance of power, unless of course it is in their favour. Ironically, given the reduction in trade union power, together with the steady decline in union membership in the United Kingdom and growth in the numbers of self-employed, it may well be that any future return towards levels of full employment would not have the effects that Kalecki argued capitalists feared.

In addition to the three political constraints identified by Kalecki, a fourth should now be added. This is the fear of inflation. This has probably become the most powerful constraint in turning governments and policy makers away from concern with the goal of full employment, and so powerful has its impact become that even left-leaning governments place the inflation target on at least an equal footing with that of employment. Why has this occurred? In part the reason is historical. Kalecki's argument was developed at a time when memories of the Great Depression and falling prices were strong. The inflationary spectre was not a serious threat. It is also consistent with Kalecki's understanding of how a developed capitalist economy functions. A key part of his theoretical apparatus is that, up to the level where labour *and* equipment are scarce, 'short period supply curves are horizontal or mildly rising for most commodities' (Kalecki, 1944, p. 361). Consequently, it follows that, if government demand creation 'stops short of increasing effective demand over the full employment mark, there is no need to be afraid of inflation' (Kalecki, 1943a, p. 348). Such insouciance in connection with inflation was borne out by the experience of economies such as the United Kingdom's during the 1950s as high levels of employment were not accompanied by serious levels of inflation. Events of the 1970s, triggered by the oil price shocks and reinforced by the breakdown of social consensus between labour and capital, meant that both the threat and actuality of inflation became much more real, and the New Right acceded to power in the United Kingdom on a platform which emphasized this.

There is, however, a further reason that plays a part in accounting for this shift. Kalecki's original argument is couched largely in terms of the opposition of *industrial* capital to achieving and maintaining full employment. It emphasizes opposition to the impact of state intervention on private industrial interests and the negative consequences on opportunities for real investment. There is brief reference to the maintenance of full employment operating contrary to the interests of the rentier class in terms of rising prices (Kalecki, 1943a p. 355). However, the thrust of his argument remains that full employment alters the balance of power, undermines '"discipline in the factories" and "political stability"' (ibid., p. 351) and means that 'workers would "get out of hand" [so that] the "captains of industry" would be anxious to "teach them a lesson"' (ibid., p. 355).

The United Kingdom has witnessed a significant decline in the size of manufacturing and related sectors alongside a growth in the absolute size of the financial sector. As Wells (1995) shows, employment in the industrial sectors of the United Kingdom fell considerably from the mid-1960s onwards, while at the same time employment in services, particularly financial services, grew rapidly. Measured in output terms, from 1983 to 1996, banking, finance and business services grew by 46.7 per cent compared to 28.9 per cent and 27.1 per cent for construction and production industries, respectively.[2] Finance capital thus became much more important. The role of financial markets as barometers of confidence has grown with the growth of the sector and economic policy has increasingly been framed within the context of the reactions of financial markets rather than in terms of impact on industrial confidence. An important criterion of policy formulation becomes its credibility as viewed by financial markets. Adverse reactions by these markets to signs of rising inflation, often associated with publication of data showing falls in unemployment, place a constraint on governments' ability to pursue full employment and give precedence to anti-inflation measures. This is particularly important in an economy with large and international financial markets such as the UK economy. The result is a strengthening of opposition to inflation as the result of, in Kaleckian terminology, the captains of *finance* as distinct from captains of *industry*, who have a vested interest in low inflation. Given changes in the structure of the United Kingdom and in particular the decline of manufacturing and the growth of the financial sector, this is a powerful new fourth constraint of a political nature which makes governments less likely to pursue policies aimed at reducing employment.

This distinction between the two types of capital should not be exaggerated, as the interests of industrial capital also suffer from inflation even in a Kaleckian world in which the pricing of goods determined by the degree of monopoly enables wage rises to be passed on and profit margins re-established. Retained corporate earnings suffer from increased taxation at given rates of corporation tax, given the use of essentially historical cost methods in determining tax liability. This will impinge upon corporate ability both to distribute dividends and to finance investment. The former will have an impact on those who hold equity-based wealth, a group in which higher income earners predominate. Michl (1995) discusses this issue citing US studies which indicate that the costs of inflation weigh most heavily on upper income groups. Given that these groups are also likely to be more socially influential, and include significant representation from the captains of industry, we have another argument leading to the emergence of the fear of inflation as the fourth political constraint on full employment.

THE MEANS TO ACHIEVING FULL EMPLOYMENT

As already indicated, Kalecki discussed three broad categories of policy aimed at generating full employment: state investment, encouraging private sector investment and the encouragement of consumption. These areas will now be discussed in terms of the experience in the UK economy, specifically since 1979.

State Investment

The government that came to power in 1979 was elected on a manifesto which, inter alia, promised to 'roll back the state', diminishing the extent to which government intervened in the operation of the markets. It was thus clearly by implication wedded to the notion underlying Kalecki's first political constraint. A major aspect of economic policy over the period has been to withdraw from government economic activity and, with it, to lose control over a significant element of investment decision making.

Possibly the most important manifestation of this has been the policy of privatization, commencing with Amersham International in the early 1980s and running throughout the period of Conservative government to embrace a wide range of public utilities and government activities traditionally run on a more obviously commercial basis. Central government has thus effectively relinquished much of the control it has had over levels of investment in many key sectors. In other domains where it has retained such control, for example road construction, there has been a scaling down of programmes. In addition, there has been the attempt to shift the investment out of the public sector by inviting joint private/public ventures (Private Finance Initiative).[3] Classic examples of unwillingness to invest in key infrastructure projects are the rail link to the Channel Tunnel, where procrastination and concerns over the impact of the investment on public finances have delayed construction of the link, and the much-debated cross London rail link from east to west. Similarly, the retirement of the state from active involvement in house building in the 1990s has further reduced the ability to have a direct impact on a cyclically sensitive area of investment spending. Rather than using such investments as a way of creating employment, state involvement has been replaced by a determination to pursue a policy of fiscal conservatism and to control public expenditure. Conservative policy has thus been to shrink the domain of public investment, in a way which is diametrically opposed to what Kalecki argued was necessary. This has had the consequence of making it more difficult for the UK economy to move towards full employment even under boom conditions (see Skuse, 1995).

Kalecki clearly foresaw a limit to the range of economically justified projects that the state would be able to undertake, and it was this that made him guarded about the possibility of using this area of aggregate demand as the basis for creating full employment. But is the range necessarily so restricted? Sawyer (1995b) has clearly made the point that unemployment 'causes clear hardship and waste' and is hardly consistent with a view of society that posits scarcity as the key economic problem. Unemployment remains a social waste because it means unsatisfied needs/wants. We are not yet at the point where scarcity has ceased to be a problem. As Wells (1995) argues, community, social and personal services have created a steady increase in the number of jobs and, despite Conservative hostility, 'employment in public services expanded ineluctably on account of the public s aspirations for improved services' (Wells, 1995, p. 118). In what is merely an extension of a well known argument (Galbraith, 1958), many of the more pressing needs of advanced capitalist society contain the characteristics of public goods that make private provision problematic, such as transport and environmental questions. The range of viable public sector investments that is not competitive with, but rather complementary to, private sector interests may be less of a constraint than Kalecki feared. In other words, if the notion of viability does not just mean a straight private sector profit evaluation but perhaps a broader concept. The question reverts back to what Kalecki feared in terms of the constraint being in the political/ideological realm. It is no longer a strictly economic argument. Furthermore, many of the areas where the public sector has shrunk are precisely those which, in providing infrastructure such as transport, potentially enhance private sector profit rather than encroaching on its investment opportunities.

Encouraging Private Investment

The performance of private sector investment in the United Kingdom during the 1980s and 1990s is entirely consonant with Kalecki s forecast: it has taken place at levels inadequate to move to anything like full employment even at the height of boom periods such as the latter half of 1990. This has been particularly true of investment in the manufacturing sector. Kalecki foresaw the difficulty of using interest rates on a long-term basis as a means of encouraging investment, given what he argued was a secular tendency of investment to occur at an inadequate level.

The position has been exacerbated by the emphasis on using interest rate policy as the key variable in promoting anti-inflation policy since the collapse of the Medium Term Financial Strategy in the mid-1980s. With occasional glaring exceptions, such as the attempt to use the interest rate to shore up a faltering exchange rate in 1992, interest rate policy has been driven by the need to establish a credible anti-inflationary stance. Throughout the period since 1985 interest rate policy has been governed largely by the exigencies of monetary policy and the desire to stifle even the first signs of inflationary pressure, with little attention to its impact on investment and employment. The willingness to raise rates in 1994 in order to stifle any incipient signs of inflation, despite the fragile nature of recovery, is one example of this, as is the continuing conflict between the chancellor of the exchequer and the governor of the Bank of England over interest rate movements in 1996. The granting of quasi-autonomy to the Bank of England in terms of interest rate determination in May 1997 is a further step along this road. This unwillingness to use interest rates in a countercyclical way is entirely consistent with Kalecki's argument that fiscal policy to such an end would also be eschewed, so as to allay fears of any crowding out of private investment.

In a Kaleckian world, the rate of interest is only one determinant of the level of investment. A second important influence is the availability of finance which in an oligopolistic world involves retained earnings by firms, reflecting the fact that such firms are, to a significant degree, financially self-contained and less sensitive to interest rate changes in terms of real investment behaviour. This is particularly true of the UK economy, where this independence is high relative to many other European countries where the role of bank finance in private investment is greater. The policies of the Conservative government since 1979 have created a climate propitious to investment in this regard, yet, despite this, investment has not provided the motor to achieving or maintaining high levels of employment, the manufacturing sector again being the most obvious failure in this regard.

Encouraging Consumption

Given his concern that investment would fail to produce sufficient levels of aggregate demand, Kalecki considered measures to encourage consumption, either through direct subsidy or through redistribution of income to those more likely to spend. In this area, the period since 1979 has borne out his worst fears in terms of such policies being ideologically unacceptable.

A variety of changes has worked in entirely the opposite direction to the subsidy of consumption in any form and caused a movement towards consumers paying directly for what they consume. A consequence of the attachment to market ideology has been the emphasis on the consumer bearing the full market cost of a wider range of goods and services consumed. Examples of such policies have included the ill-fated attempt to reform municipal taxation (the so-called 'Poll Tax') to relate payment more directly to the number of consumers; changes in charges within health care to make consumers pay a greater proportion of actual costs, notably in optical and dental care; ill-advised pressure to make private pension provision rather than relying on state-run schemes; and consistent rises in public transport tariffs above the rate of inflation to move the provision to a more nearly commercial basis and remove the element of subsidy.

In addition to these removals of what are effectively subsidies on consumption, other aspects of fiscal policy have worked in a way that discourages rather than encourages consumption. Here examples include failure to index pensions and social security benefits in line with inflation and increases in duties on certain goods, such as alcohol, petrol and tobacco, at levels greater than the rate of inflation. While these may be desirable as initiatives to control consumption of specific goods, they clearly have an impact on aggregate demand.

The examples cited have been driven by a mixture of an ideological commitment to market forces and the associated desire to control public spending. The former motive is a complete vindication of Kalecki's comments that consumption must be based on the notion that '"you shall earn your bread in sweat"– unless you happen to have private means' (Kalecki, 1943a, p. 351). The aim of controlling public spending has clearly had quite the reverse effect to Kalecki's suggestion of subsidizing consumption.

A counterinfluence to the above has come as a consequence of the privatization policy. One of the objectives of this policy has been to introduce greater competition into the provision of telecommunications, gas, electricity and so on with attendant benefits in terms of prices to consumers. In several of these industries the cost to the consumer of the goods or services concerned has fallen in real terms. Interestingly, this has been as much due to the regulatory regime under which these erstwhile public utilities have been required to operate.[4] Though it is true that competition has been introduced into telecommunications in a significant way, even in this instance it is the pricing formula enforced by the regulatory agency that has played a major role in restraining British Telecommunication's prices. In other areas such as gas and electricity, where the extent of competition is to date more restricted, the cost reduction is almost entirely due to the regulatory body in the industry concerned. In these instances, in spite of ownership having passed to the private sector, the government has indirectly produced a result in keeping with Kalecki's requirement of encouraging consumption without the need for subsidy.

As an alternative to straight subsidy, Kalecki argued that an effective way of boosting aggregate demand would be redistribution through taxation policy from high to low income earners, thus raising the aggregate propensity to consume. There is clear evidence that, despite the political rhetoric of the Conservative governments since 1979 being the governments of 'low taxation', the overall burden of taxation over that period as a proportion of GDP actually increased, taking all forms of taxation into account. What has happened is clearly a shift from (potentially progressive) direct taxation such as income tax to greater reliance on (regressive) indirect taxation, notably VAT. Thus, in 1979, government revenue from taxes on expenditure amounted to 77 per cent of the revenues raised by taxes on income; by 1996, the figure was 116 per cent.[5] Such a shift is in itself likely to produce the reverse result to that for which Kalecki argued. Coupled with this has been evidence that there has been a significant redistribution of income and wealth since 1979, partly as the result of changes in taxation (see, for example, the 1995 Rowntree Commission report). Not surprisingly, the redistribution has been entirely in the wrong direction, in that it has increased the degree of inequality and has redistributed income to those with lower propensity to consume.

The basis of tax policy has been to concentrate entirely on the supply side of the economy as a basis for restoring employment levels, emphasizing the need to restore incentives, notably by the reduction in the degree of progression in direct tax rates, so trying to produce an effect through a route diametrically opposed to that suggested by Kalecki. It is effectively relying on a version of Say's law, in that easing supply-side restrictions/constraints is held to be sufficient to expand activity and employment.

A further distributional effect that moves away from full employment follows from the use of interest rate policy as the key instrument to control inflation. It has been suggested (Arestis and Howells, 1991) that high interest policies together with changes in the floating rate indebtedness of the personal sector of the United Kingdom have had the effect of redistributing income away from households with high spending propensity towards those sectors more likely to save. High interest has thus had a double effect both in stifling demand directly and through an 'intersectoral redistribution from spending to saving' (ibid., p. 269).

CONCLUSION

It seems difficult to avoid the conclusion reached by Kalecki that institutional change within a developed capitalist system is a necessary precondition for any realistic chance of returning to a world of full employment and maintaining it on a consistent basis. Does this mean, therefore, that we have to accept abandoning full employment as a realistic objective?

What do we mean by full employment? 'Full employment meant everyone working who wanted to work at a wage equal to but not necessarily more than his or her marginal product' (Eisner, 1996). Is this still an operational definition of full employment? Can we even think in terms of a definition that indicates some global match between those seeking work and the number of vacancies available, ignoring any mismatch between the nature of the vacancies and the labour available? Or should we, following Sawyer, accept that full employment does not mean a job for everyone of working age, but that full employment implies some limit on the length of frictional employment suffered by any one job seeker (Sawyer, 1995a). Consideration must also be given to the idea that the supply of labour may itself be influenced by demand and that long periods of unemployment may themselves cause the reduction in the supply of labour as people cease seeking work. What possibly appeared to Kalecki in 1943 as a precisely definable concept is clearly not capable of unambiguous definition. This becomes particularly important in a situation where flexible labour markets cause the creation of low-paid, poor-quality, often part-time jobs (see Wells, 1995). How do we interpret the decision of people not to offer themselves for such employment: are they *choosing* not to work in a meaningful sense of that term or would they prefer to work if an appropriate position was available?

Full employment thus becomes a fluid concept, difficult to define precisely. It seems that, like Sawyer (1995b), we should accept a definition that involves matching vacancies and offers subject to an arbitrary maximum period in unemployment, bearing in mind that this already begs some questions. Even on this definition, it is clear that the United Kingdom, along with other capitalist economies, has not achieved full employment for many years.

It would seem that Kalecki's prescient forecast in 1943 is of continuing relevance today. Full employment depends on some form of institutional change. Since 1979, UK policy has concentrated on reducing rigidities in the labour market as the means to increase employment. The requirements emanating from Kalecki's insight are for much more radical change in the institutions of capitalism as a precondition for full employment, taken by many post Keynesian economists to include Keynes's own suggestion of the socialization of investment. It is easy to charge this latter position with being utopian, requiring changes in institutions that are not acceptable. Are they any more utopian or unrealistic than the changes that are required to establish a society that conforms to the models of the competitive market economy? Or is the argument there really only in terms of ultraflexibility in the labour market thereby pushing the cost of unemployment, and responsibility for it, onto the shoulders of labour and maintaining the market as a disciplinary force?

NOTES

1. Versions of this chapter have been presented to the erstwhile ESRC Post-Keynesian Economics Study Group, South Bank University and University of East London. All have provided helpful comments, as has, in particular, Philip Arestis. The usual caveat concerning author's responsibility applies.
2. Office for National Statistics, *Economic Trends: Annual Supplement*, no. 22, London: HMSO, 1996/97.
3. This is a situation in which private sector finance is involved in financing public sector projects so that it bears some or all of any risks. (See F. Terry, 'The Private Finance Initiative – Overdue Reform or Policy Breakthrough?', *Public Money and Management*, Jan.–Mar. 1996, pp. 9–16.)
4. See Price Waterhouse, 'Regulated Industries: The UK Framework', *Centre for the Study of Regulated Industries Regulatory Brief No. 2*, London: CIPFA, 1996.
5. Based on figures from Office for National Statistics, *Financial Statistics*, London: HMSO, various dates.

REFERENCES

Arestis, P. and Howells, P.G.A. (1991) 'Financial Innovations and the Distributional Effects of Interest Rate Changes in the UK', *Eastern Economic Journal*, **XVII** (3), 263–71.

Arestis, P. and Marshall, M.G. (eds) (1995) *The Political Economy of Full Employment: Conservatism, Corporatism and Institutional Change*, Aldershot: Edward Elgar.

Arestis, P. and Skuse, F.E. (1989) 'Austerity policies and the new right: recent UK experience', *Economie Appliquée*, **XLII** (1) 171–202.

Britton, A. (1996) 'The Goal of Full Employment', *National Institute of Economic and Social Research*, Report Series, no. 10, London: NIESR.

Dow, J.C.R. (1964) *The Management of the British Economy 1945–60*, Cambridge: Cambridge University Press.

Eisner, R. (1996) 'The retreat from full employment', in P. Arestis (ed.), *Employment. Economic Growth and the Tyranny of the Market: Essays in honour of Paul Davidson*, Vol. 2, Cheltenham, UK/Brookfield, US: Edward Elgar.

Galbraith, J.K. (1958) *The Affluent Society*, London: Hamish Hamilton.

Kalecki, M. (1943a) 'Political Aspects of Full Employment', *Political Quarterly*, **14** (4), reprinted in J. Osiatynski (ed.) (1990).

Kalecki, M. (1943b) *Studies in Economic Dynamics*, London: Allen & Unwin.

Kalecki, M. (1944) 'Three Ways to Full Employment', *The Economics of Full Employment: Six Studies on Applied Economics*, Oxford: Blackwell; reprinted in J. Osiatynski (ed.) (1990).

Kalecki, M. (1945) 'Full Employment by Stimulating Private Investment?', *Oxford Economic Papers*, NS, **7**, 83–92 reprinted in J. Osiatynski (ed.) (1990).

Keynes, J.M. (1936) *The General Theory of Employment, Interest and Money*, London: Macmillan.

Lindbeck, A. and Snower, D.J. (1987) 'Union Activity, Unemployment Persistence and Wage–Employment Ratchets', *European Economic Review*, **31**, 157–67.

Michl, T.R. (1995) 'Assessing the costs of inflation and unemployment', in P. Arestis and M.G. Marshall (eds), *Political Economy of Full Employment.*

Osiatynski, J. (ed.) (1990) *Collected Works of Michael Kalecki Vol. 1*, Oxford: Clarendon Press.

Sawyer, M.C. (1985) *The Economics of Michal Kalecki*, London: Macmillan.

Sawyer, M.C. (1995a) 'Obstacles to full emplyment in capitalist economies', in P. Arestis and M.G. Marshall (eds), *Political Economy of Full Employment*.

Sawyer, M.C. (1995b) 'Overcoming the barriers to full employment in capitalist economies', *Economie Appliquée*, **48** (1) 185–218.

Skuse, F.E. (1995) 'Thatcherism and unemployment in the UK', in P. Arestis and M.G. Marshall (eds), *Political Economy of Full Employment*.

Wells, J. (1995) 'Unemployment: job creation and job destruction in the UK since 1979', in P. Arestis and M.G. Marshall (eds), *Political Economy of Full Employment*.

3. Post Keynesian economic policy: continuing relevance

Philip Arestis and Murray Glickman

INTRODUCTION

As Bernard Corry and Maurice Peston would doubtless readily agree, the match between economic realities and *conventional* policy prescriptions could hardly be better than it is at present. Nation states have striven endlessly to outbid one another in providing 'business-friendly' legislative and fiscal regimes and infrastructural conditions. The labour force, universally, has been docile, 'flexibility' its watchword. The involvement of the state in the production of goods and services has been progressively retrenched. Energy has been cheap and supplies have been assured. Most significant of all, the world is in the midst of a technological revolution which, in its capacity for unleashing sheer productive power in every sector of the economy, dwarfs anything that has preceded it.

And yet this seemingly unprecedentedly favourable set of conditions has produced strikingly poor results. In fact, among the world's mature economies a yawning gulf now exists between actual and potential economic performance, as Bernard Corry and Maurice Peston have been amongst the first to point out. This chapter is written to pay tribute to their work to draw attention to this sorry state of affairs and to support their outstanding efforts to bring about change for the good in economic policy.

We begin with a brief review of the stylized facts of the recent and not so recent economic experience of the OECD countries, followed by an excursion into the economic policies we think are capable of taking us to full employment and keeping us there. A final section summarizes and concludes.

STYLIZED FACTS

The growth performance of OECD countries in recent years stands in unmistakable contrast to the pre-1973 era, as Table 3.1 makes clear. Even the relatively sluggish United Kingdom and United States did significantly better between 1966 and 1972, and especially between 1955 and 1964, than they did between 1985 and 1994. For OECD Europe, growth rates in both of these earlier periods were more than double and, for the OECD as a whole, approaching double those witnessed in recent years.[1] The overall picture is one of secularly declining growth as the post-Second World War era recedes into the past. What is more, growth in the earlier years was not only higher but, between 1966 and 1972 in particular, distinctly more stable too.

Table 3.1 Annual percentage growth rates of real GDP in OECD countries

		OECD		UK	USA
	Total	Main 7	Europe		
Average					
1955–64	4.0	n/a	4.7	2.9	3.1
1966–72	4.7	4.6	4.5	2.5	3.5
1985–94	2.5	2.5	2.2	2.1	2.5
Standard deviation					
1955–64	1.74	n/a	1.21	1.81	2.29
1966–72	0.90	1.07	0.96	0.76	1.95
1985–94	1.08	1.13	1.16	2.01	1.62
SD/Average					
1955–64	0.44	n/a	0.26	0.63	0.73
1966–72	0.19	0.23	0.21	0.31	0.55
1985–94	0.43	0.45	0.52	0.98	0.64

Source: OECD, *Main Economic Indicators*.

Table 3.2 shows, not surprisingly, that inflation rates were lower and more stable in 1985–94 than in the oil crisis era (1966–75). But, more tellingly, it also reveals that average inflation rates were nowhere significantly higher in the *pre*-oil crisis period, 1963 to 1972, than in 1985–94 and, indeed, that in the OECD as a whole, as well as in OECD Europe, inflation was clearly better under control then than it has been recently. Furthermore, with the exception of the USA, price indexes behaved less unstably in the period before the oil crisis than they have done recently.

The evidence of Table 3.2 therefore suggests that economies guided primarily by market forces have managed to suppress inflationary tendencies. The term 'suppression' is appropriate here because the picture that emerges of continuing and highly variable upward movement in consumer prices gives little reason to suppose that inflation could have been contained effectively had plentiful spare capacity not existed.

Table 3.2 Annual percentage inflation rates in consumer prices in OECD countries

	Total	OECD Main 7	Europe	UK	USA
Average					
1963–72	4.1	3.9	4.6	5.0	3.3
1966–75	6.5	6.3	7.0	8.9	5.5
1985–94	4.7	3.5	6.2	4.8	3.6
Standard deviation					
1963–72	1.09	1.13	1.16	2.11	1.57
1966–75	3.39	3.38	3.89	6.21	2.55
1985–94	1.40	1.21	1.64	2.40	1.07
SD/Average					
1963–72	0.27	0.29	0.25	0.43	0.47
1966–75	0.52	0.54	0.56	0.70	0.46
1985–94	0.30	0.35	0.26	0.50	0.29

Source: OECD, *Main Economic Indicators*.

The other side of this particular coin is that joblessness stalks whole continents. This is the message of Table 3.3, in which the most dramatic differences of all between recent experience and the pre- 1973 period are to be found, notwithstanding systematic understatement of unemployment in official statistics that take inadequate account of part-time and casual working, diminishing activity rates and underuse of skills. Unemployment between 1985 and 1994 was more than 40 per cent higher in the United States than it had been in the period 1964 to 1972 (when the US rate had itself been significantly above the OECD average). For the OECD as a group, unemployment more than doubled and, in OECD Europe as a whole and in the United Kingdom in particular, more than trebled over the same time span. What is more, unemployment rates were as stably low in the earlier period as they have been immovably high in the most recent decade.

Beyond the purview of standard economic indicators, manifestations of mass poverty are everywhere to be seen, in material deprivation, criminality, alienation and cultural *lumpen*ness (as well as in fiscal crisis). The accumulation of impressionistic evidence is increasingly being confirmed by the findings of quantitative research. The *Independent on Sunday* referred to a study which showed that in the United Kingdom the incomes of the poorest tenth of the population fell by almost 20 per cent between 1979 and 1993 (Lean and Cooper, 1996). The OECD (1996) has found evidence that the real wages of the lowest paid are falling in Australia, New Zealand and the United States.[2] Furthermore, although the focus of this chapter is on the world's mature economies, the economic failures which concern it may have global significance. Another recently published report (United Nations Development Programme, 1996) suggests that economic decline or stagnation in 100 countries has had the effect of reducing the real income of one-quarter of the world's population over the last 15 years and that the average income is lower than it was in 1980 in 70 countries and lower than in 1970 in 43 countries.

Table 3.3 Annual percentage standardized unemployment rates in OECD countries

	Total	OECD Main 7	Europe	UK	USA
Average					
1964–72	2.9	3.1	2.6	2.9	4.4
1966–75	3.3	3.4	2.9	3.2	4.9
1985–94	7.3	6.9*	9.3	9.2	6.3
Standard deviation					
1964–72	0.41	0.40	0.41	0.61	0.85
1966–75	0.75	0.77	0.51	0.59	1.42
1985–94	0.87	1.50*	1.24	1.44	0.72
SD/Average					
1964–72	0.14	0.13	0.16	0.21	0.19
1966–75	0.23	0.23	0.17	0.18	0.29
1985–94	0.12	0.22*	0.13	0.16	0.12

Note: * 1986–94.
Source: OECD, *Main Economic Indicators*.

That such should have been the outcome of macro conditions so beneficent in conventional theory terms comes as little surprise from the vantage point of post Keynesian economics, which sees the capitalist system as essentially unstable and attributes this instability to a range of inherent obstacles and constraints and, in particular, to the behaviour of private investment. Low levels of unemployment, it suggests, are likely to be the exception rather than the rule in economies governed by markets. And, if this much is true, so much the more difficult is achievement of the central policy objective of *sustaining* full employment simultaneously with reasonable price stability and healthy rates of economic growth.

The present chapter argues that reinstatement of the role of government intervention focused on the management of aggregate demand is a necessary precondition for the revival of any hope of attaining this central goal. It attempts to show that post Keynesian analysis provides a basis on which a set of policies complementary to, and supportive of, demand management – involving intervention in the capital accumulation process, a social consensus approach to macroeconomic management and measures to assert control over international financial markets – can be developed that together offer the prospect of significantly better performance than has been achieved in recent international experience. Pivotal to the whole discussion, and indeed its starting point, is the role of investment in an advanced economy with a large oligopolistic sector and the difficulty within it of maintaining a rate of capital formation capable, on the one hand, of sustaining demand at a high enough level and, on the other, of eliminating supply constraints at a fast enough rate, to enable the growth momentum that government intervention can initiate to be maintained.

The historical context of the discussion is that in reality no completely 'free' market system has ever existed.[3] Government intervention and appropriate institutions have evolved universally with the specific aim of reducing the fluctuations that are inherent in a 'free' market system. At the same time, no set of general prescriptions for government intervention exists in the abstract that can be applied in all circumstances and regardless of the specific prior macroeconomic experience of a given economy. Policy choice depends on concrete situations and here historical background as well as sociological characteristics matter crucially.

Furthermore, while full employment is a prime objective of post Keynesian economic policy, it also seeks to promote a more equal distribution of market power, income and wealth, both as a desirable goal in its own right and as a vehicle for increasing general prosperity. As Keynes (1936) remarked, 'The outstanding faults of the economic society in which we live are its failure to provide for full employment and its arbitrary and inequitable distribution of wealth and incomes' (p. 372). It seems that today's economists are close to discovering the truth of this statement for themselves. 'The future prosperity of OECD countries depends', the report cited above (OECD, 1996) asserts, 'on reducing social and economic exclusion in the forms of high unemployment, non-participation in the labour market ... and, in some instances, growing inequalities in earnings and incomes.' Meanwhile research at a global level seems to have identified 'a positive correlation between economic growth and income equality' (United Nations Development Programme, 1996).

POLICY FOUNDATIONS: INCOMES POLICIES AND SOCIALIZATION OF INVESTMENT

We begin with the standard income identities expressing the deficit/surplus relationship between the various sectors of the economy:

$$(G - T) = (S_o - I_o) + (S_r - I_r) + (Q - X) \tag{3.1}$$

where the symbols have their usual meanings, that is, G = government expenditure, T = taxes, S_o = savings of the oligopolistic sector, I_o = investment expenditure of the oligopolistic sector, S_r = savings of the rest of the economy, I_r = investment expenditure of the rest of the economy, Q = imports and X = exports.

We now assume that expansion is initiated through an increase in government expenditure (or a reduction in taxes) to achieve full employment. The deficit faced by the government sector implies a surplus in either the oligopolistic sector or the 'rest of the economy' or a deficit in the foreign sector, or some combination of all these. The public sector deficit will constrain the growth rate of the economy, a consequence which can only be avoided if the government incurs further deficits. The upshot is a state of affairs in which the government sector must be prepared to tolerate ever-mounting debt if the economy is to remain on a higher output growth path, not one that is likely to persist for very long.[4] Alternatively, provided that the deficit in the foreign sector were somehow contained, the higher growth rate could be maintained without rising public sector debt *if* domestic surplus sectors were prepared to increase their investment–output ratios or reduce their saving–income ratios, or both. We have shown elsewhere (Arestis, 1986; Arestis and Driver, 1984) that there is a great deal of doubt whether they will behave in a way conducive to this result, and we have questioned the scope for influencing their behaviour using conventional policy methods. We concluded that substantial investment in productive capacity is exactly what is required to produce a major reduction in unemployment (see also Rowthorn, 1995; Cosh *et al.*, 1995).

The need to create an appropriate investment momentum suggests that the principle of an active industrial policy merits consideration. Such a policy is in our view as critically important today as when the director of the now disbanded National Economic Development Office wrote, a decade and a half ago, 'only the government can be relied upon to concern itself with the survival of a modern and relevant industrial base' (Stout, 1981, p. 123).

Furthermore, we shall argue, a policy towards incomes might have a reasonable chance of success if it were intrinsically different from incomes policies of the past in that (1) it operated in tandem with industrial policy so that the effects of the two policies could be mutually supportive, (2) it applied to all forms of incomes without freezing their existing distribution,[5] and (3) it was accepted rather than imposed. Such a policy would need to be seen to be fair and to involve progressive redistribution of income over time. It would need to be shown that permanently holding down labour's income share was no part of its purpose. The participative support it would need from trade unions and other economic groups implies that non-governmental agents would have a substantial role to play in the formation of overall economic strategy.

The need to link appropriate industrial policies with action to regulate incomes emerges from our preceding analysis. Were the latter to bring about a decrease in S_o sufficient to produce full employment, firms would be operating in the peak capacity range. But if they were convinced that the trend output growth rate had risen, they would surely wish to return to a lower rate of capacity utilization, in order to maintain entry barriers. Restoring excess capacity, however, would involve a rise in the investment function,[6] which might be difficult to fund out of depleted savings. Furthermore, credit availability might be particularly constrained at this phase of the cycle. Firms would thus be caught between the actual decrease in S_o and the desire to increase I_o in line with the aim of securing market dominance (Arestis and Driver, 1984). Even if policy measures acting on incomes had the effect of persuading market leaders that higher investment–output ratios were desirable, they might therefore be an inadequate instrument on their own for ensuring that the economy did actually shift onto a higher investment path. On the other hand, oligopolists might in any case prefer a short period at peak capacity rather than seeking to commit themselves to faster secular growth. A tendency towards caution would be reinforced by the prospect that future governments, uncommitted to maintaining buoyancy in demand, might be in power during the critical payback period of the investments. Experience in the UK in 1963, 1972 and again in the late 1980s testifies to the reluctance of industry to risk responding to consumer-led booms either with sustained capital investment or, for that matter, with price restraint. It is doubtful that such behaviour could be changed drastically purely by a putative incomes agreement.

Industrial policy might offer a unique way out of this impasse. It might take many forms, depending on historical and social background and institutional and sociological factors (witness the range of experience in South Korea, Japan, Germany and Sweden, to name a significant few). An approach to industrial policy which sits comfortably with the analysis pursued in this chapter and also addresses the problems it identifies in a direct and systematic way derives from Keynes's observation that 'a somewhat comprehensive socialisation of investment will prove the only means of securing an approximation to full-employment; though this need not exclude all manner of compromises and of devices by which public authority will co-operate with private initiative' (1936, p. 378).

In Keynes (1980b) this notion is made more explicit: there he calls for two-thirds to three-quarters of total investment in the economy, representing 7.5 to 20 per cent of net national income, to be influenced by public or semi-public bodies, whose activities would be guided by 'private exchange' and 'technically social' motives (pp. 322–3). A stable long-term programme operating along such lines, he suggests, should be capable of reducing the potential range of fluctuations to much narrower limits than formerly, when a smaller volume of investment was under public control and when even this part tended to follow, rather than correct, fluctuations of investment in the strictly private sector (p. 322). In this way, socialization of investment could not only fill the gap left by private investors but encourage private investment by helping to create a more stable environment.[7] It is arguably a policy that has never been more relevant than in the conditions prevailing in the United Kingdom and other mature economies today, where neither rising consumer confidence, when it materializes, nor the whole panoply of market-oriented policy initiatives undertaken in recent years seem capable of energizing the will to invest. Table 3.4 makes clear the significant deterioration in investment performance in OECD economies since 1979. It also testifies to the instability of capital formation in the mature economies (most evident in the United Kingdom and United States) over the same period.

Table 3.4 Average annual percentage change in real gross fixed capital formation in OECD countries

	Total	OECD Main 7	Europe	UK	USA
1966–72					
Average	5.4	5.5	4.8	2.5	3.5
Standard deviation	1.63	1.86	2.26	1.88	4.09
SD/Average	0.30	0.34	0.47	0.76	1.16
1979–95					
Average	2.5	2.5	2.0	1.9	2.6
Standard Deviation	3.04	3.25	3.51	6.30	5.63
SD/Average	1.22	1.31	1.72	3.30	2.20
1986–95					
Average	2.8	2.6	3.0	2.1	2.2
Standard deviation	2.44	2.37	3.94	6.42	3.93
SD/Average	0.87	0.90	1.30	3.03	1.82

Source: OECD, *Economic Outlook*.

Socialization of investment constitutes a long-term policy, turning the state into a direct player. It might be implemented in a variety of ways. In this chapter, three approaches discussed in the literature will be reviewed. The first emanates from Keynes's (1982) call for the establishment of a National Investment Board (NIB) which would aim to achieve full employment by strategically regulating the aggregate flow of investment, pooling and redirecting funds accumulated in the hands of public and semi-public bodies created for the purpose. The NIB would ensure 'an adequate demand for [the funds], partly by making them available at a rate which would attract a sufficient demand and partly by stimulating the undertaking of particular investment propositions' (ibid., p. 137). A variant on this approach is the employee investment funds idea developed in Sweden (Arestis, 1986).

A second conception, also originating in Keynes's writings, envisages a separate 'capital budget' for government, distinguishing sharply between investment and consumption expenditures (see, for example, Kregel, 1985). Government should aim to produce surpluses in the ordinary budget which are then 'transferred to the capital Budget, thus gradually replacing dead-weight debt by productive or semi-productive debt'. At full employment, cyclical fluctuations should not be compensated 'by means of the ordinary Budget' but via this capital budget (Keynes, 1980b, pp. 277–8). This interpretation of socialization of investment is concerned with the composition of government expenditures and not with any increase in the share of government in the total spending of the economy. At the same time, though, public capital expenditure should be sufficient to enable government to stabilize aggregate investment spending over the business cycle. Keynes (1936) is explicit on this point when he suggests that 'State action enters in as a balancing factor to provide that the growth of capital equipment shall be such as to approach saturation-point at a rate which does not put a disproportionate burden on the standard of life of the present generation' (p. 220). Clearly, this proposal differs radically from the NIB approach.

The third interpretation of socialization of investment is the idea of 'industrial economic regulation', which again implies a long-term perspective and aims at economic regulation to foster industrial development through 'public investment in an extended infrastructure fuelling endogenous development via supportive services' (Cowling and Sugden, 1993, p. 84). The case for giving government a role of this kind arises out of the analysis expounded above and from the identification of systemic deficiencies such as those considered in Cowling (1990): multinationalism (multinational corporations dominate economies and impose their strategies upon them which threaten their development), centripetalism (the tendency for higher value economic and other activities to gravitate to the centre and away from the periphery) and short-termism (pursuit of short-term profits, a problem particularly acute in the case of multinational corporations). In seeking to tackle these deficiencies, government should adopt a 'developmental' role. This implies, in the first place, that it should actively promote an appropriately 'democratic market structure' in concert with the interest groups involved, especially employees. Cooperatives are a case in point (Cowling and Sugden, 1993, p. 89). This role should include restructuring of the financial system, possibly through a national bank to provide the main source of corporate finance and thus promote long-termism (Kitson and Michie, 1996).

The precise form 'industrial economic regulation' might take would depend on the structure of the economy in question. The institutional frameworks developed by the Japanese, other East Asian states and the 'social corporatist' countries of Europe which have successfully implemented policies of this type differ greatly from one another. But the role of the financial sector has been central, as banking experience in Germany, France and Japan, amongst other countries, testifies. For the institutional structure of an economy critically affects the impact of a given policy (for a similar view, see, for example, Eichengreen, 1996).

A clear limitation of Keynes's NIB proposal is that interest groups, crucially trade unions and cooperatives, are excluded from the participation in the process of socializing investment which is, we would argue, a *sine qua non* of its success. This is a still more serious criticism of the second, 'capital budget', conception. In this respect the industrial economic regulation approach constitutes progress on Keynes's perspective. Trade unions would, however, be far more likely to cooperate if they were to be involved in collective bargaining, which is in turn predicated upon a firm commitment to full employment. On the other hand, a social compromise of such a kind is likely to be more durable if there is successful economic restructuring of the type described here. Unemployment has been lower in countries (Austria, Finland, Norway and Sweden) in which commitment to full employment has been part of a broad consensus between trade unions, industry and the state (Glyn and Rowthorn, 1988). Furthermore, those countries which practise collective bargaining, either centralized or decentralized but with coordinated industrial relations, have a superior pay–jobs trade-off (Soskice, 1993; Rowthorn, 1992). Cross-section evidence suggests a positive relationship between collective bargaining and investment, whilst time series analysis provides no evidence that unionization adversely affects investment (Metcalf, 1993).

Evidence from the United States, the United Kingdom and Japan seems to suggest that, although decentralized wage bargaining may increase the influence of intrafirm productivity and profit trends,[8] it also encourages some workers to rent-share where their employers operate in imperfect product markets (Metcalf, 1993; Okun, 1981). This implies that decentralization favours a small minority of workers at the expense of the majority, increasing wage dispersion and, critically from the point of view of this chapter, undermining industrial relations.[9]

CONSTRAINTS AND OBSTACLES

Post Keynesian economic policy analysis openly recognizes the obstacles to interventionist policies of this type. Political and social pressures impose significant constraints. Very early on, Kalecki (1943) expressed scepticism about prospects for permanent full employment. Although governments could gear the economy to full employment, the 'power of vested interests', with their dislike of government interference, would offer resistance. Kaldor (1983) gave further support to these ideas: he contended that the changes in the power structure of society generated antagonism towards the Keynesian economic policies which produced them. As an example of such hostility, he refers (Kaldor, 1982, p. xxi) to the early postwar cheap-money policies which constrained the freedom of banks and City institutions and to which they objected, calling for a more 'active' monetary policy on the usual grounds of 'sound money'.

A different type of constraint is emphasized in the work of Myrdal (1957): his theory of 'circular and cumulative causation'. This is based on the dynamic interplay between investment and productivity growth, which reinforces inequalities and regional disparities. 'Cumulative causation' in economic terms generates inequalities in non-economic terms: regions which are relatively rich dominate, not just economically but also politically. They are in a position to impose a policy culture which accords with their own conceptions on less powerful regions, so that the distinctive institutions of the latter are put under severe threat. The policy implication of this model is intervention at a regional level via assistance to companies to locate production in depressed areas and through financial activism such as the promotion of regional banking.

The fact that these policies demand social cooperation and consensus between the state, industry and labour constitutes a further area of difficulty. But the conspicuous success of some countries with economic policies that relied on consensus (Sweden, Norway, Australia and Austria) is encouraging.[10] Indeed, there exists overwhelming evidence to suggest that, at the level of the firm, the degree of participation is one of the key determinants of productivity and that firms which involve workers in decision making experience superior profitability, sales, growth and better performance overall than similar firms which do not pursue policies of this nature (Knight and Sugden, 1989). However, in economies in which the effect of government policy has been to undermine the potential for consensus – the United Kingdom is a prime example – post Keynesian alternatives have the additional and difficult task of recreating it. It would be an advantage for industrial policies, as well as operating to achieve macroeconomic objectives, also to encourage economic activity to develop at regional and local level in a way which involved genuine community participation (Cowling and Sugden, 1993).

The operations of transnational corporations and international financial capital imply a further serious constraint. The actions of transnationals in the short run could jeopardize expansion and, indeed, UK experience indicates how real this possibility is. In the long run it can be anticipated that these firms would undertake a greater volume of investment once the economy had achieved a sustained expansionary path. In the short run, however, control over their operations would need to be established. Fiscal measures could be used to promote domestic rather than foreign investment, although the evidence here is that transnationals might easily evade the impact of measures of this type. The experience of other countries is revealing. Japan, the United States, France, Canada and, most notably, a number of developing countries have all adopted policies towards transnationals. These have ranged from monitoring their activities, and taking positive steps to discriminate in favour of domestic firms where there are fears of multinational dominance, to tighter and more direct regulation of their activities. Sugden (1989) suggests that a *transnational unit* with sufficient muscle to enable it to monitor the activities of transnationals effectively is essential. Most importantly, it would scrutinize inward and outward investment activity. This monitoring should become part of overall strategic planning (Cowling, 1987).

Similarly, policy makers can, and should, attempt to have an impact on international financial capital and trade flows. Keynes (1980b, p.52) envisaged strict capital controls to deal with situations in which the centres of international financial capital became untameable. He argued that capital controls, both inward and outward, should be permanent. Indeed, he went as far as to propose extending the idea of planning to embrace the whole of the international economic system. Hicks (1985) reinforces this view, advocating concerted action on the part of a number of the more 'important' countries. Tinbergen (1989) concurs, proposing close cooperation between the European Union (EU) and Japan.

The prospect for successful adoption of capital controls by countries like the United Kingdom would be enhanced if such measures were taken at the European level. A recent proposal (Arestis, 1993; Arestis and Sawyer, 1996) for a European Clearing Agency (ECA), in place of the European System of Central Banks, is highly relevant in this context.[11] It is predicated on the achievement of high levels of economic activity and full employment, based on the construction of a supportive EU financial system, the core element of which is a fixed, but adjustable, exchange rate system. Another proposal which sits comfortably with the idea of ECA is that of taxes on foreign exchange transactions aimed at containing speculative capital movements (see, for example, Eichengreen *et al.*, 1995). In the absence of financial costs on transfers of funds from one currency to another, even minor adverse movements in interest differentials can precipitate crises by causing large-scale shifts out of a troubled currency. A transaction tax increases the scale of interest rate movement that the system can tolerate before speculative activity is triggered, and can help contain it.[12] However, the possibility always exists that such a tax could be passed on by speculators and that it could lead to foreign exchange transactions being driven offshore. The effectiveness of a transaction tax would be greater if it covered a wider grouping of countries than just the EU. Ideally, it would be introduced under the aegis of a revamped international monetary system.

Recent developments in the world economy, such as the movement towards the reduction and elimination of exchange and credit controls, have caused the interests of finance capital and international industrial capital to converge ever more closely, increasing the power of the latter, even though conflicts of interest between finance capital and domestic industrial capital remain (Radice, 1989). In this context, collaborative measures, involving groups of countries, of the kind discussed in the preceding paragraph assume greater significance. For controlling the activities of international capital, both industrial and financial, in the new environment has become even more difficult when attempted in isolation. Globalization has weakened the economic and political basis for effective policy action at the level of individual economies, but at the same time it has created the impetus for a genuine internationalist programme. The inevitable conclusion is that the way ahead lies in the direction of explicitly and firmly 'internationalist' policies (Harcourt, 1994), what we may call 'global Keynesianism'.

SUMMARY AND CONCLUSIONS

This chapter opens with the claim that actual economic performance in the world's mature economies today signally fails to match potential. The distinctively post Keynesian common threads running through the discussion which follows it are (1) a conviction that this state of affairs is in large measure attributable to a dominant mind-set in influential policy-making circles the world over which rejects any approach lacking first-order reliance on the workings of atomistic competition, and (2) a related belief in the potential of policies based on principles of regulation, cooperation and collaboration from the supranational level down to that of the firm. The chapter calls for an industrial policy inspired by Keynes's conception of the socialization of investment. It would be based on a social consensus between the state, industry and the trade unions which would also aim to avoid wage pressures that could damage profitability and accumulation and so make it possible to reinstitute and preserve a commitment to full employment.

The approach is in the spirit of analysis and policy discussion to be found in Keynes (1936, 1980a, 1980b) and Kalecki (1971) and draws on the ideas of many influential post Keynesians. Keynes might have defended it as 'the only practicable means of avoiding the destruction of existing economic forms in their entirety and as the condition of the successful functioning of individual initiative' (Keynes, 1936, p. 380).

NOTES

1. Over the whole period between 1945 and 1973, the average annual growth rate of real GDP in OECD countries was no less than 5.9 per cent (Adelman, 1991; see also Davidson, 1996).
2. The same study questions any correlation between increased inequalities of the kind implied by these falling real wages and lower unemployment.
3. Despite attempts in certain countries to 'roll back the frontiers of the state' (the UK in the 1980s is a good example), the trend in the twentieth century has been towards more government intervention, as Sawyer (1989, p. 302) argues. Using the crude indicator of public expenditure as a proportion of GDP, he shows that for a range of developed capitalist countries this ratio has increased in each of the decades since the 1950s, including even the 1980s.
4. A budget deficit is seen as unsustainable if it leads to a spiralling national debt–GDP ratio. However, so long as the growth rate of the economy exceeds the post-tax rate of interest (whether expressed in nominal or in real terms), budget deficits need not lead to a rising debt–GDP ratio (Arestis and Sawyer, 1996). The difficulty in relation to budget deficits which has arisen in recent years is simply that real rates of interest have been at historically unprecedently high levels whilst economic growth has been sluggish. These high interest rates are attributable to the pursuit of tight monetary policies aimed at dampening down inflation. We would also make the obvious point that, insofar as the budget deficit is in effect mopping up any excess of private savings over investment, the Keynesian alternative to running a deficit would be the stimulus of investment and the discouragement of savings.
5. It is admittedly the case that incomes policies have so often failed precisely because the attempt has been made to apply them to *all* forms of incomes. A further complication in this context arises from the problems associated with the measurement of productivity in some sectors, the service sector being the obvious example.
6. Furthermore, the incremental capital – output ratio would tend to rise if capital goods were produced with more capital-intensive technology than output as a whole.
7. Which, if the post Keynesian thesis that investment behaviour is inherently unstable is correct, macroeconomic policies based on adherence to pre-announced rules will inevitably fail to achieve.
8. A study by Holmlund and Zetterberg (1991) found that, in comparison with Norway, Sweden, Finland and Germany, industrial wage setting in the United States was considerably less dependent on 'outside', economy-wide, influences and much more dependent on price and productivity conditions within industries themselves. In contrast, the Scandinavian countries' 'inside' influences on wage levels were found to be negligible.
9. Rowthorn (1992) supports this view and offers evidence which shows that centralized collective bargaining, following the Nordic model, is associated with low wage dispersion and, as already noted, better employment prospects.
10. The case of Sweden is very interesting in that, although economic policies of the type discussed here were successful for a long period, they appear to have worked less satisfactorily recently. The problems of the Swedish model may not be entirely due to weaknesses of the consensus approach but also to mistakes in the conduct of macroeconomic policy by the government in response to the globalization of the economy.

11. The ECA proposal is firmly rooted in Keynes's (1980a) International Clearing Union and, even more so, in Davidson's (1992–3) International Money Clearing Union The latter is in the spirit of Keynes but without the requirement for am international central bank.
12. A further possible advantage of the tax is that it can be a source of revenue to the government, but the essential role of the tax is to contribute to an orderly realignment of currencies when necessary.

REFERENCES

Adelman, I. (1991) 'Long Term Economic Development', *Working Paper No. 589*, Giannini Foundation of Agricultural Economics, Berkeley, California.

Arestis, P. (1986) 'Post-Keynesian Economic Policies: The Case of Sweden', *Journal of Economic Issues*, **20**(3), 709–23.

Arestis, P. (1993), 'An Independent European Central Bank: A Post-Keynesian Perspective', paper delivered at the 11th Keynes Conference, University of Kent, 19 November.

Arestis, P. and Driver, C. (1984) 'The Policy Implications of Post-Keynesianism', *Journal of Economic Issues*, December.

Arestis, P. and Sawyer, M.C. (1996) 'European Monetary Integration: A Post Keynesian Critique and Some Proposals', in P. Arestis (ed.), *Keynes, Money and the Open Economy: Essays in Honour of Paul Davidson*, Vol. 1, Cheltenham, UK/Brookfield, US: Edward Elgar.

Cosh, A., Coutts, K. and Hughes, A. (1995), 'Manufacturing, the Balance of Payments and Capacity', *Working Paper No. 12*, ESRC Centre for Business Policy, University of Cambridge, September.

Cowling, K., (1987) 'An Industrial Strategy for Britain: The Nature and Role of Planning', *International Review of Applied Economics*, November.

Cowling, K., (1990) 'The Strategic Approach to Economic and Industrial Policy', in K. Cowling and R. Sugden (eds), *A New Economic Policy for Britain*, Manchester: Manchester University Press.

Cowling, K. and Sugden, R. (1993), 'Industrial Strategy: A Missing Link in British Economic Policy', *Oxford Review of Economic Policy*, **9**(3), 83–100.

Davidson, P. (1992–3) 'Reforming the World's Money', *Journal of Post Keynesian Economics*, **15** (2), Winter, 153–79.

Davidson, P. (1996) 'Policies for Fighting Speculation in Foreign Exchange Markets: the Tobin Tax vs. Keynes's Proposals', paper presented at the Second International Conference on Keynes, Knowledge and Uncertainty, University of Leeds, March.

Eichengreen, B. (1996) 'Explaining Britain's Economic Performance: a Critical Note', *Economic Journal*, **106**(434), January, 213–18.

Eichengreen, B., Tobin, J. and Wyplosz, G. (1995) 'Two Cases for Sand in the Wheels of International Finance', *Economic Journal*, **105**(432), June, 162–72.

Glyn, A. and Rowthorn, R.E. (1988) 'West European Unemployment: Corporatism and Structural Change', *American Economic Review*, Papers and Proceedings, **78**(2), May, 194–9.

Harcourt, G.C. (1994) 'A 'Modest Proposal' for Taming Speculators and Putting the World on Course to Prosperity', *Economic and Political Weekly*, **XXIX**(38), 17 September, 2490–92; reprinted in G.C. Harcourt (ed.), *Capitalism, Socialism and Post-Keynesianism: Selected Essays of G.C. Harcourt*, Aldershot: Edward Elgar, 1995.

Hicks, J.R. (1985) 'Keynes and the World Economy', in F. Vicarelli (ed.), *Keynes's Relevance Today*, London: Macmillan.
Holmlund, B. and Zetterberg, J. (1991) 'Insider Effects in Wage Determination: Evidence from Five Countries', *European Economic Review*, **35**(5), 1009–34.
Kaldor, N. (1982) *The Scourge of Monetarism*, Oxford: Oxford University Press.
Kaldor, N. (1983) 'Keynesian Economics After Fifty Years', in D. Worswick, and J. Trevithick (eds), *Keynes and the Modern World*, Cambridge: Cambridge University Press.
Kalecki, M. (1943), 'Political Aspects of Full Employment', *Political Quarterly*, October–December.
Kalecki, M. (1971) *Selected Essays on the Dynamics of the Capitalist Economy, 1939–70*, Cambridge: Cambridge University Press.
Keynes, J.M. (1936) *The General Theory of Employment, Interest and Money*, London: Macmillan.
Keynes, J.M. (1980a) *Activities, 1940–1944: Shaping the Post-War World: The Clearing Union, The Collected Writings of John Maynard Keynes*, Vol. XXV, London: Macmillan.
Keynes, J.M. (1980b) *Activities, 1940–1946: Shaping the Post-War World: Employment and Commodities, The Collected Writings of John Maynard Keynes*, Vol. XXVII, London: Macmillan.
Keynes, J.M. (1982) *Activities, 1931–1939: World Crises and Policies in Britain and America, The Collected Writings of John Maynard Keynes*, Vol. XXI, London: Macmillan.
Kitson, M. and Michie, J. (1996) 'Britain's Industrial Performance since 1960: Underinvestment and Relative Decline', *Economic Journal*, **106**(434), January, 196–212.
Knight, B. and Sugden, R. (1989) 'Economic Democracy and a Company Act for the Twenty-First Century', in *Beyond the Review: Perspectives in Labour's Economy and Industrial Strategy*, Industrial Strategy Group, University of Edinburgh.
Kregel, J.A. (1985) 'Budget Deficits, Stabilisation Policy and Liquidity Preference: Keynes's Post-War Proposals', in F. Vicarelli (ed.), *Keynes's Relevance Today*, London: Macmillan.
Lean, G. and Cooper, Y. (1996) 'Too much for them, not enough for us...' *Independent on Sunday*, 21 July.
Metcalf, D. (1993) 'Industrial Relations and Economic Performance', *British Journal of Industrial Relations*, **31**(2), June, 255–83.
Myrdal, G. (1957) *Economic Theory and the Underdeveloped Regions*, London: Duckworth.
OECD (1996) *Employment Outlook*, 14th edn, London: HMSO.
Okun, A.M. (1981) *Prices and Quantities: A Macroeconomic Analysis*, Washington, DC: Brookings Institution.
Radice, H. (1989) 'British Capitalism in a Changing Global Economy', in A. MacEwan and N.T. Tabb (eds), *Instability and Change in the World Economy*, New York: Monthly Review.
Rowthorn, R.E. (1992) 'Centralisation, Employment and Wage Dispersion', *Economic Journal*, **102** (May), 506–23.
Rowthorn, R.E. (1995) 'Capital Formation and Unemployment', *Oxford Review of Economic Policy*, **11**(1), 26–39.
Sawyer, M.C. (1989) *The Challenge of Radical Political Economy: An Introduction to the Alternatives to Neo-Classical Economics*, Hemel Hempstead: Harvester Wheatsheaf.

Soskice, D. (1993) 'Wage Determination: The Changing Role of Institutions in Advanced Industrial Countries', *Oxford Review of Economic Policy*, **6**(4), 36–61.

Stout, D.K. (1981) 'The Case for Government Support of R&D and Innovation', in C. Carter (ed.), *Industrial Policy and Innovation*, London: Heinemann.

Sugden, R. (1989) 'The International Economy: Britain at the Mercy of Transnationals?', *Beyond the Review: Perspectives in Labour's Economy and Industrial Strategy*, Industrial Strategy Group, University of Edinburgh.

Tinbergen, J. (1989) 'How to Reduce Unemployment', *Review of Political Economy*, **1**(1), March, 1–6.

United Nations Development Programme (1996) *Human Development Report* 7th edn, New York: Oxford University Press.

PART II

The Independent Central Bank

4. The privatization of monetary policy

Keith Bain and Peter Howells

INTRODUCTION

Those of us old enough to have taught macroeconomics during the 1970s owe a considerable debt to Maurice Peston for his *Theory of Macroeconomic Policy* (1982), a book whose two editions were notable for their clarity of exposition and for the insights which came from Maurice's own experience of being at the heart of macroeconomic policy making. It is an indication of the scale of change that has taken place in macroeconomics that no such text is thought necessary today and that those of us who wish to explain to students that government behaviour may still have some impact on real aggregates have to call upon the diminishing number of copies of Maurice's excellent book.

This chapter documents the demise of one strand of macroeconomic stabilization policy. In doing so, it demonstrates the ability of ideas, at one time seemingly dead and buried, to re-emerge, sometimes in more virulent form. In this way it relates also to an area of economics which has always been of interest to Bernard Corry – the historical development of economic ideas and the relationship between this and political change. This interest was shown in Bernard's first book, *Money, Saving and Investment in English Economics, 1800–1850* (Corry, 1962), and most recently in his paper, 'Politics and the Natural Rate of Unemployment' (Corry, 1996).

The 'privatization of monetary policy' is a phrase we have used before.[1] The phrase summarizes two ideas. The first is that what has happened in monetary policy in recent years can best be understood as part of the general attack on the role of government in mixed capitalist economies which has dominated mainstream economics over the past two decades. On this view, what has happened to monetary policy is comparable to the process of privatization of the nationalized industries. The second idea is that recent theory and practice represent a more extreme version of the pre-Keynesian norm that economic policy, even when nominally controlled by governments, should be conducted in the interests of the most powerful groups in the economy.

Putting these two ideas together, it is easy to draw the conclusion that monetary policy has completed a full circle since the late nineteenth century, passing through a brief period of democratic management before returning to the longer-term orthodoxy of central banks acting independently of government and people. This is broadly true, but misleading in some interesting details. For example, we will show that while monetary policy prior to Britain's second departure from the Gold Standard in 1931 was effectively in the hands of finance capital, there was considerable resistance to the existing policy and great concern was expressed in many quarters regarding the effects of policy and the power of the Bank of England. The present enthusiasm for independent central banks (ICBs) has, by contrast, been accompanied by much less critical debate.[2] The triumph of international finance capital over democratically elected governments appears far more complete than ever it was in the gold standard era. Just as privatization in the industrial sector has represented a good deal more than the 'denationalization' of a few industries, the privatization of monetary policy has taken us to new levels in the private control of that policy.

The notion of a private monetary policy encompasses two elements: the nature of the institution determining the policy and the purposes the policy serves. Until the First World War, and during the period 1925–31,[3] these two elements went together. Adherence to the gold standard ensured that British monetary policy was in the hands of the Bank of England, a privately owned bank which conducted a policy favourable to its owners and directors. The advice of industrialists was largely ignored. There can be no doubt that the concentration on the avoidance of inflation and the maintenance of London as a leading financial centre in relation to the low importance attached to employment and the balance of trade were particularly favourable to finance capital and that there were a large number of losers in the rest of the economy.

The (re-)constitution of independent central banks in recent times, however, involves a deliberate and conscious act by (more or less) democratically elected governments to give power away. Furthermore, the power is being transferred to institutions which remain publicly owned and whose constitutions must therefore be carefully designed to protect them from the pressure of democratic choice. Consequently, far greater intellectual effort has been required to mount the case for (modern) independent central banks than was ever necessary under the gold standard. Much of this effort has been directed at persuading the majority, with little to gain from 'institutionalized deflation', that all other options are worse.

The present chapter is organized on broadly historical lines. The next section provides a detailed account of the operation of monetary policy from 1870 to 1939. We will see that frequent doubts were expressed about the consequences for the real economy, and for the balance of interest between rentier and worker, of following the gold standard's imperatives. Losers there most certainly were, but they were clearly recognized as such and they did not go down without a struggle.

In 1946, following the Beveridge plan and the elevation of full employment to an objective of macroeconomic policy, monetary policy could be said to have been nationalized, along with the Bank of England. The third section considers this period. By 1976, changes were under way and the 1980s and 1990s saw crucial alterations in both the approach to policy and in institutional arrangements. The fourth section deals with this period, highlighting the weakness of opposition to these developments. The final sections conclude by attempting to explain modern developments and considering how they might be understood in terms of the theory of macroeconomic policy.

MONETARY POLICY IN BRITAIN PRIOR TO 1939

Like most indispensable phrases, the 'gold standard *system*' can mislead. As Drummond has pointed out 'no one designed it, ... no international agency administered it, or brooded about it. Each country did what it liked, taking its own decisions about monetary matters' (1987, p. 9). Furthermore, while most of the world's trading countries were on the gold standard from 1900 to 1914, it is impossible to date the start of the 'system' since countries joined at different times and held to it with varying degrees of commitment and success (Bordo and Schwartz, 1996).

In spite of the fact that par values had been fixed with no reference to the balance of payments or to degrees of international competitiveness, this system of fixed exchange rates worked well from 1870 to 1914 for the major trading countries. Traditionally, 'worked well' has been understood to mean that world trade expanded rapidly, with few suspensions or devaluations (outside Latin America at least). More recently, however, research has followed the recent ICB literature in seeking to show that the pre-1914 gold standard functioned as a contingent rule (Bordo and Kydland, 1995) and that those countries which adhered most consistently to the standard enjoyed a reputational advantage which enabled them to raise long-term capital at rates of interest which incorporated lower risk premia (Bordo and Rockoff, 1996).

For many years, the smooth functioning of the system was ascribed to the specie-flow mechanism outlined by David Hume. It was essentially this mechanism that contemporaries had in mind in giving evidence to the Cunliffe (1918) and Macmillan (1931) committees. However, this consensus began to break down in the 1950s and rival explanations began to emerge, as described in Drummond (1987). Just as the benefits have come to reflect the recent ICB literature, so too has the mechanism. True to the spirit of our times, the most recent work stresses the importance of expectations and credibility. Jeanne (1995) uses monthly data in a structural VAR in order to trace the linkages between a gold outflow and domestic monetary variables. The results suggest that an outflow of gold led automatically to a rise in market interest rates because markets knew that the Bank of England was credibly committed to a fixed exchange rate and confidently expected interest rates to be raised if necessary.

Whatever may have been the mechanism, the instruments of monetary policy were few, simple and, crucially, in the hands of the central banks. Central banks, not government treasuries, held the gold reserve and they alone had the power to impose interest rate changes and to make them effective. The power and independence that this gave to central banks, which lies at the core of the commitment literature referred to here, was widely recognized by contemporary and later commentators.

The organization of the Bank of England and the way in which it exercised its power were subject to considerable contemporary criticism. For example, Bagehot's *Lombard Street*, which first appeared in 1873 and is often cited as the first textbook on central banking, was critical of some procedures, in particular the Bank's 'rules of thumb' by which it determined the size of the reserves that it needed to hold and of the practice, established 'by old usage', whereby the directors of the Bank could not themselves be 'trade bankers'. This bothered Bagehot because he felt it excluded from representation the majority of interests which were affected by the Bank's decisions; it is also the origin of the criticism often made of the parity decision in 1925 that it was made by bankers whose interests lay narrowly in overseas finance and not in the domestic economy.

The Bank's independence was a source of recurring irritation also to Gladstone:

> From the time I took office as Chancellor of the Exchequer (1852) I began to learn that the State held, in the face of the Bank and the City, an essentially false position as to finance ... The hinge of the whole system was this: the Government itself was not to be a substantive power in matters of finance but was to leave the Money Power supreme and unquestioned. In the conditions of that situation, I was reluctant to acquiesce, and I began to fight against it. (Morley (1903), *Life of Gladstone*, vol. I, p. 518)

As Clapham points out in his history of the Bank of England, most of Gladstone's disputes with the Bank concerned aspects of debt management and coupon payments (Clapham, vol. II, 1944, pp. 251–6) but they embraced interest rate policy as well. Chapter 8 contains a sustained commentary on the mechanical response of bank rate to gold flows 'while the Court or the Governor operated without explanation or self-justification' (ibid., p. 387). This behaviour is confirmed in Sayers' later history:

> the accepted doctrine both inside and outside the Bank was that its most important action was the fixing of Bank Rate, announced each week before the Court of Directors proceeded to less important business. In this regular and public action the

> pre-1914 generation regarded the Bank of England as exercising its power as the central bank.... Despite the significance attached, through decade after decade, to this regular function of the Bank, there is not the slightest indication in the court or Committee of the Treasury records of the reasoning on which each week's action was based. The Court merely minuted its acceptance of the Governor's proposal. (Sayers, vol. I, 1976, pp. 28–9)

The *Report* of the Cunliffe Committee has long been recognized as a valuable source of information on the way contemporaries thought monetary policy under the gold standard worked. Writing in 1935, Sir Charles Morgan-Webb produced a very hostile treatise on the conduct of monetary policy between 1922 and 1932 (a period dominated by the short-lived return to gold) using material from the Cunliffe *Report* as evidence that bankers knew the effects upon industry that a bank rate policy in support of a fixed exchange rate would have, and that they felt such effects to be necessary and inevitable (Morgan-Webb, 1935, pp. 57–60). The same point is made by the biographer of Montagu Norman (governor from 1920 to 1944).

> Among the thousands of diary entries referring to many and varied cares of office, there are less than half a dozen oblique allusions to the specific problems of domestic unemployment and industrial stagnation. By and large, Norman believed himself to be above such issues. (Boyle, 1967, p. 142)

Norman's attitude to his relationship with parliament is shown clearly by entries in the diary of Emile Moreau, governor of the Bank of France. Moreau mentions plans on the part of Norman and other leading financiers to make London the leading international financial centre, an objective which has often been cited as one reason for the determination to return to gold quickly and at $4.86. The diary continues:

> Apart from all issues of centralization, he wants more than anything else to witness the setting up of links between the various Banks of Issue, even without his initiative.... In his view politicians and political institutions are in no fit state to direct with the necessary competence and continuity this task of organization which he would like to see undertaken by central banks. (Moreau, quoted in Boyle, 1967, p.205)[4]

In Pollard's view (Pollard, 1970), this ambitious plan failed only because no other central bank enjoyed the Bank of England's dominance over political authority.

Since our argument is that the gold standard mechanism itself was largely instrumental in giving control over monetary policy to central banks, it is interesting to look at the key moments of movement onto and off gold. The official departure from the gold standard occurred in March 1919 and by July the governor of the Bank of England, Brian Cokayne, was writing to the chancellor of the exchequer, Neville Chamberlain, that 'We regard it as urgent in the public interest that power to control the market should at once be restored to the Bank'[5] and again in September, '*If the Bank had been free to exercise their* [sic] *proper functions* they would long ago have taken steps to raise the value of money in the Country in order to protect the exchanges'.[6] Susan Howson, in her detailed study of British monetary policy between the wars, also makes the point that 'in 1919 control of monetary policy rested with the Treasury rather than the Bank of England' (Howson, 1975, p. 11)[7] and emphasizes in a more recent paper that abandoning the short-lived return to the Gold Standard (1925–31) had the effect of moving power over monetary policy *back* to the Treasury (Howson, 1988, p. 548).

Clearly, then, the operation of the gold standard gave considerable independence to the Bank of England, an independence recognized at the time and widely accepted by commentators to the present day. But what evidence is there that this independence was viewed more critically at the time than similar independence is viewed in the current ICB literature? Although historians of the Bank have simply documented the independence without comment, many of those who commented on the independence of central banks in the gold standard era did so from a position of anxiety. As we have already seen, this is apparent in Gladstone, and in two of Norman's biographers. Many other voices were quite explicit about the objectionable nature of a monetary policy operated by central banks responding to the dictates of the gold standard. The most frequently cited objective was the 'institutionalization of deflation', to borrow a phrase used in the current ICB literature (Parley, 1996), though when it came to details the cost of this was seen by some as favouring creditors over debtors and by others as giving priority to exchange rate stability over stability of output and employment.

Favouring creditors over debtors was a theme throughout the later nineteenth century and a leading propagandist was W.J. Bryan who insisted that 'Mankind has been crucified on a cross of Gold' (Bryan, 1896), a phrase that was taken up by both sides in the argument.[8] Pamphlets circulated in the United Kingdom and in continental Europe arguing that the adoption of the single metallic standard had (or had not) benefited the rentier class at the expense of workers. Writing in Belgium in 1897, Alphonse Allard alleged that 'Faithful to this duty – the duty of keeping and increasing their fortunes – the financiers of our age have found the means, hitherto unknown, of increasing their riches' (Allard, 1897). It was attacks like this that led to the formation of the Gold Standard Defence Association (president, Sir John Lubbock MP) which retaliated with a series of pamphlets, conferences and letters to the press.[9]

The second theme, the preference for a stable exchange rate over a stable real economy, understandably came to the fore in the later period surrounding the decision to return to gold in 1925, in circumstances of a major slump in the United Kingdom's export industries. Keynes's fulminations about the workers having to bear the 'adjustments' required by the decision to overvalue sterling in 1925 are well known (Keynes, 1931) but attempts to suggest that his was a lone voice (for example, Sayers, 1960) are not now sustainable (Pollard, 1970). The British Association issued a *Report* in 1921, with contributions from Clapham, Guillebaud, Lavington and Robertson debating the choice of exchange rate (British Association, 1921) and as the return to gold became imminent, G.D.H. Cole, John Wheatley and even Philip Snowden were amongst well-known figures on the left raising objections in the press and in parliament (Adams Brown, 1929, ch. 10).

But more fundamental objections were raised. One might have expected objections of principle to emanate from the left, and it seems to be true that the Trades Union Congress (TUC) was more radical on this issue than the Labour Party itself (Pollard, 1969). However, the most explicit questions about the balance between internal and external stability and between the interests of rentier and worker implied by a fixed exchange rate regime 'managed' by the Bank of England came from sections of industry and, perhaps most surprisingly, from the retail banking sector of the City. 'The Mond–Turner Conferences, which were in part responsible for the Macmillan Committee, made the protest against the gold standard one of their main concerns' (Pollard, 1970, pp. 6–7), while Sir Alfred Mond himself raised the objection to having monetary conditions in Britain dictated by external factors in the debate over return in March 1925, referring this time to the British economy being 'hanged [*sic*] on a cross of gold' (182 *HC Deb. 5s*, pp. 786–7).

The *Bankers' Magazine* was consistently hostile to the Cunliffe *Report*, regularly complaining that it had not paid aufficient attention to those voices which had argued repeatedly over the years for reform of the Bank Charter Act and the gold standard (*BM*, 106, 1918, pp. 523–4). The same observation was made by *The Times* (30 October 1918). The fundamental objection lay with the frequency of bank rate changes required by the combination of the 1844 Act with the gold standard and this was a theme which was kept before the public by Felix Schuster and E.H. Holden, respectively chairman of the Union Bank of London and managing director of the London, City and Midland Bank. The campaigns organized by the two men and the supporters that they attracted are detailed in Hume (1963) (see also Clapham, vol. I, 1944 pp. 366–415 and *The Economist*, 1 February 1919, pp. 145–7). The criticism of the whole system continued, however, in the pages of *The Economist* and in reports from the Federation of British Industries, which called repeatedly between 1921 and 1924 for a new committee to be established to look at alternative ways of conducting monetary policy (Hume, 1963, pp. 131–3, 139–44).

The United Kingdom's commitment to the gold standard ended on 20 September 1931. Bank rate was raised to 6 per cent but a series of reductions during 1932 took it to 2 per cent in July, where it remained until August 1939. The most detailed (and contrasting) discussions of the origin of this cheap money policy have been provided by Nevin (1953) and Howson (1975), the former stressing low interest rates as a by-product of foreign exchange policy, the latter stressing evidence that the Treasury had wanted low interest rates from as early as 1926, specifically for recovery purposes. Furthermore, according to Howson (1975, ch. 4 and p. 142), the Treasury had occasionally 'managed' the currency in practice in the late 1920s but was frustrated because the principle of management was in conflict with the 'automatic' mechanism which was supposed to operate under the gold standard. If this is true, it suggests that, by 1930, scepticism about a monetary policy conducted independently of elected representatives penetrated right to the heart of the administrative system. In its 1931 *Report*, the Macmillan Committee endorsed this scepticism: 'in the case of our financial, as in the case of our political and social, institutions we may well have reached the stage when an era of conscious and deliberate management' is justified (Committee on Finance and Industry, 1931, para. 9).

THE NATIONALIZATION OF MONETARY POLICY

After 1945, monetary policy became just one instrument to be used in conjunction with others in the attempt to achieve jointly a set of goals. The choice of goals and, where choices had to be made, the weights attached to them were clearly influenced by the desire of governments to be re-elected. By and large, politicians acted to provide the sort of monetary policy voters appeared to want. In this picture, experts were held to be subject to the political will and to practise their positive economics within the normative framework determined by the elected government. Markets were required to operate within this framework and were subject to government control. In other words, monetary policy was partly a reflection of the operation of democracy.

The word 'partly' is important here. After all, between 1945 and 1972, monetary policy was again constrained by membership of a fixed exchange rate system. That there remained, in contrast to the Gold Standard period, scope for other influences was due to four factors. Firstly, although Britain was forced on several occasions towards the peak of trade cycles to place the maintenance of balance of payments balance ahead of other policy goals, the United States as leader of the Bretton Woods system could not be said to have imposed consistent deflationary pressure on other countries. Secondly, Britain increased its freedom to choose its own monetary policy through the devaluations of 1949 and 1967, though the pressure from finance capital against devaluations ensured that no others occurred and that the two which did take place were delayed as long as possible. Thirdly, the restrictions on international capital flows, especially up to the introduction of non-resident convertibility in 1958, allowed British interest rates to be kept lower than would otherwise have been possible without jeopardizing the exchange rate. In Britain, direct controls over the money supply continued to have some purchase until the 1960s and this too provided some extra freedom in the setting of domestic interest rates. Finally, the view that monetary policy and fiscal policy should work together (aided later by incomes policy) allowed monetary policy to play a part in an overall economic strategy influenced to some extent by all groups in the economy.

In the immediate postwar period, it was felt that 'in spite of the need to borrow heavily from North America to cover the balance-of-payments deficit domestic monetary policy could, because of extensive controls, be conducted without much regard for external considerations' (Howson, 1988, p. 558). This freedom was used to maintain the cheap money policy which had been in existence until 1939. Dalton, the first Labour chancellor, assumed that interest rates could be set wherever the authorities wanted them. Early doubts arose, however, about the ability of the authorities to control long-term interest rates and from early 1949 the Bank of England regarded a rise in short-term interest rates as essential, sooner or later, to curb bank lending. This was resisted by the Labour government, but the Bank finally got its way following the Conservative election victory in October 1951. The cheap money policy disappeared and the ability of the authorities to control interest rates was steadily eroded. Nonetheless, there was an attempt to keep interest rates stable because this was thought to be required for debt management at least in the short run – and direct controls were maintained on the growth of bank advances to help to achieve this. These, however, were undermined by the growth of non-clearing banks and then of non-bank financial intermediaries which operated outside the controls. In the 1970s, monetary policy concerns took on a much higher profile as indicated by the institution in 1976 of targets for the rate of growth of the money supply. Although direct controls over bank behaviour continued for much of the period, the rhetoric of the time was in favour of the use of the interest rate as the instrument of control of the money supply and the institution of greater competition within money markets.

In countries later characterized as 'wet' or 'soft on inflation', high employment levels were accompanied during the postwar period by marked movements towards more equitable income distributions, while inflation remained at politically acceptable levels. This apparent democratization of economic policy could not last. The rapid increase in international capital mobility through the 1960s caused the fixed exchange rate system to bite more ferociously as the United States came under consistent pressure from financially conservative governments to restrict the outflow of dollars. In Britain, financial institutions grew in strength and found it increasingly easy to bypass direct monetary controls. The interest rate was more and more required to protect the fixed exchange rate and so could less easily be used for domestic policy purposes. The control of monetary policy had begun to move towards financial markets and away from the political system.

THE PRIVATIZATION OF MONETARY POLICY

The process of privatization of monetary policy in Britain has been drawn out and somewhat uneven, largely because institutional developments have been slow to catch up with the realities of policy. The movement towards the privatization is probably best dated from 1979 with the removal of all controls over foreign exchange transactions since this destroyed any possibility that the British economy could be partly isolated from the effects of the vast amount of capital moving around the world, largely in search of profits from purely financial transactions. Steadily, limitations on capital mobility were removed in other countries, with a major step being the acceptance of full capital mobility as part of the Single European Market.

Theoretical developments within mainstream economics, discussed below, emphasized the idea that markets generally, but financial markets in particular, now dominated governments. Since the principal concern of financial markets was, for obvious reasons, the maintenance of low inflation, all that was seemingly left to policy makers was to demonstrate the credibility of their anti-inflation policies and build up anti-inflation reputations. Following the failure of a short-lived dash for lower unemployment in France in the early 1980s, political opposition to deflationary policies faded away.

Policy disagreements centred on mechanisms. The debate over UK membership of the European Monetary System (EMS) and economic and monetary union (EMU) could be expressed in terms of a choice between fixed and floating exchange rates, with floating rates giving the government control over its own monetary policy. But if that monetary policy were to be placed in the hands of an independent central bank which needed to follow deflationary policies, the choice would be more apparent than real. Despite the heat that the EMS/EMU debate has produced, it has lacked importance from the perspective of monetary policy to the extent that monetary policy has been dominated by the need to achieve and maintain anti-inflation credibility in the eyes of the markets. Amidst major redistributions of income in many countries, the losers largely disappeared from sight.

The ideas triumphed amongst academic economists. High unemployment rates became 'natural' and hence seemingly unchallengeable. The financial markets came to be seen as so powerful and resourceful that governments could not hope to resist. Economists (for example, Garber and Taylor, 1995) stressed the impossibility of modest proposals to reassert some control over financial markets such as the 'Tobin tax' (Eichengreen *et al.*, 1995). Belief in the invisible hand of the market became absolute, but these were no longer the perfectly competitive markets of economic theory but markets dominated by large financial institutions whose activities were at best only tenuously related to the real economy.

In institutional terms, the Bundesbank became the symbol of austerity policies, even though it did not always follow its own caricature. Despite the fact that politicians everywhere showed themselves willing to accept the dictates of the markets, they remained unreliable and the notion strengthened that monetary policy had to be removed from their control and be placed in the hands of politically independent central banks modelled on the Bundesbank. Experts (bankers and economists) were no longer held to act within a normative framework provided by elected governments. Indeed, this model had been neatly reversed. The framework was to be provided by the markets and bankers and elected governments needed to be held in check by the constraints so provided. In practice, this meant that the normative decisions were taken by the financial markets. An independent central bank also only has power to the extent that its policy is held to be credible. This is freely acknowledged by the Bundesbank itself:

> Against the growing globalization of the financial markets, Germany was unable to disengage itself from the international interest rate trend, it is true, but, given the credible anti-inflationary thrust of monetary policy, interest rates in Germany rose less than in most other countries .... an aggressive interest-rate-cutting strategy on the part of the central bank ... would have been doomed to failure. It would have risked causing mistrust in the future movement of the domestic and external value of the currency, and in the final analysis would probably have led to higher, rather than lower, capital market rates. (Deutsche Bundesbank, 1995, p. 71)

MONETARY POLICY AND THE THEORY OF MACROECONOMIC POLICY

For much of the postwar period, the study of macroeconomics included the theory of macroeconomic policy based on the work of Tinbergen (1952) and Theil (1964).[10] This sought to provide a theoretical basis for government intervention in the macroeconomy. It is of interest to relate the developments we have discussed above to that theory and to its demise.

We have seen above that the privatization of monetary policy requires the decentralization of macroeconomic policy, with monetary policy being placed in the hands of a separate institution (the central bank) which is given the predominant task of achieving a single goal of policy (the control of inflation). In terms of the standard theory of macroeconomic policy, to be able to do this should require:

1. that the chosen instrument be efficient with respect to the chosen target, in the sense that only a small change in the instrument variable is needed to produce a significant impact on the target variable;
2. that changes in the instrument variable not have important effects on other policy targets; and
3. that the instrument be capable of being controlled independently of other policy instruments.

In line with the discussion above, we will assume that our target variable is the rate of inflation either directly or indirectly through the maintenance of a fixed exchange rate. In Britain, the instrument has always been the rate of interest: the money stock has been either a by-product of the fixed exchange rate or a rather uncertain indicator of the required change in interest rate.

In a world of highly mobile capital, the interest rate is only an efficient instrument for the maintenance of a fixed exchange rate when financial markets judge that the existing peg is sustainable. Any speculative pressure against that peg requires extremely high short-term interest rates if there is to be any hope of the pressure being resisted. In other words, the interest rate can only function effectively if used in conjunction with policies which ensure that strong speculative pressure against the currency does not occur. Where the exchange rate is variable and the target becomes the rate of inflation itself, recent experience has demonstrated that the rate of interest is anything but an effective instrument, again unless it is supported by other policies. Once inflationary pressure exists in an economy, interest rates need to be raised up very sharply in order to have an effect on the desire of consumers and firms to borrow and spend. The impact is long-drawn-out and the usual outcome of the ultimately very high interest rates is to send the economy into a sharp decline, recovery from which may be very slow. This hardly provides support for the interest rate as a decentralized instrument of policy.

This last point also means that the interest rate fails our second requirement since, even though the effects may occur only slowly, interest rates do have a significant impact on real variables, largely because of the impact of high interest rates on the confidence of consumers and firms. Further, we have seen that the growth in the number of mortgagees in the personal sector, together with various aspects of financial innovation, have increased the ultimate impact of interest rate policy on the real sector as well as on the distribution of income (Arestis and Howells, 1992).

Finally, the acceptance of the budget constraint by economists calls the third requirement strongly into question. It remains possible to operate monetary and fiscal policies which work in opposite directions. For example, it is possible, as the United States demonstrated in the early 1980s, to combine a tight monetary policy with a loose fiscal policy, but the high interest rates push up the exchange rate and increase the cost of financing the public debt, causing future problems for fiscal policy. An independent central bank at odds with a government could easily generate a series of back-and-forth uncoordinated actions, causing target variables to fluctuate around their target values with increasing amplitude. In short, there appears to be little basis for support from the theory of macroeconomic policy for placing the interest rate in the hands of an independent central bank.

Plainly, this problem disappears if there is only one target of macro policy and one effective instrument. This was provided in the classical model with its separation of the real and monetary sectors. It, however, was overly dependent on assumptions of fully flexible prices. In practice, the real effects of tight monetary policies associated with the maintenance of the gold standard were only too obvious. Further, as Bernanke (1995) notes, countries who left the gold standard earlier recovered from depression during the 1930s more rapidly than those who did not. More imaginative support for the privatization of monetary policy was clearly necessary.

Modern Theoretical Support for the Privatization of Monetary Policy

Attacks in the 1950s and early 1960s on the ability of governments to operate monetary policy were practical in nature, concentrating on the existence of time lags of variable length and the inability of economists to construct models which would forecast accurately. These arguments were later strengthened by the Lucas critique of forecasting models (Lucas, 1976). Such forms of attack, however, left open the possibility that even imperfect attempts at discretionary policy might produce outcomes preferable to those which would arise from a failure to intervene.

Thus the principal aim of the theoretical attack was switched to the denial of the existence of a trade-off between inflation and unemployment. But the initial argument, based on the expectations-augmented Phillips curve, related only to the long run. A trade-off still existed in the short run and, since the short run was merely an expression of a period in which an economy was not in equilibrium, it could represent a significant period of calendar time – certainly long enough from the point of view of voters to justify operating economic policy as if there were a trade-off. Clearly, more support was needed for the *laissez-faire* case.

This came with the application of rational expectations to the market-clearing neoclassical model, leading to the construction of policy ineffectiveness models in which governments could not hope to increase employment even in the short run. Since there were now no real benefits to offset the costs of higher inflation, we no longer (it seemed) had to worry about calculating the costs of inflation. The control of inflation had become once more the only target of macro policy.

Of course, there were problems associated with the realism of rational expectations: the fact that the market-clearing equilibrium at the heart of the new classical model was just a theoretical construct, and inconvenient continued failures to provide empirical support for the natural rate hypothesis (Cross, 1995) or to demonstrate an actual link between lower rates of inflation and higher rates of economic growth. However, as Corry suggests (Cross, 1995), the victories of new paradigm models are seldom, if ever, related to empirical 'refutations' of the replaced paradigm and often owe much to political acceptability. The argument for the privatization of monetary policy came to rest entirely upon the importance of credibility and reputation. Tight monetary policies, it was held, would only cause problems for the real sector of the economy to the extent that they were not held to be credible. Lack of credibility derived in turn from a poor reputation in the control of inflation and institutions which placed the levers of monetary policy in the hands of politicians (and hence the voters – we are back to the theory of the knaves). Semi-miraculously, independent central banks with a reputation for low inflation restore the position of money as only a veil over the real economy.

In such a model, interest rates must be an efficient instrument for an independent bank with a good inflation reputation, since the central bank virtually needs to do nothing to maintain its low inflation other than to maintain the confidence of the markets by keeping interest rates aufficiently high, moving them up in the face of inflationary shocks. If government macroeconomic intervention can have no positive effects, there is no need for a theory of macroeconomic policy. Politicians and voters had been eclipsed in economic theory as well as in practice.

CONCLUSION: THE ABSENCE OF OPPOSITION

We have seen that the privatization of monetary policy has returned the operation of monetary policy to its position under the Gold Standard, nominally under the control of an independent central bank but with policy in effect determined by the financial sector through its ability to put pressure on exchange rates and interest rates through the movement of capital. This ensured the dominant position of the control of inflation as a target of policy. We saw, however, that in the Gold Standard period this view was vigorously challenged, and it was accepted that there would be many losers from it. Modern economic theory has returned us to the classical position in which there are no real losers through the effective separation of the real and monetary sectors of the economy. In fact, as we have noted, the impact of monetary policy on the real economy has, if anything, increased. The link between the real and monetary sectors is accepted by the financial markets themselves. Thus any indication of tightness in labour markets causes the financial markets to fear inflation. Capital leaves the economy putting downward pressure on the exchange rate and increases still further the fear of inflation. A credible independent central bank will push up interest rates and, in expectation of this, stock prices fall. It is a familiar story. The puzzle is to explain the lack of opposition from those who have, indeed, lost.

One possible explanation can be found in industrial decline and the great reduction in the strength of industrial capital relative to finance capital. A second lies in the increased centralization of both government and private sector institutions. In the United Kingdom, a third lies in the repeated failure of the Labour Party to be elected, together with the increased sophistication of the analysis of marginal voters and the factors likely to influence them. Thus it has been decided that British elections hang on the votes of a small number of middle-income voters in relatively affluent constituencies who are more worried by inflation than by the prospect of unemployment and are assumed to be likely to vote for the party with the tougher anti-inflation stance. The economic stance of the Labour Party in opposition (including support for an independent central bank) can then be seen as an attempt to overcome its past reputation of being 'soft' on inflation (Milesi-Ferretti, 1995). This analysis suggests that, in a modern representative democracy in which, for the majority of voters, the choice they face is between voting for the party they have always supported or not voting at all, the views of the majority are largely irrelevant.

The worry must be that the lack of opposition to the independence of central banks (and all that this implies in terms of policy choices) derives from an increased acceptance among workers, industrialists, politicians and voters (and, increasingly, non-voters) of their inability to influence the real economy.

NOTES

1. In a paper given at the conference to mark the tenth anniversary of the publication of *Economies et Sociétés*, Série 'Monnaie et Production', held at the Faculté Jean Monnet, Université de Paris Sud, Paris, April 1996.
2. On 6 May 1997 (after the drafting of this chapter), the newly-elected UK Labour government announced its decision to pass responsibility for interest rate determination to the Bank of England. The announcement was met with overwhelming enthusiasm, even securities markets *rising* in response to the prospect of higher interest rates.
3. In practice, the determination of the City to ensure the return to gold meant that monetary policy between 1919 and 1925 was carried out with the return to gold largely in mind. Thus it cannot be compared with the period after 1931.
4. These plans are a major theme of an intensely hostile biography of Norman written by John Hargrave. There is no date of publication but details suggest that it must have been published between 1940 and 1943. On p. 66, Hargrave describes Norman's plan as 'A bankers' league-of-nations, built up quietly, without any fanfare of trumpets'. See also ch. 10.
5. Public Record Office, Treasury Files, box no. 172 (Chancellor of the Exchequer's Office – Miscellaneous Papers) file no. 1059, letter from Governor to Chancellor.

6. PRO Cab. 27, Cabinet Committees, vol. 72, Finance Committee, letter from Governor to Chancellor, 25.9.19; emphasis added.
7. Though she goes on to say that the Treasury was scarcely in control either, policy being dictated by Prime Minister Lloyd George and cabinet colleagues.
8. See, for example, the pamphlet, *Unemployment and the Gold Standard* by T.B. Johnston, chairman of a number of major west country firms. Critical of the gold standard system in principle, it used the quotation from Bryan on its cover.
9. The full story of this organization has yet to be told and would obviously repay further research. One of the pamphlets (no. 31), was written by Lord Farrer and entitled 'Has the Gold Standard made the Rich Richer and the Industrious Poorer?'
10. See, for example, Peston (1982).

REFERENCES

Adams Brown Jr, W. (1929) *England and the New Gold Standard, 1919–26*, New Haven: Yale University Press; reprinted in S. Pollard (ed.) (1970).

Allard, A. (1897) *Démocratie Rurale*, Brussels: n.p.

Arestis, P. and Howells, P.G.A (1992) 'Institutional Developments and the Effectiveness of Monetary Policy', *Journal of Economic Issues*, **XXVI**, March.

Bagehot, W. (1904) *Lombard Street*, London: Kegan Paul, Trench, Trübner and Co.

Bernanke, B.S. (1995) 'The macroeconomics of the great depression: a comparative approach', *Journal of Money, Credit and Banking*, **27**(1), 1–29.

Bordo, M.D. and Kydland, F. (1995) 'The Gold Standard as a Rule: an Essay in Exploration', *Explorations in Economic History*, **32**, 423–64.

Bordo, M.D. and Rockoff, H. (1996) 'The Gold Standard as a "Good Housekeeping Seal of Approval"', *Journal of Economic History*, **56**(2), 389–428.

Bordo, M. D. and Schwartz, A.J. (1996) 'The Operation of the Specie Standard: Evidence for Core and Peripheral Countries, 1880–1890', in B. Eichengreen and J. Braga de Marcedo (eds), *Historical Perspectives on the Gold Standard: Portugal and the World*, London: Routledge.

Boyle, A. (1967) *Montagu Norman*, London: Cassell.

British Association (1921) *Monetary Policy: The Report of a sub-committee on Currency and the Gold Standard*, London: British Association.

Bryan, W.J. (1896) 'Speech to the Democratic Convention', quoted in P. Studenski and H.E. Grooss, *Financial History of the United States*, New York: McGraw Hill, 1952.

Clapham, J.H. (1944) *The Bank of England*, 2 vols, Cambridge: Cambridge University Press.

Committee on the Currency and Bank of England Note Issues (Bradbury Committee) (1925) *Report*, Cmd 2393, London: HMSO.

Committee on Currency and Foreign Exchanges after the War (Cunliffe Committee) (1918) *First Interim Report*, Cmd 9182, London: HMSO.

Committee on Currency and Foreign Exchanges after the War (Cunliffe Committee) (1919) *Final Report*, Cmd 464, London: HMSO.

Committee on Finance and Industry (Macmillan Committee) (1931) *Report*, Cmd 3897, London: HMSO.

Cross, R. (ed.) (1995) *The Natural Rate of Unemployment: Reflections on 25 Years of the Hypothesis*, Cambridge: Cambridge University Press.

Deutsche Bundesbank (1995) *Annual Report 1994*, Frankfurt am Main: Deutsche Bundesbank.

Drummond, I.M. (1987) *The Gold Standard and the International Monetary System, 1900–39*, London: Macmillan.

Eichengreen, B., Tobin, J. and Wyplosz C. (1995) 'Two cases for sand in the wheels of international finance', *Economic Journal*, **105**(428) January, 162–72.

Rt Hon. Lord Farrer (1898) 'Has the Gold Standard made the Rich Richer and the Industrious Poorer?', Gold Standard Defence Association, pamphlet no. 31, London: Cassell.

Garber, P and Taylor, M.P. (1995), 'Sand in the wheels of foreign exchange: a sceptical note', *Economic Journal*, **105**(428), January, 173–80.

Howson, S. (1975) *Domestic Monetary Management in Britain, 1919–38*, Cambridge: Cambridge University Press.

Howson, S. (1988) 'Socialist Monetary Policy: monetary thought in the Labour Party in the 1940s', *History of Political Economy*, **20**(4), 543–64.

Hume, L.M. (1963) 'The Gold Standard and Deflation: Issues and Attitudes in the 1920s', *Economica*; reprinted in S. Pollard (ed.) (1970).

Jeanne, O. (1995) 'Monetary Policy in England, 1893–1914: a Structural VAR Analysis', *Explorations in Economic History*, **32**(3), 302–26.

Keynes, J.M. (1931) 'The Economic Consequences of Mr. Churchill', *Essays in Persuasion*, London: Macmillan.

Lucas, R.E. (1976) 'Econometric policy evaluation: a critique', in K. Brunner and A.H. Meltzer (eds), *The Phillips Curve and Labour Markets*, Carnegie-Rochester Conference Series on Public Policy, Amsterdam: North-Holland.

Milesi-Ferretti, G. (1995) 'The disadvantage of tying their hands: on the political economy of policy commitments', *Economic Journal*, **105**(433), 1381–1402.

Morgan-Webb, C. (1935) *Ten Years of Currency Revolution, 1922–32*, London: Allen & Unwin.

Morley, J. (1903), *Life of Gladstone*, London: Macmillan.

Nevin, E. (1953) 'The Origins of Cheap Money, 1931–1932', *Economica* ; reprinted in S. Pollard (ed.) (1970).

Peston, M. (1982) *The Theory of Macroeconomic Policy*, 2nd edn, Oxford: Philip Allan.

Palley, T.I. (1996) 'The institutionalization of deflationary monetary policy', *Economies et Sociétés* (Monnaie et Production), **10**(2–3), 247–68.

Pollard, S. (1969) 'Trade Unions' Reactions to the Economic Crisis', *Journal of Contemporary History*, **4**(4); reprinted in S. Pollard (ed.) (1970).

Pollard, S. (ed.) (1970) *The Gold Standard and Employment Policies Between the Wars*, London: Methuen.

Sayers, R.S. (1960) 'The Return to Gold, 1925', in L.S. Pressnell (ed.), *Studies in the Industrial Revolution*, London: Athlone Press.

Sayers, R.S. (1976) *The Bank of England, 1891–1944*, 2 vols, Cambridge: Cambridge University Press.

Theil, H. (1964) *Optimal Decision Rules for Government and Industry*, Amsterdam: North-Holland.

Tinbergen, J. (1952) *On the Theory of Economic Policy*, Amsterdam: North-Holland.

5. Emergency changes in monetary policy

John Grahl

My many debts to Bernard Corry and Maurice Peston, as teachers, colleagues and friends over many years, include my first sustained encounter with modern economic theory, and its application to policy. The present chapter does not make formal use of economic theory, but it does attempt to discuss an important policy issue while drawing on the Keynesian tradition to which both Bernard and Maurice have given a continuing, if critical, allegiance.

One of the factors responsible for the marked eclipse of Keynesian influence from the 1970s is perhaps the relative neglect of monetary problems by many mainstream Keynesians in the previous decades. This neglect is, of course, an irony because Keynes was above all a monetary theorist; what seems to have happened is that Keynes's own relatively contingent pessimism about the value of monetary policy as a response to the unemployment of the 1930s was gradually promoted to an article of doctrine. This weakness became particularly important in the post-Bretton Woods world of flexible exchange rates in which the prominence of monetary factors in the main theories opposed to Keynesianism became a decisive strategic disadvantage for the latter.

Such neglect was, of course, never universal, and the work of post Keynesians, in particular, has done much to correct it (for a recent survey of post Keynesianism, see Arestis, 1996). One significant theme in this work concerns the role of the central bank. From the work of Minsky (1982, 1986), as representative of the post Keynesians, and Kindleberger (1978, 1987), perhaps representing an original Keynesian generation for whom it was inconceivable to relegate monetary issues to secondary status, one can draw a view of the central bank which calls into question the extremely fashionable opinions that monetary policy can be assigned, without any fundamental difficulties, to the target of price level stabilization, and that the best way to secure such an assignment is by means of *central bank independence*.

The purpose of the present contribution is simply to insist that there is a great deal of evidence for the Keynesian contestation of these current orthodoxies, whose (perhaps dangerous) influence can be detected both in the design for a European Central Bank (Grahl, 1997, ch. 8) and in the recent reform of the Bank of England. While mainstream concern about such proposals focuses directly on the possible destabilization of employment, the post Keynesian work referred to above, without neglecting employment effects, emphasizes the potential problem of *financial stability*. It is held that the situational logic of central banks gives them an inescapable responsibility for financial stabilization which may well conflict with the straightforward assignment of monetary policy to the war against inflation. Below, the reasoning behind these doubts is sketched briefly before the nature of the evidence is indicated. The evidence is of three kinds: the lessons of history; the analogy between current proposals for purely monetary disinflation and the completely failed project of monetary base control; and lastly, and of greatest significance, several recent episodes in national and international policy formation which directly exemplify the conflict in question.

THE LENDER OF LAST RESORT

The basic argument need not be developed in great detail. The issue of money is seen as arising through the workings of the private credit system. Credit relations tend to take a hierarchical form, with lower-level agents depending on those at higher levels for accommodation. The central bank is at the apex of this structure, with an obligation to refinance major intermediaries and credit markets when this cannot be done in a stable way through purely private transactions. This obligation can constrain, and even impede, the orthodox assignment of central bank money issue to the single objective of price level stability.

The key questions are whether this conflict of responsibilities is necessarily, or only contingently, linked to the position of the central bank within the credit system as a whole and what the conditions are under which the potential conflict becomes actual. Two examples of the first issue are the possible role of fiscal policy in financial stabilization and the ability of private sector agents, acting collectively, to provide the emergency refinance which might be required. The second question essentially hinges on the stability of private credit relations. Can disturbances be held at a microeconomic level without significance for the conduct of macroeconomic policy? Are widespread refinancing requirements always the consequence of previous policy errors? Are there forms of prudential supervision which can prevent these kinds of policy dilemma? It will be briefly suggested that, although such considerations certainly situate the problem, they by no means eliminate it.

One can consider first the issue of other agents: can either fiscal policy instruments or private sector insurance relieve central banks of the responsibility for financial stabilization? The answer, in both cases, seems to be, 'Yes, but not completely.' Minsky himself, in his characterization of the financial stabilization problem, repeatedly states that it is transformed by 'big government' (that is, a high share of public expenditure in GDP and an active fiscal policy) which provides an alternative, and in some ways more effective, stabilizer of the financial system and thus mitigates the conflicting pressures on the central bank. Two factors, however, might limit the ability of the fiscal authority to replace the monetary one in this context: firstly, the question of speed – government may be unable to act as fast as the central bank because it is not continuously present in the same way in financial markets or the banking system; and more fundamentally, the government's own need for financial support – effective fiscal intervention in a financial emergency may presuppose strong support for public debt instruments by the monetary authority itself. In both cases, the fiscalization of the necessary intervention does not change its essential nature, although it will affect its tactics and timing.

Can private sector institutions take over the role of financial stabilization? It is easy to be ironical about the notion of privatizing lender-of-last-resort functions, which starts to approach some of the more radical notions of free banking, but the issue surely deserves to be taken seriously. Schwartz (1986) has pointed out that in the United States powerful private coalitions have tried, sometimes with success, to stabilize a crisis-struck banking system. (On this basis, she argues that the lender-of-last-resort function might be largely privatized, although, unlike the free bankers, she regards the issue of high-powered money as an essentially public function; she argues, in addition, that if monetary policy is properly conducted it should not give rise to financial crises.) Such an argument stands on an alternative reading of the same kind of historical evidence as is advanced by Kindleberger, for instance: if some of today's central banks evolved *from* private institutions which acquired systemic stabilization functions, is there any reason why a *return* of some functions to private responsibility should be ruled out in an era which has found many possibilities of privatizing erstwhile public activities? There do seem, however, to be such reasons, which arise from the public good aspect of stabilizing behaviour. Although any strongly perceived public interest may on occasion be internalized by a powerful group of private agents, there exists a tendency for competition to prevent an adequate response within the private sphere, since the most socially responsible agents may put themselves at a cost disadvantage. In the present context this would correspond to the lower yields obtained by, for example, a major bank which held a large portfolio of liquid assets with a view to defending, not only its own position, but that of the financial sector as a whole.

If a very complete degree of portfolio diversification were available on a purely market basis then private insurance would become easier. But, for two reasons, diversification is an incomplete solution: firstly, investigation of asset prices in a very wide range of financial markets – for foreign exchange, bonds and equities – can only give a realistic account of price movements by invoking substantial risk premia, which shows that the real opportunities for diversification must be limited in practice; secondly, there is general recognition of system-wide risks which implicate such a wide spectrum of assets that diversification can only be a partial defence against financial distress (see below).

Both moral hazard and non-internalized interdependence among agents may prevent the emergence of sufficient insurance against financial distress on a purely market basis. This is not to deny that some such insurance can, and usually does, take place; indeed the existence of localized or sectoral stabilization commitments by private banks or organized financial markets was part of the description of the problem above. However, the reinsurance of these private stabilizers themselves may pose problems of coordination which exceed, in principle and practice, the capacities of the private sector.

The second group of problems concerns the *scale* of instabilities in private sector finance. If the problem of financial stability is real, is it large enough to constitute a significant constraint on the workings of monetary policy? It is certainly true that there are cases of financial distress which may involve externalities great enough to raise questions of public interest without being so widespread as to imply generalized refinance of the banking and credit system as a whole. In this case the lender-of-last-resort function would be a genuine public responsibility but it would be separable from the macroeconomic objectives of the central bank. Goodhart and Schoenmaker (1993) point out that institutional evidence on this issue is mixed: in some countries the detailed supervision of financial agents is traditionally seen as a central bank function; in others, Germany for example, it is undertaken by quite separate agencies. There are mixed cases, such as the complex overlap of micro and macro functions in the United States, and recently proposed reforms in Britain show that institutions may change character in this respect.

One suspects, however, that among the main motives behind intervention into local or sectoral financial distress are the fear that the problem may spread and the associated desire to nip what are potentially system-wide dislocations in the bud. The possibility of *pre-empting* the need for generalized refinance – whether this is to be done by close regulation or by rapid microeconomic intervention – cannot be independent of the historically conditioned nature of particular financial systems. Where private finance is extremely robust, as (at least prior to unification) in Germany, the scope for forestalling general emergencies may be so wide as to permit an effective partition between financial and price level stabilization.

At least in theory, this kind of separation seems fragile. There are logical interactions between such preventative action, on the one hand and, on the other, the pressure for emergency changes in general monetary policy which it is intended to avoid. Financial agents may be more easily subjected to prudential supervision if this is the price of access to emergency refinance, while defence of the room for manoeuvre in central bank policy provides at least one set of principles by which supervisory mechanisms might be designed. Similarly, if possible 'contagion' (or other forms of interdependence among financially distressed agents) is feared largely because of the constraints on macroeconomic policy to which it might lead, then the evaluation of these risks cannot be divorced from the assessment of monetary policy as a whole – the importance of a particular line of policy and the costs involved in departing from it. For example, it is sometimes suggested that variations in short-term interest rates are more damaging in Britain than in other European countries; this would increase the need to avoid financial disturbances with system-wide implications. As for the third form of pre-emption, that is the use of tight credit as a disincentive to the adoption of exposed positions, in this case the inseparability of the conflicting functions of monetary and financial stabilization becomes a tautology, since it is acknowledged that financial fragility is a continuous constraint on credit policy.

This glance at the structure of the problem will have served its purpose if it suggests that serious conflicts between overall monetary control and financial stabilization can hardly be excluded on a priori grounds. It follows that some consideration of the evidence might be relevant. The following sections by no means attempt to examine the record in a systematic way; they aim only to indicate that there is a range of pertinent experience which is not accorded its due weight in typical discussions of macroeconomic policy.

HISTORY AND TRADITION

The historical evidence of the need, recurrently, to assign central bank policy to the imperative task of financial stabilization and, hence, to divert it from other tasks such as the defence of a currency standard is well known and need not be rehearsed in detail. A particularly unequivocal reading of the record is given by Hawtrey (1932) who asserts that the central bank obtains control over the supply of money *because* it is the lender of last resort. The Bank of England is often taken as a paradigmatic example of this necessity because its evolution, from a commercial bank *primus inter pares* to a public body, first in practice and then, also, in law can be taken to indicate a logic of situation which clarifies both the need for a central instance of monetary control and the specifically financial responsibilities which that instance tends to acquire. Two aspects of Bank of England history can be mentioned which are compatible with the view that there may exist fundamental conflicts among the objectives of monetary policy (for two readings of central bank evolution, see Aglietta, 1992; Goodhart, 1988).

The first is precisely the failure to separate the functions of defending the monetary standard and providing emergency accommodation to important financial agents. Under the influence of bullionist theories (without going into a detailed assessment of the doctrines of the Currency School one can ask whether it is simplistic to interpret these as a kind of protomonetarism) the Bank Charter Act of 1844 attempted just such a separation by the construction of a chinese wall between the issue and banking departments of the Bank of England. The impracticality of this strategy was then demonstrated by the repeated suspension of the Act in times of financial emergency, when the banking (or financial) arm had to be granted irregular recourse to issue department credits. (Evans, 1859, gives an account of one such suspension, in 1859, complete with the formal indemnification of Bank officials for breaches of the Act which became an almost ritualized declaration of financial emergency.)

A second pertinent aspect of nineteenth-century experience was the evolution of an operational distinction between external and internal drains of specie from the central bank: the first came to be interpreted as a monetary problem in the narrow sense, requiring restrictive policies in defence of the Gold Standard, while the second might be the symptom of a loss of confidence, associated with disturbed credit relations, to which the best response was abundant central refinance. Thus Disraeli commented:

> A foreign drain is a very unimpassioned, calculating transaction .... But the moment you come to a domestic drain you have to encounter elements of a very different character. The moral quality, as well as the material element, enters into the calculation of the domestic drain. The passions of fear and hope govern mankind; the mart and the exchange are not free from the influence of those passions, and when you have circumstances in which a whole nation is panic struck you cannot hope by the aid of economic science successfully to encounter them. (Cited in Evans, 1859, p. 209)

It will certainly not be claimed here that the lessons of history are either obvious or univalent. The institutional forms of modern economic life are extremely plastic. But it might be argued that the US central bank also emerged in ways which indicate the primacy of financial stability over other aspects of monetary policy. Throughout the nineteenth century, there was intense political resistance to any centralized controlling instance in monetary affairs, Andrew Jackson's eventual triumph over the Bank of the United States being an illuminating example. When, despite the Americans' basic antipathy to central control, the Federal Reserve System was established, the key imperative was not monetary stability – in the sense of a stable monetary unit – but the need for a powerful agency for *financial* stabilization whose absence, it was thought, had aggravated crises like that of 1907.

The original design of the Fed was based on the assumption that this stability could be secured on a regionally differentiated basis, but all commentators agree that this was unrealistic from the start because of the very high degree of financial integration among the states of the Union; thus Federal Reserve policy is always interpreted as that of a unitary central bank. Policy is made in

Washington and implemented in New York, with the other regional banks of the system acting as mere branches. This pattern calls into question the design of the European Central Bank, which necessarily centralizes monetary policy but leaves issues of financial stability to be dealt with, according to the famous doctrine of subsidiarity, on a national basis. Clearly, the adequacy of this design depends on the degree of financial integration in Europe (already high and expected by all commentators to rise). It depends also on the scale of the financial disturbances which may arise: if these can be dealt with on a national level then the functional separation of financial and monetary responsibilities will presumably be efficient; otherwise, there may be problems in the formulation of centralized monetary policy. It is argued by Miron (1989) that the early policy of the Federal Reserve displayed a clear preoccupation with stable credit and this is quite consistent with the view that central banks are typically confronted with complex financial constraints (although it should be noted that Miron's own view is that this preoccupation was excessive).

Of course, it can be thought that the stabilization problems of the modern economy are quite different from those of the nineteenth century, which were only the infantile disorders of the market system, rather than early signs of inescapable and intrinsic limits to market organization in any pure form. Opinions on such issues are themselves cyclical. However, the sanguine assumption of inherent stability in private credit systems which prevailed in much economic discourse until recently might be interpreted as an ironic misreading of postwar experience, by which the stability achieved through large and powerful interventionist regimes in advanced countries was, quite erroneously, attributed to market relations as such, and thus helped to fuel the assault on interventionism. All that is suggested here is that the historical record is sufficiently complex and ambivalent to justify doubt on the question and that, in consequence, an examination of more recent experience may be of relevance (for a historically informed account of the current forms of financial crisis, see Aglietta *et al.*, 1990, ch. 5). It would be a major task to undertake such an examination in any systematic way. What follows is merely a brief description of two bodies of evidence which, prima facie, merit some attention.

BASE CONTROL: AN ISOMORPHISM?

As a technical problem of monetary policy design, the issue of monetary base control has been extensively debated. The consensus which has gradually emerged might be characterized as follows: in *operational* terms monetary base control does not work; it is interest rates in those short-run credit markets where the central bank is present which must be regarded as the immediate, and to a considerable extent discretionary, instruments of policy; however, this does not affect the *strategic* content of policy, which can still be assigned, in an unproblematic way, to price stability, whether the latter is a direct target or is approached via some quantitative aggregate such as nominal GDP. This dualism has marked the policy of the Bundesbank, for example, since it began monetary targeting in 1974 and is to be transferred to the European Central Bank after the introduction of the Euro.

The aim here is not to reopen the debate on base control, which can be taken as settled, but to ask whether the issue has wider implications. In many ways it seems to be a microcosm, or high-frequency analogue, of the general problem of monetary control versus financial stabilization. Of course there are obvious differences: in the case of base control the positions which may require refinance are largely in what, from a wider point of view, would be considered very liquid assets: short-run government paper or close substitutes for it, such as short-term placements on the inter-bank market, held by commercial banks. Nevertheless, short run volatility in interest rates, aimed at stabilizing *monetary* variables, seems to have led to acute strains in financing even these liquid portfolios.

In practice, thoroughgoing quantitative control over the monetary base seems only to have been approached, never achieved, a fact which may itself indicate that it poses insuperable problems of stability. In the early years of Paul Volcker's tenure at the Federal Reserve, quantitative limits were introduced for, essentially, open market operations ('free reserves') but discount policy continued to provide a relatively elastic supply of funds to the commercial banks ('borrowed reserves'), although recourse to the discount window was associated with certain disadvantages for the borrowing banks. Even this partial implementation of the quantitativist programme seems to have made for extreme volatility in short-run credit relations, and the procedures were abandoned around the summer of 1982. In Britain opposition from financial practitioners was intense and no use of the narrow or central bank money stock as an instrument took place even during the most radical phase of counterinflationary rigour. Attempts to target broader aggregates with precision over rather short time intervals seem to have been the nearest British approach to such an experiment; even so, a variety of technical problems arose which suggested that financial malfunctions and credit market tensions increase rapidly as policy moves closer to strict quantity control (for a detailed examination, see Dow and Saville, 1990).

The point to be made here concerns the wider significance of these experiments. One interpretation, perhaps dominant in academic discussion, is that the issue is essentially technical and has no implications for the wider project of monetary disinflation as this is conventionally conceived. Thus Cuikerman (1992) attributes the problems of base control to the need for 'interest rate smoothing', but this conclusion is situated in a broad view of central bank independence which would still assign lower frequency variations in interest rates (over quarters, say, rather than day-to-day) to the target of price stability without seeing any fundamental problems of financial stability. Goodhart's (1995) survey of the issue, on the other hand, is rather more open. He writes, 'in an analytical sense the debate also mirrors a fundamental, continuing discussion about the process of money supply determination. Central bankers, and their supporting economists, see the driving force of monetary expansion as deriving from the demand from the public and private sectors for *credit*.'

Such a view makes any assignment of monetary policy conditional on the stability or otherwise of credit relations. If there is a reliable and regular link between credit demand and money expenditures of the kind presupposed by standard IS–LM models, then a straightforward counterinflationary approach to monetary policy is still valid. If one is less sanguine, a variety of constraints emerge which call that view into question. In some circumstances, a restrictive stance might be desirable: not to limit the growth of money GDP or some such aggregate, but to avoid the accumulation of fragile or overexposed balance sheets; on the other hand, widespread financial distress might force the authorities to adopt an accommodating stance even though price level developments in themselves do not justify it. In other words, the classical separation of money and credit proposed by Ricardo would be inapplicable. For Ricardo, monetary policy – a public function – controls purchasing power; credit relations – a set of essentially private transactions – redistribute that purchasing power among agents. The logic of this distinction, reproduced in so much theory, is unassailable; what is at issue is the extent to which actual economic structures allow it to be used as an operational basis for policy.

The suggestion here is that there is at least an analogy between the high frequency case of base control, where the tension between financial stability and monetary control seems to become absolute, and the same tension over longer time periods. Prior to a convincing analytical account of the problem it is speculative in the extreme to say more than this. Such a full analysis seems to be unavailable at present because one of the key issues in the monetary control of inflation is still far from being understood; this is the question of the source of nominal price rigidities. Blinder (1994) points out how far the competing academic accounts of price rigidity are both from each other and from the explanations offered by business enterprises. Similarly, in the base control case, price formation is still imperfectly understood: for example, standard theories fail even to explain the price of a six month bill in terms of the prices of two successive three month bills.

It is conceivable, however, that more than an analogy is involved, that the apparently technical issue of the immediate instruments of monetary policy is identical in structure to the strategic question of policy assignment. In other words, the base control problem might be *isomorphic* with the more general problem of lender-of-last-resort operations. If this were the case, the base control debate, and its relatively clear outcome in favour of interest rates as policy instruments, would amount to significant evidence in favour of the Keynesian position on financial stability. One aspect of the pattern which may emerge is the necessity experienced by financial agents for refinancing facilities as a kind of *insurance*, which must to some extent be provided on a centralized basis for reasons involving both moral hazard, limiting the efficiency of private markets, and spillovers, which can, under adverse circumstances, transform a localized into a macroeconomic emergency.

However that may be, a third body of evidence can be adduced for the existence of potentially acute conflicts between the role of monetary policy as guarantor of financial stability and any unproblematic assignment of the same policy to the imperative of disinflation. Such conflicts can be directly observed, in recent experience and in several countries. The next section gives some pertinent examples.

RECENT EMERGENCIES

Standard empirical procedures can have a distorting effect on the interpretation of economic data. What is relevant to the present discussion is no more than a series of *episodes*. The construction of macroeconomic models, however, usually tries to establish regularities over time within a given economy and the tendency is to absorb a short period of exceptional behaviour into the residuals of the model rather than to focus on the period as a specific explicandum. As a result, the recurrence of similar phases of emergency in several economies is not accorded the significance which may be due.

Of course, the somewhat more regular fluctuations in price and output variables which are the concern of business cycle theory are the focus of a whole branch of macroeconomics, but there is no clear relation between the two problems. Episodes of acute financial distress may, but certainly need not, characterize business cycle downturns, which are typically explained by relatively smooth variations in flow and stock variables. Post Keynesian accounts of business cycle history tend to associate deep depressions with *uncontrolled* financial crises, and monetarist history (Cagan, 1965; Friedman and Schwartz, 1972) tends to agree, at least for the special case of monetary deflations. However, the record is difficult to read just because lender-of-last-resort operations are so common.

Nevertheless, episodes of financial stress can be seen as sufficiently common, and as sufficiently similar to each other, to merit treatment as a distinct pattern of economic events. Even though there is no way to render such episodes quantitatively homogeneous, they may display strong qualitative similarities with implications for such aspects of policy as the design of financial institutions or the conduct of disinflationary strategies.

The first example that will be offered is that of the United States towards the end of the phase of extreme monetary stringency associated with the early years of Paul Volcker's chairmanship. This episode is not yet given its due importance in the analysis of current economic and political change; it seems in particular to have triggered a decisive shift away from Keynesian intervention in the West European economies (Grahl, 1991). Institutional factors, in particular the relative ease with which economic agents can offset interest payments against tax, may have mitigated its impact in the United States itself. This was, nevertheless, severe and included two very deep recessions in rapid succession. The move away from extreme stringency (involving also a revision of operating procedures in order to smooth interest rates, as described above) took place in the summer and autumn of 1982 and seems certainly to have had an 'emergency' character. A large number of important players – both domestic, such as agribusiness interests, and foreign, such as Latin American governments – were on the brink of insolvency. It seems to have been thought that major refinancing exercises to limit the damage to debtors and creditors in such fields were inevitable and that therefore it was as well to modify policy immediately rather than wait until the scale of necessary refinance had been swollen by further disorganization. An interesting development, in the light of the currently fashionable nostrum of an independent central bank, was the intense political pressure on the Fed, which seems to have included even some threats to its status by Congress.

A second episode, this time clearly international in scope, concerns the stock market crash of October 1987. Perceived dangers included straightforward wealth effects of declining equity values on, especially, consumer spending but there was also a fear of the transmission of financial distress from the stock market to other agents (for a discussion of the possible channels by which international disturbances of this kind might be propagated, see Portes and Swoboda, 1987). It happened that international policy coordination machinery was at the time very active since G7 countries had recently agreed on substantial intervention, first to lower dollar exchange rates and then to stabilize the dollar and avoid a feared 'hard landing' from the previous correction. Thus it proved possible to organize a concerted reduction of interest rates by major OECD economies in order to compensate for possible expenditure reductions and to relieve financial tensions (Dobson, 1991).

In retrospect, it is not clear whether the policy response was necessary since the actual impact of the crash on activity levels seems to have been negligible and equity prices soon resumed their climb. This is probably a general difficulty in the assessment of lender-of-last-resort operations: to get a clear quantitative idea of their value one would have to develop very complex counterfactual scenarios of what are, almost by definition, unstable processes. But it is surely unlikely that prompt and coordinated action would have been taken unless monetary authorities had *perceived* significant risks.

A third example is furnished by the Scandinavian economies, in particular that of Sweden, in the early 1990s. Here the precipitating factor was a boom and bust in property values, arising from the mismanagement, through the 1980s, of financial liberalization. The consequence was the virtual insolvency of a large part of the commercial banking system which was faced simultaneously with massive non-performing loans in property and elsewhere and a rapid depreciation of the collateral by which they were secured. Although the main drive of policy towards a reduction in state expenditures continued, it was interrupted by what even resolute market reformers recognized to be an unavoidable rescue. To some extent this could be fiscalized in the medium term, but only because the central bank's immediate support for the commercial banking system could be taken for granted. The resulting need for monetary policy relaxation was at least an important contributing factor in Sweden's abandonment of the fixed D-mark parity which had become a key aspect of policy in the late 1980s. The complete dedication of monetary policy to the maintenance of this D-mark standard, which had been expressed in September 1992 by call money rates of 500 per cent, simply no longer made sense, as such stringency could only increase the scope and the scale of the refinancing operations which had become inevitable (OECD, 1995a). In 1992 alone, these amounted to 40 billion kronor (Lindbeck Committee, 1993).

The same pattern of real estate boom and bust was in the background of the most dramatic emergency switch of monetary policy to occur in recent times, the case of Japan in the early 1990s. In this case, however, virtually the entire range of financial assets was affected as there also took place a significant decline in stock market prices. The resulting pressure on Japanese commercial banks was exacerbated by their relatively low profit margins and was all the more menacing because of their key role in the process of industrial investment. In these circumstances the Japanese authorities were able to take full advantage of an enormously strong external position in terms of both trade flows and the stock of external assets. The scope for directing monetary policy to the task of internal stabilization without fear of uncontrollable external repercussions was wider than in perhaps any other country. Full use was made of this wide margin of manoeuvre to introduce the lowest nominal interest rates seen for a generation. Discount rates were brought down to less than 1 per cent and held at this level for several years. Since there is still some inflation in the Japanese economy, this corresponds to an extremely low real rate. In fact, discount rates do not measure the full extent of the relaxation because open market operations flooded money markets with such an abundance of cheap credit as to make recourse to discounting facilities superfluous for all but the most acutely embarrassed financial agents. The outcome is a national monetary regime with a resolutely expansionist character in the heart of a generally restrictive world system (for details, see OECD, 1995b).

Such examples could be multiplied, from the emergency refinancing of Greek commercial banks (and, indirectly their industrial debtors) in the early 1980s, to the recent bail-out of Mexico by the United States. In the developing world, it seems to be the case that public funds, especially from the World Bank, did much to replace the private credits which dried up for several years in the wake of the Volcker shock (for data, see Gilbert *et al.*, 1996). (Devaluations pose certain analytical difficulties in the general perspective of lender-of-last-resort operations: on the one hand, they may sometimes be seen as necessary preparations for emergency switches of policy, as seems to have been the case both with the Swedish depreciation which preceded the refinancing operation discussed above and the departure of the United Kingdom from the Exchange Rate Mechanism (ERM) in September 1992; on the other hand, devaluation itself may also represent a functional equivalent to refinance in the sense that it is an inflationary move which relieves pressure on the tradeable goods sector – the same UK example being a case in point. At least one can recognize that devaluation writes down the external value of domestically denominated debt, but it is not clear whether this financial effect is of quantitative significance.)

If these various episodes are not given their full weight in policy discussion, this may be because standard econometric procedures search for structural continuities within specific national economies and assimilate the sharp but usually brief discontinuities which occur as financial emergencies to the impact of random disturbances. The consequence is that the general but, almost by definition, irregular phenomena linked to increasing fragility in global financial relations are systematically neglected.

The same kind of consideration applies to standard macro-modelling procedures. One can perhaps summarize a standard IS–LM system by saying that the IS curve shows the conditions under which non-financial agents will *undertake* expenditures, while the LM curve shows the conditions under which the banking and credit system will *finance* the same. Underlying the construction are the assumptions that the two sectors can be distinguished in a meaningful way and that transactions between them follow rather stable and predictable patterns. The kind of emergency discussed here, however, will invalidate both assumptions: there is a fundamental disturbance to relations between lenders and borrowers which destabilizes both the behaviour of each and the mechanisms of financial intermediation: although it will always be possible, ex post, to specify parameter shifts which reconcile the model with the observed evolution of the economy, such an accommodation trivializes the disturbance which consists precisely in the loss of those points of reference which previously worked to define the roles and reactions of financial agents.

CONCLUSION

The considerations above should not be seen as an argument for a generally expansionary monetary regime. As the literature on the lender-of-last-resort function itself makes clear, there are insuperable problems of moral hazard associated with the regular and reliable refinancing of distressed agents. For example, one consequence of such an approach is to induce herd behaviour in financial markets: agents believe that if they stay with the crowd, they are bound to be bailed out if things go wrong. A fortiori, automatic and routine refinancing seems to lead rapidly to the soft-budget constraints which characterized the Soviet-type economies, and which still handicap their 'transitional' successors.

On the other hand, the opposite stance, that of no-bail-out rules and the maintenance of general, anti-inflationary monetary policies regardless of the width or intensity of financial distress, seems equally utopian. As indicated above, central banks do not in practice achieve such a clear separation of their financial and monetary responsibilities and the attempt even to approach it leads to unmanageable policy conflicts.

It *is* suggested, however, that it is necessary to recognize important financial constraints on monetary policy. This is the case both for phases of expansion, where the development of exposed positions cannot, in practice, be treated as a purely private responsibility, and for phases of restriction, where the avoidance of cumulative failures sets sharp limits to the speed and intensity of corrective actions. Since the project of purely monetary disinflation, now in the form of independent central banks rather than of strict quantitative targets, remains extremely fashionable, it is as well to point out that there is an important body of evidence to indicate that it is not empirically possible to separate completely the targets of monetary stability and real economic development. Progress towards efficiency and stability in such areas as employment relations, external competitiveness and investment finance will work to reduce conflicts and tensions in the pursuit of price stability.

The neglect of such objectives, on the other hand, makes it extremely probable that control of nominal variables will be compromised by the unavoidable policy swings necessitated by acute financial pressure. If a concrete instance of these risks is required, one can refer to the sang froid with which the proponents of European monetary union seem, up to the present, to have regarded the issue of financial stability within the quite unprecedented combination of monetary centralization with decentralized fiscal and structural policies which is about to emerge in the countries of the European Union.

REFERENCES

Aglietta, M. (1992) 'Genèse des banques centrales et légitimité de la monnaie', *Annales*, 3, May–June.

Aglietta, M., Brender, A. and Coudert, V. (1990) *Globalisation Financière: l'aventure obligée*, Paris: Economica.

Arestis, P. (1996) 'Post-Keynesian Economics: towards coherence', *Cambridge Journal of Economics*, **20** (1), January.

Blinder, A. (1994) 'On Sticky Prices: academic theories meet the real world', in N. Mankiw (ed.), *Monetary Policy*, London: University of Chicago Press.

Cagan, P. (1965) *Determinants and Effects of Changes in the Stock of Money, 1875–1960*, New York: Columbia University Press.

Cuikerman, A. (1992) *Central Bank Strategy, Credibility and Independence: theory and evidence*, Cambridge, Mass.: MIT Press.

Dobson, W. (1991) *Economic Policy Coordination: requiem or prologue*?, Washington DC: Institute for International Economics.

Dow, J. and Saville, I. (1990) *A Critique of Monetary Policy*, 2nd edn, Oxford: Clarendon.

Evans, D. (1859) *The History of the Commercial Crisis 1857–1858 and the Stock Exchange panic of 1859*; reprinted New York: Augustus Kelley, 1969.

Friedman, M. and Schwartz, A. (1972) *A Monetary History of the United States, 1867–1960*, Princeton NJ: NBER.

Gilbert, C., Hopkins, R., Powell, A. and Roy, A. (1996) 'The World Bank: its functions and future', *ESRC Global Institutions*, Working Paper 15.

Goodhart, C. (1988) *The Evolution of Central Banks*, Cambridge, Mass.: MIT Press.

Goodhart, C. (1995) 'Money Supply Control: base or interest rates', in K. Hoover and S. Sheffrin (eds), *Monetarism and the Methodology of Economics*, Aldershot: Edward Elgar; reprinted in C. Goodhart, *The Central Bank and the Financial System*, Basingstoke: Macmillan, 1995.

Goodhart, C. and Schoenmaker, D. (1993) 'Institutional Separation between Supervisory and Monetary Agencies', in F. Bruni (ed.), *Prudential Regulation. Supervision and Monetary Policy*, Milan: Bocconi University; reprinted in C. Goodhart, *The Central Bank and the Financial System*, Basingstoke: Macmillan, 1995.

Grahl, J. (1991) 'Economies out of Control', *New Left Review*, **185**, Jan./Feb.

Grahl, J. (1997) *After Maastricht: a guide to EMU*, London: Lawrence & Wishart.

Hawtrey, R. (1932) *The Art of Central Banking*, London: Longman; reprinted London: Cass, 1962.

Kindleberger, C. (1978) *Manias, Panics and Crashes*, New York: Basic Books.

Kindleberger, C. (1987) *The World in Depression*, rev. edn, Harmondsworth: Penguin.

Lindbeck Committee (1993) 'Options for Economic and Political Reform in Sweden', *Economic Policy*, **17**, October.

Minsky, H. (1982) *Inflation. Recession and Economic Policy*, Brighton: Wheatsheaf.

Minsky, H. (1986) *Stabilising an Unstable Economy*, New Haven: Yale University Press.

Miron, J. (1989) 'The Founding of the Fed and the Destabilisation of the Post-1914 US Economy', in M. de Cecco and A. Giovannini (eds), *A European Central bank?: perspectives on monetary union after ten years of the EMS*, Cambridge: CEPR Cambridge University Press.

OECD (1995a) *Economic Surveys: Sweden*, Paris: OECD.

OECD (1995b) *Economic Surveys: Japan*, Paris: OECD.

Portes, R. and Swoboda, A. (eds) (1987) *Threats to International Financial Stability*, Cambridge: Cambridge University Press.

Schwartz, A. (1986) 'Real and Pseudo-financial Crises', in F. Capie and G. Wood (eds), *Financial Crises and the World Banking System*, London: Macmillan.

6. Central bank independence has costs, not just benefits

Gerard Lyons

INTRODUCTION

Bernard Corry and Maurice Peston never taught me, but I learnt much from them. As a PhD student at Queen Mary College from 1983 to 1985, I came across both. Maurice would hold court in the tea-room at three o'clock. Bernard would preside over discussion in the SCR bar in the evening. Their expertise in the 'four Es' was immense: entertaining football, education, employment and of course economics. It is the last of these I wish to write on today, in the context of central bank independence and its role in economic policy making.

In May 1997, a Labour government was elected almost 18 years to the day after the Conservatives won power in 1979. Gordon Brown's first task as chancellor was to make the Bank of England independent. Having gained power, Labour gave away one of the most important levers of economic policy. Central bank independence (CBI) has become another fashionable fad in economic policy making. Here I argue why I disagree with independence and why it is a fashion that may not stand the test of time. I analyse the arguments and evidence for and against Bank of England independence, and examine the implications.

- Independence shows the Labour Government is committed to low inflation. Already this has allowed long-term gilt yields to fall, reducing debt-servicing costs and releasing government spending for other areas such as education.
- Independence may prove successful, but there is no guarantee it will. As Professor Barro wrote, in the 1995 *Bank of England Quarterly Bulletin*, 'Low inflation cannot be attained merely by instituting legal changes that appear to promise a more independent central bank.'
- The benefits from central bank independence are often overstated, the costs usually underestimated. Despite popular perception, the academic literature

is mixed: some research finds in favour of independence, other research against.

- There are four main arguments against independence: (1) there are other factors apart from independence to explain why countries achieve low inflation; (2) it does not guarantee consistency between fiscal and monetary policy; (3) the temptation for political interference in interest rates is replaced by the risk of monetary overkill, as the new policy committee seeks to establish its anti-inflationary credibility; (4) there is a lack of democratic accountability.
- The structure of the economy, as well as the individuals who make the policy decisions, will be key issues as to whether Britain achieves low inflation.
- It is good that the Bank will be accountable and its decisions transparent, but it should have been given twin objectives, like the US Federal Reserve. As Alan Blinder once said, 'A central bank that decides to concentrate exclusively on price stability is, in effect, throwing in the towel on unemployment.'
- Official interest rates rose from 6.0 per cent to 6.25 per cent alongside the announcement, ensuring that the pound remained overvalued. Rather than forecast the short-run outlook for the economy here, it is important to stress that the previous monetary mechanism worked well, and Chancellor Clarke had raised rates when necessary.

ARGUMENTS AGAINST

It is widely assumed in the financial markets that central bank independence is a good thing. This is not always so, as I explain in looking at the arguments for and against independence, based on academic research, economic theory and empirical evidence from around the world.

> Back in the 1920's, the then Governor of the Bank of England, Montagu Norman, took every opportunity to emphasise the need for all countries to establish 'autonomous' central banks. Nobody listened. At home, thirty years on, the Labour Chancellor of the Exchequer Stafford Cripps took great pleasure in describing the Bank of England as his bank. And the Treasury's bank it has remained ever since. (Majorie Deane and Robert Pringle, *The Central Banks*)

And so it remained until the first Tuesday after the election, 6 May, when the Labour chancellor Gordon Brown gave the Bank of England 'operational independence' to set interest rates. A new nine-person Bank of England Monetary Policy Committee will set interest rates. This Committee is to have a built-in majority of Bank of England officials.

Giving the Bank of England greater independence is a recipe for monetary overkill and an overvalued pound. It points to higher official interest rates, as the new Committee aims to achieve what is still a tough inflation target of 1.0 per cent – 2.5 per cent. (I have argued previously that the original 1.0 per cent – 4.0 per cent inflation target was more appropriate, and that 1.0 per cent – 2.5 per cent is too tight, particularly in a booming economy. Measurement bias of inflation could overstate inflation pressures. Hence the Bundesbank regards 2 per cent as equivalent to price stability, and even New Zealand's inflation target of 0 per cent – 2 per cent was raised to 1 per cent – 3 per cent partly to reflect measurement bias.)

Furthermore, there is every likelihood that the new Monetary Policy Committee will view 2.5 per cent as a ceiling not a target. That means the Bank could choose a lower rate of inflation, say 2 per cent, to focus on as the target, recognizing there will be times when supply shocks could push inflation temporarily up to, say, 2.5 per cent. Thus 2.5 per cent becomes the ceiling, 2 per cent the target. The announcement of independence coincided with a 0.25 per cent rate increase from 6 per cent to 6.25 per cent, and base rates now look set to head higher.

There are four main arguments against making the Bank of England independent. Most of these are not specific to the United Kingdom and can be applied generally.

The Influence of a 'Third' Factor

It is an easy way out to believe inflation depends on whether a central bank is independent. It does not. As Table 6.1 shows, there is *not* a strong correlation between independence and low inflation. As Professor Barro showed in the 1995 *Bank of England Quarterly Bulletin*, 'Low inflation cannot be attained merely by instituting legal changes that appear to promise a more independent central bank.' Central bank independence does not guarantee low inflation. Other factors could. Figure 6.1 shows recent inflation performance in Germany and Japan (note that the vertical axes are different). Germany has an independent and credible central bank, but Japan has the most *dependent* central bank in the G7, and arguably amongst industrialized countries. Despite this, Japan's inflation record has been good.

The importance of another factor to explain low inflation is highlighted by Japan, but one need not look solely at Japan. Some research (see, for instance, Hall, 1994) argues that collective bargaining is as responsible as the Bundesbank for low inflation in Germany. Certainly, Germany's collective bargaining process has, until recently, minimized the unemployment cost of an anti-inflationary policy but Hall's arguments may be more applicable to France, which also enjoyed low inflation but whose central bank has only recently been made independent.

Also great attention is focused on New Zealand's experience but, as Figure 6.2 shows, there is similarity between Australia and New Zealand's performance – possibly suggesting that external developments, such as the global competitive environment, and not the institutional structure of the central bank are the key issue.

Table 6.1 Inflation rates and central bank independence

Country	Index of independence[a]	Inflation rate 1960–90	Country	Index of independence	Inflation rate 1960–90
West Germany	0.71	0.037	South Africa	0.33	0.099
Switzerland	0.65	0.038	Nigeria	0.33	0.125
Austria	0.65	0.043	Malaysia	0.32	0.034
Egypt	0.57	0.094	Uganda	0.32	0.353
Denmark	0.53	0.069	Italy	0.31	0.088
Costa Rica	0.52	0.117	Finland	0.30	0.073
Greece	0.52	0.109	Sweden	0.30	0.067
USA	0.51	0.049	Singapore	0.30	0.034
Ethiopia	0.50	0.058	India	0.30	0.074
Ireland	0.50	0.083	UK	0.30	0.077
Philippines	0.49	0.107	South Korea	0.29	0.113
Bahamas	0.48	0.063[b]	China	0.29	0.039
Tanzania	0.48	0.133	Bolivia	0.29	0.466
Nicaragua	0.47	0.436	Uruguay	0.29	0.441
Israel	0.47	0.350	Brazil	0.28	0.723
Netherlands	0.47	0.045	Australia	0.27	0.067
Canada	0.47	0.054	Thailand	0.27	0.052
Venezuela	0.45	0.100	Western Samoa	0.26	0.112[c]
Barbados	0.44	0.075	New Zealand	0.25	0.085
Argentina	0.44	0.891	Nepal	0.23	0.084
Honduras	0.44	0.058	Panama	0.23	0.033
Peru	0.44	0.606	Zimbabwe	0.22	0.074
Chile	0.43	0.416	Hungary	0.21	0.047
Turkey	0.42	0.235	Japan	0.20	0.054
Malta	0.42	0.035	Pakistan	0.19	0.072
Iceland	0.42	0.229	Columbia	0.19	0.170
Kenya	0.40	0.082	Spain	0.16	0.096
Luxembourg	0.40	0.044	Morocco	0.15	0.055
Zaire	0.39	0.357	Belgium	0.13	0.048
Mexico	0.37	0.227	Yugoslavia	0.12	0.395

Table 6.1 continued

Country	Index of independence[a]	Inflation rate 1960–90	Country	Index of independence	Inflation rate 1960–90
Indonesia	0.36	0.366	Poland	0.12	0.293[b]
Botswana	0.36	0.076	Norway	0.12	0.066
Ghana	0.35	0.256			
France	0.34	0.064			
Zambia	0.34	0.174			

Notes:

[a] The index of central bank independence is computed from data in Cukierman (1992, ch. 19, Appendix A). The index is a weighted average of the available data from 1950 to 1989 of legal provisions regarding: (1) appointment and dismissal of the governor (weight ⅙); (2) procedures for the formulation of monetary policy (weight ⅙); (3) objectives of central bank policy (weight ⅙); and (4) limitations of lending by the central bank (weight ½). The first category is an unweighted average of three underlying variables that involve the governor's term of office and the procedures for appointment and dismissal. The second category is an unweighted average of two variable, one indicating the location of the authority for setting monetary policy and the other specifying methods for resolving conflicts about policy. The third category relates to the prominence attached to price stability in the bank's charter. The fourth category is an unweighted average of four variables: limitations on advances, limitations on securitized lending, an indicator for the location of the authority that prescribes lending terms and the circle of potential borrowers from the central bank. For each underlying variable, Cukierman defines a scale from 0 to 1, where 0 indicates least favourable to central bank independence and 1 indicates most favourable. The overall index shown in this table runs correspondingly from 0 to 1.

[b] 1970–90.

[c] 1975–90.

This table 'shows the average inflation rate from 1960 to 1990 for the 67 countries in my sample that have data on the index of central bank independence'.

'A comparison between the index and the inflation rate reveals a crucial problem: the correlation between the two variables is essentially zero'.

'This negative finding is of considerable interest – it suggests that low inflation cannot be attained merely by instituting legal changes that appear to promote a more independent central bank.'

Source: Barro (1995), Bank of England.

An Independent Central Bank Does Not Guarantee Consistency between Monetary and Fiscal Policy

For economic policy to be effective, monetary and fiscal policy should be working towards achieving the same goal. Of course, an independent central bank can act as a brake on a profligate government whose fiscal policy is too loose, but, in such an environment of tight money and loose fiscal policy, the result is usually an appreciation and overshooting of the currency.

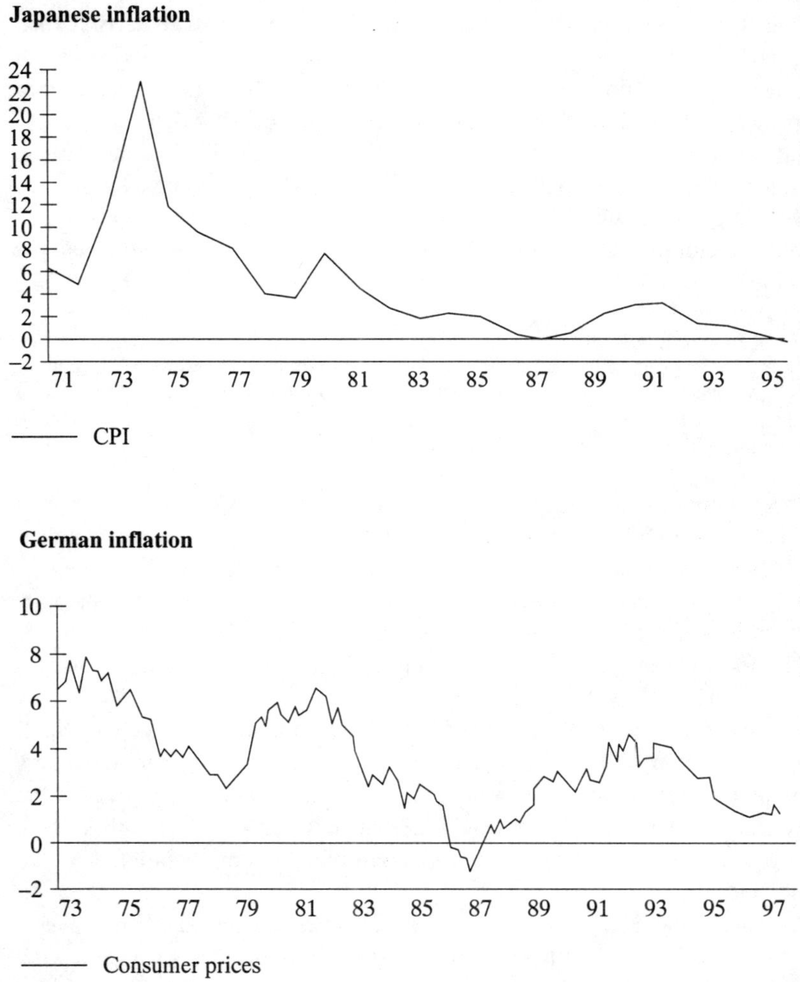

Figure 6.1 Inflation in Japan and Germany: the importance of a third factor

The academic literature on the issue of inconsistency produces mixed results, and is based on game theory and the relationship between the government and the central bank. The Labour government is committed to a tough fiscal policy and the hope has to be that the Bank of England's Monetary Policy Committee will take this into account when setting interest rates.

The Temptation of Monetary Overkill

Independence can result in monetary overkill, especially if a central bank is aiming to prove its anti-inflationary credibility. This is particularly a risk, judging from the Bank of England's behaviour in recent years and from the perception that Britain is an inflation-prone economy. This is the main criticism the previous chancellor, Kenneth Clarke, has made against independence.

Monetary policy has to strike a delicate balance, as the US Fed has shown. But even in America, where the Fed has a dual mandate, governors are seen as 'doves', and often subject to criticism, if they are seen as paying too much attention to employment. As Alan Blinder, former vice-chairman of the Fed, put it (in the *Federal Reserve Bank of Richmond Economic Quarterly*, Fall, 1996)

> The need to reduce large fiscal deficits (around the globe) dictates that budget policy remains a drag on total spending for the foreseeable future, regardless of the state of the macroeconomy. With the fiscal arm of stabilisation policy thereby paralysed, a central bank that decides to concentrate exclusively on price stability is, in effect, throwing in the towel on unemployment.

There is mixed evidence from the academic literature. Alesina and Summers (1993) found no evidence of overkill, but others have. In theory, monetary policy should be set by an authority that is more anti-inflationary than society as a whole, namely a central bank (the so-called 'Rogoff model'). But for the best outcome, the degree of central bank conservatism must not be too high, otherwise policy will be too tight and the cost of reducing inflation in terms of lost jobs and unemployment will be too high.

Even if a government's choice of officials aims to minimize this risk of overkill, there is no guarantee it will succeed, as there is a tendency for central bankers to 'go native', adopting a deflationary bias once in their new jobs. And, in the case of the new Monetary Policy Committee, there will already be a built-in Bank of England majority before the four external members are appointed by the chancellor.

Basic analytical models suggest that a central banker can be too inflation-averse and too insensitive to the possibilities of stabilizing output. As a result, the Monetary Policy Committee must be accountable in terms of providing information, being open to questioning and receptive to criticism. It is good that the United Kingdom's new set-up has many of these safeguards, in terms of accountability, but it is not clear how receptive to criticism the Monetary Policy Committee will be.

Whilst Chancellor Brown is right that monetary policy needs to be shielded from inappropriate political pressures, it also has to be sensitive to the real needs of the public, and independence does not address this dilemma. The way round this problem could have been to give the central bank twin objectives, reflecting

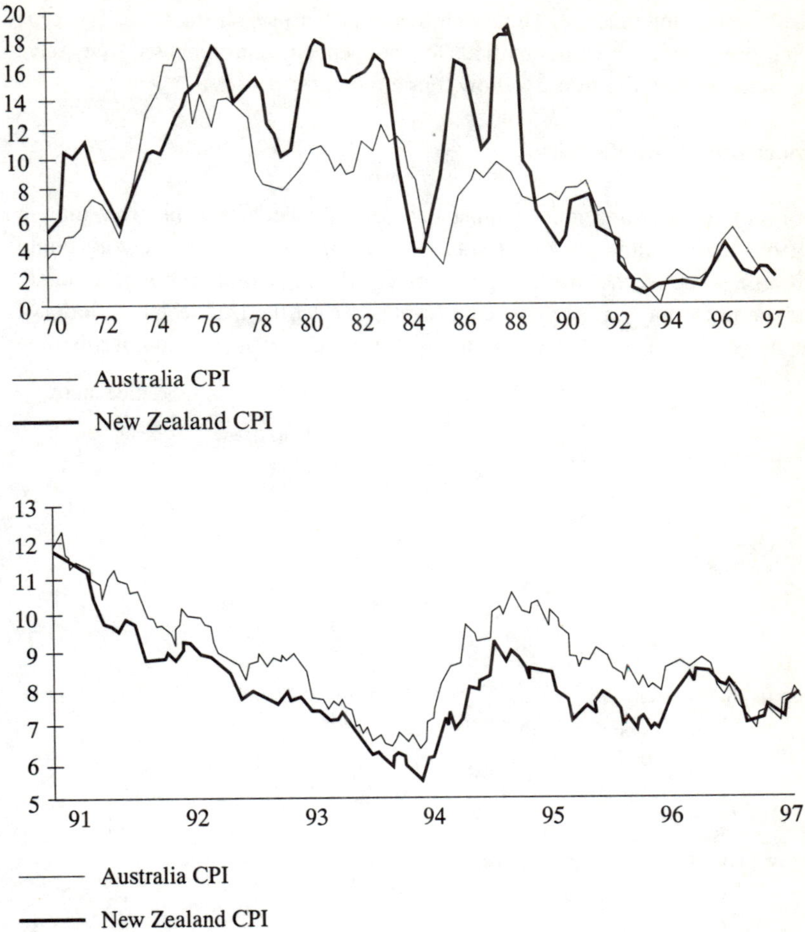

Figure 6.2 Inflation in Australia and New Zealand

the possible trade-off in policy. The US Federal Reserve not only has to achieve price stability but has to conduct policy to maintain stable employment conditions. The key issue is to try and ensure that the central bank carries out its policies in a responsible fashion. And in the absence of twin objectives this highlights the importance of the people involved.

While independence will remove political interference from interest rate decisions, it replaces this with the risk of monetary overkill. The Monetary Policy

Committee has to establish its credibility and has only one target to achieve. This risks interest rates being pushed too high. Figure 6.3 shows sacrifice ratios in recessions since 1962 against the Grilli, Masciandaro and Tabellini measure of central bank independence. The graph from Fischer (1994) suggests, 'There is no credibility bonus in labour markets for independent central banks – they have to continue repeatedly to prove how tough they are.'

Democratic Accountability

This is not the main argument against an independent central bank, even though the 1993 Roll Committee felt it was. An appropriate legal framework could overcome some of the fears. Page 30 of the Roll Committee's report stated, 'Transparency may have important advantages over the Bundesbank model of independence, which relies more on reputation and trust.' Although this may

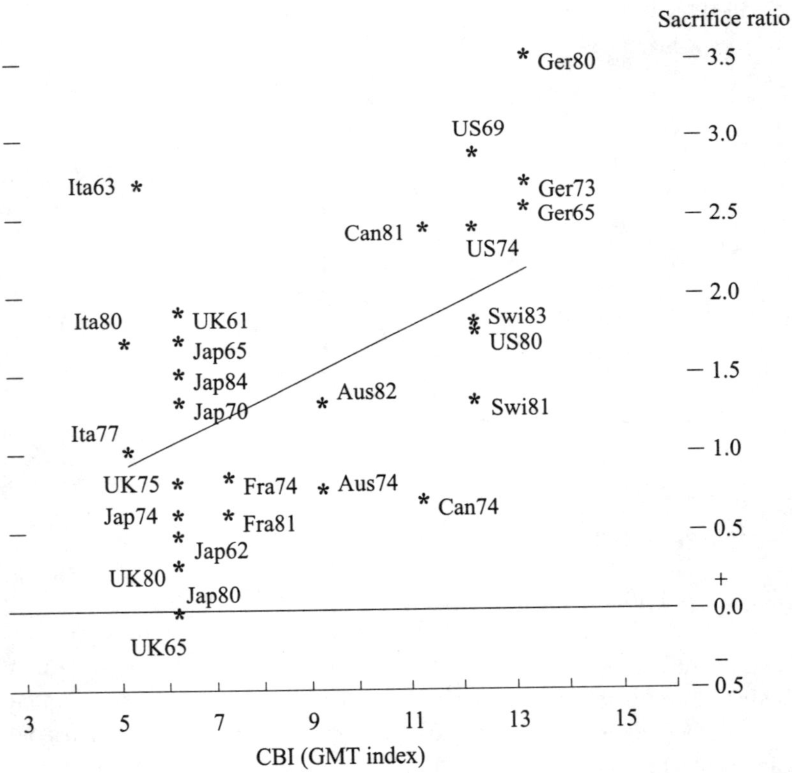

Source: Fischer (1994), Bank of England.

Figure 6.3 Monetary overkill

impose a constraint on the way a central bank conducts its policy, this is desirable and hence the accountability of the new Committee is welcome. Greater accountability should go hand-in-hand with independence and, in this respect, it should not only inform the public debate but condition the Committee to make sensible decisions.

OTHER ISSUES

Is it Necessary?

If a country wants low inflation, it is a debatable point whether this needs to be institutionalized through an independent central bank. The culture of a country and the structure of its economy are important in contributing to the inflation performance. The best way to reduce inflation is for the public to accept this. The revealed preference of people is reflected in their behaviour. Germany is committed to low inflation, because of its experience of hyperinflation. This is reinforced by the current economic climate, which suggests inflation may remain low.

Economic fashion has focused attention on the wrong issue, as the inflation environment and inflationary psychology of the 1970s and 1980s has created the desire for central bank independence. There is a tendency to think of Britain

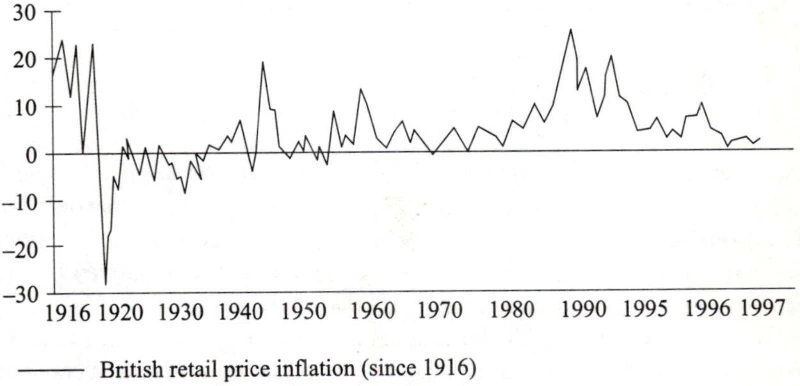

Figure 6.4 UK inflation: a low inflation era

as a high inflation country. Indeed, in the last 20 years, inflation has been high but beyond that Britain has enjoyed sustained periods of low inflation, as Figure 6.4 illustrates, which shows UK inflation since 1916. Britain's recent inflation performance has been good, reflecting the changing character of this economic cycle, where disinflationary pressures prevail.

The behaviour of the British electorate, like that of voters elsewhere, has shown a desire for cautious, anti-inflationary policies, reflected in the main parties advocating similar conservative and mainstream macroeconomic policies.

The Importance of the People Involved

This is a key issue. The Bank of England will have to be judged by its behaviour. Hence the people involved will be very important. If one has a good central bank and chancellor, the outcome is likely to be favourable. If one makes the Bank of England independent but has people who are not very good at making decisions the outcome will *not* be efficient. As the Roll Committee, itself a keen advocate of central bank independence, said,

> Because the formal degree of independence is always imprecise, the effective independence and hence credibility of a central bank is linked to its operational record. Within the same formal framework, different central banks can win differing degrees of credibility. In such circumstances, individuals can make a difference.

This is also linked to the issue of credibility. And as the US Fed chairman, Alan Greenspan (1994) said, 'Implicit in any monetary policy action or inaction, is an expectation of how the future will unfold, that is, a forecast. Ill-advised short-run perspectives on the part of a central bank lead to inflationary instabilities in the longer run.' Often the key is the individuals involved, as the successful performance of the US Fed under Greenspan has shown.

ARGUMENTS IN FAVOUR

What, then, are the arguments in favour of independence? As stated in Labour's election manifesto, 'We will reform the Bank of England to ensure that decision making on monetary policy is more effective, open, accountable and free from short-term political manipulation.' All these points were emphasized by the chancellor in handing operational independence over to the Bank.

If successful, central bank independence can be portrayed as a left-of-centre government changing its tactics and not its overall strategy, to take account of the influence of the financial markets.

Less Political Interference

There will be less political *interference*, but there will still be some political *influence*. For instance, Governor George may wish to be reappointed to his position when his current term expires in June 1998. Both deputy governors may wish to replace him. All may therefore wish to please Chancellor Brown. There is *no* reason to suggest they will, just as there was *no* sign that Ken Clarke took decisions solely on political considerations. It just highlights the point that politics can still play a role, through the power of appointment, in independent central banks.

One way to minimize this is to make very long appointments, as in the United States, where, with the exception of the chairman who stands for reappointment every four years, governors can be appointed for up to 14 years. Of course, experience shows that many do not remain for their whole term. The fact that appointments in the United Kingdom are to be for three years will allow the Chancellor to monitor closely the behaviour and consistency of the members, which should ensure that their behaviour is responsible.

Related to this point are two issues. First, why hive off just monetary policy? Surely Labour's move suggests it wants power, without responsibility? But as Deane and Pringle note in *The Central Banks* there is a particularly strong case for a government hiving off monetary policy compared with, say, energy or indeed any other area, as 'Money is the most politically sensitive commodity conceivable, its management does need some protection from political misuse.' Second, monetary policy affects the economy with a long lag. It is generally accepted that monetary policy may take up to two years before its full effects feed through and thus, the argument goes, it should be carried out by far-sighted central bankers. This is reinforced by the view that the costs of tight monetary policy are borne 'up front', while the benefits feed through with a lag.

The Conduct of Monetary Policy is Technical

Thus trained technicians, or economists, can carry out policy better than politicians. Recent experience, however, suggests that it may not always be the technicians who read the economy well. And, if they do, the goals of policy should still be set by the government.

Commitment to Low Inflation

Giving the Bank control over interest rates shows the government is committed to low inflation. This will be followed by a tough fiscal stance when Gordon Brown delivers his first budget. It is unlikely there will be any surprise tax increases, but there will be a commitment to existing tight spending plans. This has reassured the City, allowing long-term gilt yields to fall, reducing the government's debt-servicing bill and releasing money for other areas such as education. Not only will independence reduce inflationary expectations, but it is another step along the road to European Monetary Union (EMU). In view of this, the spread of longer-dated gilt yields over German bunds will narrow significantly – but gilt yields may not fall sharply until official interest rates reach their peak. There will be a convergence of spreads, but not yet.

The main argument is that independence will guarantee low inflation. This is often seen as a necessary and sufficient condition for stable, longer-term growth. Low inflation, followed *eventually* by lower interest rates, should remove the need for boom/bust economic policies. If successful, it should be followed by higher investment. Certainly, low inflation is an important aim of policy but this should not be at the expense of all other objectives. Reducing unemployment, improving living standards for those in work and boosting the United Kingdom's low level of investment are all vitally important current macroeconomic policy needs that should be directly addressed by proactive policies.

Emphasis on Longer Term

I welcome the chancellor's emphasis on the need for stable longer-term economic performance. But my concern, as stated above, is that too much emphasis may be placed on the institutional changes at the Bank of England. And, as should be clear from the foregoing, I certainly would have preferred twin objectives. Without these, much depends on the way the new committee behaves, and clearly the Bank needs to be judged on its behaviour.

The cost in the labour market could be too high (see Figure 6.3). Furthermore to minimize any adverse initial impact on investment plans, and to reverse Britain's longer-term trend of low investment, there is a need for a more proactive policy geared towards boosting investment through tax incentives. The cost to the economy of investment not occurring is greater than the price of ensuring that it does.

Reduction of Interest Rates and Debt Servicing

Entering EMU and adopting the anti-inflationary credibility of the European Central Bank could reduce the risk premium on gilts, where yields are high compared with those on the continent. But so, too, will Bank of England independence. As long-term yields fall, debt-servicing costs are reduced. The November budget Red Book showed that, in the fiscal year 1996, expenditure on net debt interest was £22.2 billion, which is 7.1 per cent of total government expenditure. As inflation expectations improve, long-term yields will decline, releasing money for other areas, such as education.

Stepping Stone towards EMU

The Labour government has adopted a welcome positive approach towards Europe, but is still someway short of endorsing a single currency. (I remain pro-Europe but anti-European Monetary Union and against the deflationary mentality of a single currency.) Independence is a stepping stone towards EMU and gives the UK greater flexibility if it wishes eventually to join a single currency.

All the above points are valid but, even after taking them into account, the arguments against independence are more compelling.

ACADEMIC EVIDENCE

I have already referred to some of the evidence above. Table 6.2 summarizes the academic literature on the issue of central bank independence. Not all papers are summarized here, just a sample. There is a tendency to think the evidence supports fully the argument for independence – but it does not.

The three most significant papers favouring independence are Rogoff (1985), Cukierman *et al.*, and Alesina and Summers (1993). Rogoff (1985) found it is best to allow monetary policy to be controlled by a conservative, anti-inflationary independent central banker. This establishes a case for independence but, as stated above, it is crucial that the central bank is not too conservative. Ensuring this balance puts much importance on the choice of individuals for the Monetary Committee. Cukierman *et al.* (1992) constructed an index of independence, extending the work of Grilli *et al.* (1991). In terms of the Cukierman index shown in Table 6.1, granting independence moves the UK from 0.3 to about 0.6, where 0 is least favourable and 1 most favourable to independence. The subsequent decision of Chancellor Brown to remove supervision from the Bank of England also, in theory, increases their degree of independence. Alesina and Summers (1993) is a seminal piece on this subject. The authors' research showed that independence reduced inflation, without any associated loss of output. On the basis of these results, there would appear to be no costs from central bank independence. Yet subsequent work by Alesina and Gatti (1995) finds that a central bank does not make a big effort at stabilizing output shocks.

As conclusive as this evidence is in favour of independence, it does not stand alone. The results from Fujiki (1996), for instance, suggests that the relationship between central bank independence and inflation or growth from Alesina and Summers is contingent on both sample periods and other variables involved in a cross-country comparison. That is, the arguments based on work by Alesina and Summers do not stand up to changes in samples and in statistical methods. If this is so, it supports the argument that there are other issues that must be taken into account.

Table 6.2 Recent academic literature on central bank independence

Year	Economist	Analysis	Conclusion and comments
1985	Rogoff	Social welfare function weighting deviations of output and inflation from optimal levels.	Best policy is to allow monetary policy to be controlled by a 'conservative' central banker, that is an institution weighting inflation deviation more heavily than in the social welfare function. But there is a downside. This reduces average inflation but increases output variability.
1991	Grilli, Masciandaro & Tabellini	Calculates a measure of central bank independence for 18 industrialized countries over 1960–92, based on five main measures: (1) appointments of officials; (2) relationship with government; (3) constitution; (4) monetary financing of budget deficit; (5) monetary instruments.	Found significant negative relationship between inflation and CBI. But the weights used in averaging the components to measure central bank independence are somewhat arbitrarily chosen.
1992	Cukierman, Webb & Neyapti	Extends above analysis using four classes of criteria to 72 countries and also constructed questionnaire-based index of CBI for 26 countries.	Found significant positive relationship between inflation and CBI. This seemed to be correlated with turnover of central bank governors. Also found distinction between the way central bankers described their independence in the questionnaire and legal CBI.
1992	Lohmann	Allows the conservative central banker of Rogoff to be overruled by the government.	This extra constraint of government involvement means the central bank responds more to larger disturbances, thus ruling out the need for the government to intervene – 'a flexible escape clause'. CBI is less inflationary and less activist. Proposes policy handed to partially (not fully) independent central bank.
1992	Waller	Looks at choice of a conservative central banker in a multi-sector model, analysing spillover effects between different sectors of the economy.	Appointment of ICB will be subject to partisan influences. Choice of conservative central banker leads to disagreement between sectors over degree of inflation reduction and output instability that should occur.

Table 6.2 continued

Year	Economist	Analysis	Conclusion and comments
1993	Alesina & Summers	Analyses data for 16 industrialized countries, 1955–88, taking into account degree of independence.	The perfect result for central bankers, CBI provides improved inflation performance but not at the expense of growth: 'The inflation benefits of central bank independence are likely to outweigh any output costs.' But takes no account of other factors accounting for cross-country differentials in inflation and growth.
1993	Blake & Westaway	Attempts to clarify some of the theoretical issues regarding Bank of England independence, analysing policy chances in the context of dynamic game theory.	'Economic grounds for delegation of monetary policy to the Bank of England may be rather weak, and indicate instead that a unified approach to fiscal and monetary policy is more likely to achieve the government's objectives.'
1993	Posen	Response to Alesina & Summers.	Relationship is not causal. Countries that are risk-averse as regards inflation develop institutions to support this. In particular, countries in which the financial sector is politically powerful become effectively inflation-averse.
1993	Roll Committee	General discussion of Bank of England discussion.	Make BOE independent to enhance credibility, with sole objective of price stability and government override possibility.
1993	Walsh; and Persson & Tabellini	Game theory approach. A principal (society) designs a contract so the agent (central bank) will act in the principal's best interests. Central bank punished if it does not achieve its target.	Central bank is assumed to have better information but much depends on how the loss function of the central bank relates to that of society. Finds this policy works well, removing inflation bias of monetary policy.
1994	Debelle & Fischer	Analyses inflation performance in terms of three factors: (1) inflation objective; (2) economic influences, such as setting official rates; (3) political influences, such as appointments.	The ability of the CB to use freely its policy instruments (i.e. (2)) is the most important influence on inflation. Inflation objective also important, but not political influences.

Table 6.2 continued

Year	Economist	Analysis	Conclusion and comments
1995	Alesina, Gatti	Isolates two sources of output variability: (1) economic variability induced by exogenous shocks that monetary policy should stabilize; (2) political variability introduced by uncertainty about future policy.	Effect of independence is ambiguous; it reduces policy-induced variability but there is increased variability 'caused by the fact that the inflation-averse central bank does not make a big effort at stabilising output shocks'.
1995	Barro	See text.	There is little correlation between CBI and inflation, but evidence for adverse effect of inflation (10 per cent higher inflation a year reduces GDP by 0.2 per cent to 0.3 per cent a year).
1995	Fischer	Discusses the theoretical basis for CBI, which he supports, and also raises some open unresolved issues.	'The most important conclusion of both the theoretical and empirical literatures is that a central bank should have instrument independence, but should not have goal independence.' But finds a central bank can be too independent.
1995	McCallum	Brief discussion and analysis of the literature.	Concludes there are two faccalies in the literature, which play down the benefits of CBI – good monetary performance and the benefits arising from contracts – even though he had concluded that contracts merely relocated and did not remove the motivation for dynamic inconsistency.
1995	Walsh	Adopts a principal (government)–agent (central bank) framework to determine how to structure the central bank and induce the socially optimal policy.	Optimal contract ties the rewards of the central bank to realize inflation and punishes the central bank when inflation deviates from the optimal level. But inflation targeting rules are suboptimal in the presence of supply shocks.
1996	Fujiki	Extends the Alesina & Summers (1993) analysis, using stricter conditions based on Barro (1991) and Romer (1993).	Results of Alesina & Summers do not prove robust under stricter econometric tests, casting doubt on their reliability as a basis for policy recommendations. For instance, 'The negative correlations between central bank independence and inflation are statistically significant in the samples of 1960–89 and 1975–89 but *not* significant in the restricted period of 1980–89.'

The issue of consistency between monetary and fiscal policy is also addressed in the literature, with the focus on game theory. Blake and Westaway (1993) consider this issue, and conclude that a unified approach to monetary and fiscal policy is better than independence per se. Professor Currie, by contrast, reaches a different conclusion.

Overall, there is something in the academic literature for everyone, but it is important to stress that the evidence is not as pro-independence as one might expect. And even some economists who are in favour of independence find strong arguments against. I do not agree that having an independent central bank is a necessary or sufficient condition for low inflation. But the Bank of England having been given independence, other measures are necessary to ensure that the policy is successful.

MODELS: TWIN GOALS NEEDED

The government had a number of role models to choose from. The German Bundesbank is given goal independence, free to choose its own inflation targets, in addition to setting interest rates. By contrast, the Reserve Bank of New Zealand is given instrument independence, allowing it to set interest rates to achieve the inflation target, which is set by the government after consultation.

The model for the Bank of England is along the lines of New Zealand. And if we are to enter a single currency, there will be a further shift to the German model. By contrast under the US Federal Reserve Act, as amended, the Fed is directed by Congress to promote 'maximum employment, stable prices, and moderate long-term interest rates'. As price stability is assumed to bring low long-term interest rates, it is referred to as the Fed's 'dual mandate'. It is disappointing that the Bank was not given twin objectives, like its US counterpart, whose role is to achieve low inflation and stable employment conditions. While independence will remove political interference from interest rate decisions, it replaces this with the risk of monetary overkill.

Table 6.3 summarizes the differences between the Bundesbank and the Reserve Bank of New Zealand, while Table 6.4 compares the new set-up for the Bank of England with those of the Federal Reserve, the Bundesbank and the Bank of Japan, which is to become independent in April 1998.

IMPLICATIONS

The question is how best to structure the institutional environment to produce the monetary policy most beneficial to society's welfare. I do not think the answer is to have an independent Bank of England. A danger is that granting independence creates an unrealistic expectation about what an independent Bank of England can do and will achieve. It is important that it does not divert attention from the need to maintain healthy employment conditions and further improve the supply side of the economy and that it is not seen as a substitute for other policy measures which are needed, particularly those aimed at boosting investment.

Bank of England independence could be successful. As we are in a disinflationary environment there should not be the need for excessive policy tightening. The prime minister described the decision to give the Bank independence as the most important economic decision since the war. The same was said the day the pound entered the ERM, and we all know the consequences of that. It is to be hoped that Bank of England independence will not end in tears, but much depends on how responsible the new nine-person Monetary Policy Committee is in setting interest rates.

Table 6.3 Alternative approaches to central bank independence

	Constitutional/ reputational	Legal/performance contract
Example	*Deutsche Bundesbank*	*Reserve Bank of New Zealand*
Main objective		
Price stability	Primary objective	Sole objective
Supporting government economic policy	Secondary objective	—
Government override	Only implicit (new law)	Statutory provision in current law
Main targets		
Obligatory	No	Yes
Agreed with government	No	Yes
Escape clauses	No	Yes
Time horizon	No	Three years
Responsibility		
Laid upon:	Board	Governor
Monitoring	Only implicit	Dismissal of governor for failure

Table 6.4 Comparison of central banks

	Germany[a]	America[b]	Japan[c]	Britain[d]
Independent	Yes, very	Yes	Spring 1998	Yes (called operational independence, but effectively full independence)
Operational set-up	Council directorate	FOMC governors regional members	Policy Board regional presidents	Nine-person Monetary Policy Committee: governor deputy governors other BOE officials outside economists
Appointment	Council members tend to rise through the ranks	Mixture, but strong political interference over governors	Political control over Policy Board members	By government/chancellor
Policy Goal	Single goal: low inflation (in theory, Bundesbank is supposed to support government's economic policy)	Twin objectives: inflation employment	Twin objectives, but emphasis is low inflation; credit system the other	Tough inflation target set by the government. Currently 1 per cent–2.5 per cent. And, without prejudice to that price objective, to support the government's economic policy, including its objectives for growth and employment
Accountability	Little accountability	Very accountable, and this helps prevent monetary overkill	Halfway house, six-monthly report, via finance minister, to parliament	Independent, but will have to report to parliament's Treasury and Civil Service Committee
Meetings	Every two weeks	Eight times a year	Like the Bundesbank, every two weeks	Monthly monetary meeting
Minutes	No	Yes	Yes	Yes

Notes:
[a] Bundesbank (blueprint for European Central Bank).
[b] Federal Reserve Board.
[c] Bank of Japan (proposal from April 1998).
[d] Bank of England (following Labour's changes).
Source: Capie et al. (1994), Bank of England.

REFERENCES

Alesina, A. and Gatti, R. (1995), 'Independent central banks: low inflation at no cost?', *AEA Papers and Proceedings*, Vol.85, No.2, May 1995, 196–200.

Alesina, A. and Summers, L.H. (1993), 'Central bank independence and macroeconomic performance: some comparative evidence', *Journal of Money, Credit and Banking*, 25 May, 151–62.

Barro, R. (1995), 'Inflation and economic growth', *Bank of England Quarterly Bulletin*, Vol.35, No.2, May 1995, 166–76.

Blake, A. and Westaway, P. (1993), 'Should the Bank of England be independent', *Natural Institute Economic Review*, No.143, February 1993, 72–80.

Blinder, A. (1996), 'Central Banking in a Democracy', Vol.82, No.4, *Federal Reserve Bank of Richmond Economic Quarterly*, Fall 1996, 1–14.

Capie, F., Goodhart, C., Fisher, S. and Schnadt, N. (1994), *The Future of Central Banking*, The Tercenterary Symposium of the Bank of England.

Cukierman, A. (1992), *Central Bank Strategy, Credibility and Independence: Theory and Evidence*, Cambridge MA: MIT Press.

Cukierman, A., Webb, S. and Neyapti, B. (1992), 'Measuring the independence of central banks and its effect on policy outcomes', *The World Bank Economic Review*, **6**, 1992, 353–98.

Currie, D., Levine, P. and Pearlman, J. (1992), 'European monetary union or hard EMS?', *European Economic Review*, **36**, 1185–1204.

Deane, M. and Pringle R. (1994), *The Central Banks*, London: Hamish Hamilton.

Debelle, G. and Fischer, S. (1994), 'How independent should a central banker be?', *Federal Reserve Bank of Boston.*

Fischer, S. (1994), 'Modern central banking' in Capie et al., 262–308.

Fischer, S. (1995), 'Central bank independence revisited', *AEA Papers and Proceedings*, Vol.85, No.2, May 1995, 201-11.

Fujiki, H. (1996), 'Central bank independence indexes in economic analysis: a reappraisal', *Bank of Japan Monetary and Economic Studies*, December 1996, 79–101.

Greenspan, A. (1994), 'Discussion of conference proceedings', in Capie, F. *et al.*, pp. 241–45.

Grilli, V., Masciandaro, D. and Tabellini G. (1991), 'Political and monetary institutions and public finance policies in the industrial economies', Economic Policy, **13**, October, 341–912.

Hall, Peter A. (1994), 'Central bank independence and coordinated wage bargaining: their interaction in Germany and Europe', *German Politics and Society*.

Lohman, S. (1992) 'Optimal commitment in monetary policy: credibility versus flexibility', American Economic Review, Vol.82, No.l, March 1992, 273–84.

McCallum, B.T. (1993), 'Specification and analysis of a monetary policy rule for Japan', *BOJ Monetary and Economic Studies*, Vol. 11, No.2, November, 1993, 1–45.

Persson, T. and Tabellini, G. (1993), 'Designing institutions for monetary stability', *Carnegie Rochester Conference Series Public Policy*, **39**, December 1993, 53–84.

Posen, A. (1993), 'Central bank independence does not cause low inflation: the politics behind the institutional fix', Harvard University.

Rogoff, K. (1995), 'The optimal degree of commitment to an intermediate monetary target.', Quarterly Journal of Economics, November 1995, **100**(4), 1169–90.

Roll, E. (1993), 'Independent and accountable – A new mandate for the Bank of England', The Roll Committee report of an independent panel, Centre for Economic and Policy Research.

Waller, C.J. (1992), 'The choice of a conservative central banker is a multi-sector economy', *American Economic Review*, Vol.82, No.4, September 1992, 1006–12.

Walsh, C.E. (1993), 'Central bank strategies, credibility and independence: a review essay', *Journal of Monetary Economics*, **32**, 1993, 287–302.

Walsh, C.E. (1995), 'Optimal contracts for central bankers', *American Economic Review*, Vol.85, No.1, March, 1995, 150–67.

7. What are the central bank's and the private sector's objectives?

Charles A.E. Goodhart and Haizhou Huang*

INTRODUCTION

Maurice Peston and Bernard Corry have always been concerned with public policy issues, and in particular with the political and practical realism of the economic analysis being developed. The structure of models, and the choice of assumptions, however, are all too often dictated by mathematical convenience and tractability, rather than by empirical evidence, or even by common sense.

In our example of that syndrome in this chapter, taken from the game-theoretic approach to central banking, the crucial form of the monetary authorities' utility function is set up in the standard formulations on a remarkably flimsy basis, while the private sector's own objectives and utility are hardly motivated at all. Even more important, the *political* interactions between the private sector and the monetary authorities, whereby the satisfaction of the public with the policies pursued by the authorities impinges directly on those authorities (and not just indirectly via changing expectations and nominal wage demands), is rarely explicitly modelled. It is our purpose here to try to inject more political realism into this formal model. We hope, and believe, that Maurice and Bernard will approve.

To recapitulate, in the time inconsistency literature, dating back to Kydland and Prescott (1977), the central bank can use its monetary policy instrument instantaneously to affect output. Hence, with the private sector's inflation expectations given at any time, there will be an incentive for the monetary authorities to expand output, even if the authorities have tried to commit themselves not to do so. Indeed, the problem of time inconsistency is often held to explain much of the inflationary bias in recent decades.[1] A large proportion of the theoretical literature on monetary policy and central banking has been taken up with elaborating this analysis (for example, Cukierman, 1992) and with trying

* For helpful comments and suggestions on the previous draft of the paper, we thank Peter Clark, Francesco Lippi, Kenneth Rogoff, Riccardo Rovelli, Eric Schaling, Guido Tabellini and Carl Walsh. Needless to say, we are solely responsible for all the remaining errors and omissions.

to suggest partial remedies, ranging through reputable central banks (Barro and Gordon, 1983) to the appointment of conservative central bankers (Rogoff, 1985), to independent central banks (Fischer, 1994) and to specially designed contracts for central bankers (Walsh, 1995; Persson and Tabellini, 1993).

The above strategic interactions between the monetary authorities and the private sector were first analysed in a game-theoretic model by Barro and Gordon (1983), which has since become the standard game-theoretic model employed to analyse the time inconsistency issue in monetary analysis, which has been such a fertile and fruitful field in recent years. However, there remain a number of respects in which the current generation of models outlining this game are implausible and unrealistic. To some extent, such shortcomings have been inevitable, given the need to keep such models relatively simple and mathematically tractable. Nevertheless, we believe that it should be possible to align several features of the structure of such models more closely to reality without making the whole exercise impossibly complex.

One of our main concerns here as regards the present structure of these models is that the utility functions of both the monetary authorities and the private sector are not motivated with sufficient realism. The purpose of this chapter is to provide a more realistic motivational basis for the actions of the main players, that is, the monetary authorities and the private sector, while remaining within the context of the standard game-theoretic analysis.[2]

The private sector's sole function in most of the current games in the literature is to select a level of nominal wages and prices, conditioned on its expectations of future inflation, which in turn depend on its perceptions of what the monetary authority will subsequently want to do. Insofar as this sector's utility function is represented at all, it is usually only a (symmetric) function of the deviation of actual from expected inflation. Usually (though not in all such exercises) the private sector is assumed not to care about unemployment, but, even when it does do so, such concern is immaterial for the game, because the private sector's only role lies in setting nominal contracts, prior to the monetary authority's determination of its monetary instrument.

In contrast to the private sector, which usually either does not care about, or cannot influence, the level of employment, the monetary authority is supposed to wish to achieve a level of employment above the equilibrium natural rate. But since the private sector either does not care about unemployment or cannot punish the authorities for high unemployment, the motivation for this preference is rarely clear. In most cases, the 'critical ingredient responsible for the inflationary bias result is the notion that due to the existence of distortionary labor taxes, the natural level of employment ... is lower than the desired rate' (Cukierman, 1992, p. 35). The artificiality of this argument is evidenced by the paucity of studies trying to give an empirical basis to a relationship between the inflationary bias and the extent of such tax-produced distortion. Moreover, Cukierman himself argues that 'a competitive equilibrium view of the labor market does not deliver an inflationary bias even in the presence of distortionary labor taxes and nominal contracts' (ibid., p. 38) and retreats to a more complicated labour market involving both unionized and competitive sectors. Even here, employment is only a decreasing function of the real wage rate under some quite complex conditions, which Cukierman assumes rather than tests. Thus the 'social welfare' basis for the inflationary bias remains somewhat tenuous and obscure.[3] In much of the literature it gets slipped in early as an assumption, which serves to allow the modelling exercise to proceed, without much, or any, justification – certainly not empirical justification.

In the more descriptive accounts of the basis for an inflationary bias and for time inconsistency, if not in most of the formal models, the reason for that bias is clearly stated as being to please the electorate (the 'feel-good' factor) in the short run. Time inconsistency is thus related to the political business cycle, though even here empirical evidence for the actual existence of this latter (Alesina, 1989) is much more sparse than is widely believed. But if politicians want to expand employment to become more popular among voters, a desire for employment above the natural rate must enter into the utility function of the private sector.

There are, indeed, several reasons why this might be so, for example connected with the fact that most agents cannot choose their optimal amount of work effort along a continuously differentiable function. Moreover, a decrease in unemployment is consistently treated as 'good news'. It is, we assert, a stylized fact of modern economies that less unemployment is always preferred to more. Thus we express the private sector's (*P*) utility function as:

$$UP_t = -\phi(y_t - y^*)^2 - (\pi_t - \pi^*)^2, \tag{7.1}$$

where y^* is maximum attainable output in logarithm (and can also be expressed as $y^* = ky_n$, where k is a positive, possibly constant, coefficient greater than unity, and y_n is the natural rate of output), and the second term represents the standard formulation whereby the costs of inflation are represented by the deviation of inflation, symmetrically given the quadratic form, from the desired level, π^*, which may be zero.[4]

The private sector's level of utility is, however, irrelevant to the monetary authorities in most of the social welfare explanations of the inflationary bias, since the private sector's only function in such models is to set nominal wages and prices. In the more realistic political models, however, the private sector's utility does enter the utility function of the political authorities, since at the time of elections the politicians will be removed from power if the electorate becomes unhappy.

Thus, if the monetary authorities are dominated by the decisions of the political authorities, with central bank subservience, then their utility function will depend on the satisfaction rating which they are receiving from the private sector. Hence the monetary authorities' utility function will respond to, and in a sense incorporate, the utility function of the private sector (Goodhart, 1994). This does not, of course, prevent the monetary authorities from placing a differing weighting on employment and inflation depending on differences in position, information and tastes. Hence we may write for the monetary authorities (*M*), a utility function:

$$UM_t = -\gamma\phi(y_t - y^*)^2 - \xi(\pi_t - \pi^*)^2 - 2\psi\pi_t, \tag{7.2}$$

where γ and ξ are positive coefficients, which may be greater, or less, than unity, depending on the differences between the politicians' and the private sector's objective weightings; γ and ξ may be time varying, for example over the electoral cycle, as a result of political pressure from the private sector. The additional term, $\psi\pi_t$, is entered to account for the possibility, explored by Walsh (1995) and Persson and Tabellini (1993), of penalizing the monetary authorities for inflationary outcomes, in such a way as to counteract their inflationary bias. Again ψ is a positive coefficient, whose size depends on the incentive structure imposed on the authorities.

Granting the central bank independence (Fischer, 1994), with a mandate to achieve price stability (von Hagen, 1995), appointing a conservative central bank governor (Rogoff, 1985) and/or penalizing the monetary authorities for inflationary outcomes through an incentive contract (Walsh, 1995; Persson and Tabellini, 1993) are institutional ways to lower γ towards zero and to raise ξ and ψ. Even with full independence, however, γ is never likely to reach zero. There remain several routes through which the feeling of the general public will influence central bankers. At the minimum, no one likes to be criticized and reviled, and such criticism is likely to lead to some reconsideration. Beyond that, no institutional change can ever be irrevocable, however much that may be denied. What one generation has established and promulgated a succeeding generation can reverse and undo. The central bank has no more divisions than the Pope. The central bank's position and influence ultimately depend on persuading those who have delegated power to it (in a democracy that is the public at large) that it is undertaking its delegated responsibilities in a satisfactory manner (Minford, 1995). However independent the central bank may be through act of government, treaty, statute, and so on, it cannot ignore its various constituencies: the public at large, the financial sector (Posen, 1995), the political parties, and so on. So, constitutional changes to the status of the central bank may well, and are so intended to, change the coefficients in the monetary authority's utility function, but do not, in our view, change its functional form.

This more realistic formulation with the feature of a Walsh-type inflation penalty imposed on the authorities does not cause much complication. In fact it is very close to the standard format of the Barro–Gordon, or Cukierman, game structure. As shown in the next section, the basic results of this game include an inflationary bias, unless the weight ψ on the central bank's disutility from inflation is raised sufficiently to offset the inflationary bias. This latter is the key finding of the recent work by Walsh (1995) and by Persson and Tabellini (1993). In this respect, our results remain identical to those of recent work in this field. However, the basic causation of the inflationary bias here is totally different. It arises, not because the authorities want to fool the people for their own good into working harder, but because the general public wants a boom, an expanding economy, and the politicians do not have the strength to resist what the public wants. As we note further in the next section, this throws a somewhat different light on the contrainflationary success of the Bundesbank, and implies that constitutional change towards central bank independence may be more problematical than is sometimes suggested by the more standard exercises.

In later sections we also present several other interesting findings. If the central banker is subject to an optimal compensation contract, it should be no more or less conservative than the private sector and, more importantly, although its utility increases proportionally with the relative weight the private sector places on employment, as a result of political pressure, this political pressure factor is actually irrelevant to its decision on monetary policy. On the other hand, without an optimal compensation contract, the central banker should always be more conservative than the private sector, regardless of whether the inflationary penalty on the central banker is too strong or too weak. In this case, the divergence between the private sector's and the central banker's objectives increases if the private sector cares deeply about unemployment, and/or puts more political pressure on the central banker to counter unemployment, or if monetary policy has more effect on unemployment.

The organization of the rest of the chapter is as follows. The next section delivers the basic model and briefly discusses its main features; the third section discusses the optimal degree of conservativeness; the fourth section deals with the divergence between the monetary authority and the private sector's utility levels; the fifth section, on the optimal strength of political pressure, is followed by the concluding section.

THE MODEL AND ITS FEATURES

The basic model consists of the private sector's and the monetary authority's utility functions, already described, the Lucas supply function and the effect of the monetary authority's instrument on inflation. These functions are stated in equations (7.1) to (7.4) below: the private sector's utility function,

$$UP_t = -\phi(y_t - y^*)^2 - (\pi_t - \pi^*)^2; \tag{7.1}$$

the monetary authority's utility function,

$$UM_t = -\gamma\phi(y_t - y^*)^2 - \xi(\pi_t - \pi^*)^2 - 2\psi\pi_t, \tag{7.2}$$

the Lucas supply function,

$$y_t - y_n = \alpha(\pi_t - E\pi_t) + u_t, \tag{7.3}$$

where α is a positive coefficient; and finally, the effect of the instrument on inflation,

$$i_t - \pi_t = \delta_t, \tag{7.4}$$

where $i_t = \Delta m_t$, and δ_t, is assumed to be zero.[5]

So, by substitution,

$$UM_t = -\gamma\phi[y_n + \alpha(i_t - Ei_t) + u_t - y^*]^2 - \xi(i_t - \pi^*)^2 - 2\psi i_t, \tag{7.5}$$

which transforms into

$$UM_t = \alpha^2\gamma\phi[i_t - Ei_t - (y^* - y_n)/\alpha + u_t/\alpha]^2 - \xi(i_t - \pi^*)^2 - 2\psi i_t. \tag{7.6}$$

Maximizing utility with respect to the monetary instrument, i_t, gives

$$-2\alpha^2\gamma\phi[i_t - Ei_t - (y^* - y_n)/\alpha + u_t/\alpha] - 2\xi(i_t - \pi^*) - 2\psi = 0. \tag{7.7}$$

For this to be so,

$$(\alpha^2\gamma\phi + \xi)i_t = \xi\pi^* + \alpha^2\gamma\phi Ei_t + \alpha\gamma\phi(y^* - y_n - u_t) - \psi. \tag{7.8}$$

Taking expectations on both sides leads to

$$Ei_t = \pi^* + [\alpha\gamma\phi(y^* - y_n) - \psi]/\xi, \tag{7.9}$$

$$\pi_t = i_t = \pi^* + [\alpha\gamma\phi(y^* - y_n) - \psi]/\xi - [\alpha\gamma\phi/(\alpha^2\gamma\phi + \xi)]u_t. \tag{7.10}$$

The inflationary bias is higher the greater is α, the effect on output of the surprise expansion; γ, the monetary authorities' dislike of unemployment; ϕ, the private sector's dislike of unemployment; and $y^* - y_n$, the size of the gap between the maximum possible and equilibrium output. The bias is lower, the greater is ξ, the monetary authorities' dislike of inflation, and ψ, the extra penalty imposed on them for allowing inflation. Clearly, by setting this penalty accurately, so that

$$\psi^* = \alpha\gamma\phi(y^* - y_n) = \alpha\gamma\phi(k-1)y_n, \qquad (7.11)$$

the inflationary bias could be eliminated, as in the Walsh contract.[6] Thus all that would seem necessary to eliminate inflation would be an institutional mechanism to give the monetary authorities, for example an independent central bank, the right incentive structure in their contract. While we do believe that establishing a good incentive structure is desirable, in reality things are not quite that simple.[7]

The other point that we want to emphasize is that, once the private sector's utility is properly imbedded into that of the monetary authorities, γ and ϕ always appear in joint form. It is impossible for any outsider to distinguish whether low inflation is due to the priority that the private sector gives to price stability (relative to unemployment), or to the relative preferences of the authorities, because the two are so closely interrelated.

OPTIMAL DEGREE OF CONSERVATIVENESS

Because the private sector's utility function is an integral part of our model, wherein the private sector also cares about unemployment, we can use our formal model to assess its preference for the optimal degree of central bank conservativeness, that is the value of ξ that maximizes its own utility. In this respect we can extend the model of Rogoff, in which the private sector does not have an explicit utility function in which concern for employment enters.

From equations (7.3) and (7.10), we have,

$$y_t = y_n + \frac{\xi}{\alpha^2\gamma\phi + \xi}u_t. \qquad (7.12)$$

Substituting into equation (7.11) and manipulating leads to

$$UP_t = -\phi\left[(k-1)y_n - \frac{\xi}{\alpha^2\gamma\phi + \xi}u_t\right]^2 - \left[\frac{\alpha\gamma\phi(k-1)y_n - \psi}{\xi} - \frac{\alpha\gamma\phi}{\alpha^2\gamma\phi + \xi}u_t\right]^2. \qquad (7.13)$$

Taking expectations leads to

$$EUP_t = -\phi\left[(k-1)^2 y_n^2 + \frac{\xi^2}{(\alpha^2\gamma\phi+\xi)^2}\sigma_u^2\right] - \left[\frac{\alpha\gamma\phi(k-1)y_n - \psi}{\xi}\right]^2 - \left(\frac{\alpha\gamma\phi}{\alpha^2\gamma\phi+\xi}\right)^2\sigma_u^2. \tag{7.14}$$

Then $\partial EPU_t/\partial\xi = 0$, if and only if

$$\frac{\alpha^2\gamma\phi^2(\xi-\gamma)}{(\alpha^2\gamma\phi+\xi)^3}\sigma_u^2 = \frac{[\alpha\gamma\phi(k-1)y_n - \psi]^2}{\xi^3} \tag{7.15}$$

From this, the optimal level of ξ for the private sector can be obtained, which becomes,

$$\xi^* = \gamma + \frac{[\alpha\phi(k-1)y_n\gamma - \psi]^2}{\alpha^2\phi^2\sigma_u^2\gamma}\left(1+\frac{\alpha^2\phi\gamma}{\xi^*}\right)^3. \tag{7.16}$$

This somewhat messy equation is depicted more easily in diagrammatic form in Figure 7.1 below:[8]

If $\psi = \psi^*$, then the second term in equation (7.16) becomes zero, and the optimal level of conservativeness for the private sector, $\xi^* = \gamma$; that is, that the authorities' additional weighting on unemployment (additional, that is, to the private sector's), should be exactly equal to their additional weighting on inflation. In other words, if the contract enables zero inflation on average to be delivered, the private sector would like their own balance of preferences between unemployment and inflation to be respected.

In this case, with $\xi^* = \gamma$ and $\psi = \psi^*$, the utility function of the monetary authorities becomes

$$UM_t = -\gamma\phi(y_t - y^*)^2 - \gamma(\pi_t - \pi^*)^2 - 2\psi^*\pi_t = \gamma[UP_t - 2\alpha\phi(k-1)y_n\pi_t]. \tag{7.17}$$

This result has two implications. First, the central banker, whose characteristics optimize the welfare of the private sector, should be no more or less conservative than the private sector if it is subject to an optimal compensation contract; and second, and more important, although the central banker's utility increases proportionally with γ, the relative weight it places on employment (perhaps as a result of political pressure from the private sector electorate), is actually irrelevant to the decision of monetary policy.

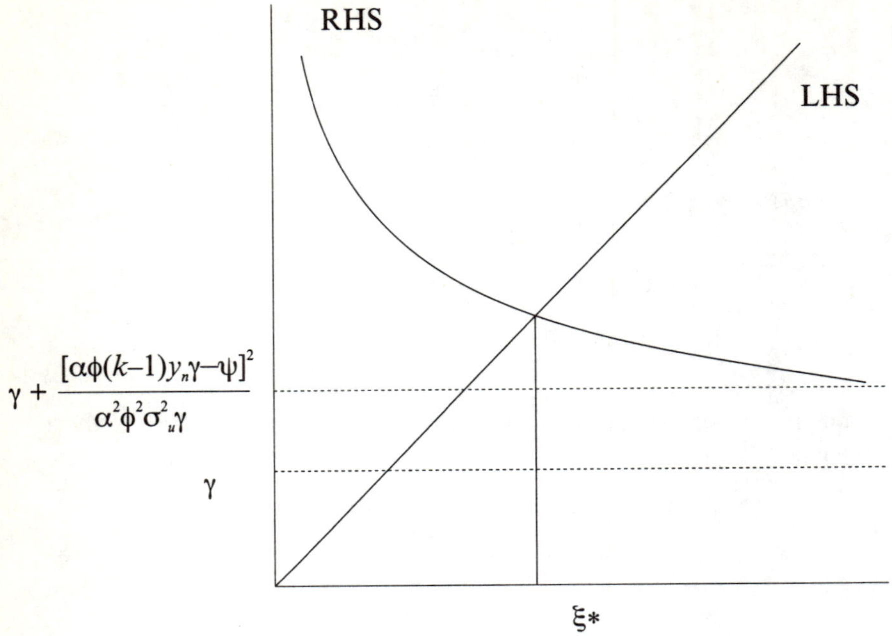

Figure 7.1 Optimal degree of conservativeness

For $\psi \neq \psi^*$, we have to revert to equation (7.16), which leads to the inequality

$$\infty > \xi^* > \gamma + \frac{[\alpha\gamma\phi(k-1)y_n - \psi]^2}{\alpha^2\gamma\phi^2\sigma_u^2}. \tag{7.18}$$

Note that the second term on the right-hand side is always positive for $\psi \neq \psi^*$; thus we will always want a (finitely) conservative central banker if the central banker does not have an optimal (linear) deflationary incentive. This is the same result as Rogoff (1985) obtains. The need for conservativeness is decreased by a higher variance in supply shocks, σ_u^2.

As in Rogoff, the upper bound of the optimal degree of conservativeness is infinite, while unlike Rogoff, our lower bound is a positive number defined in (7.18). Another difference from Rogoff is that when $\alpha\gamma\phi(y^* - y_n) > \psi$, that is the penalty disincentive on inflation for the central banker is too small (probably the usual case), then ξ^*, the optimal degree of conservativeness, will rise with α, ϕ, and k, and fall with ψ (the effect of γ is ambiguous). When the penalty disincentive is too great, the signs are reversed, but now ξ^* rises with γ.

If $\psi = 0$,

$$\xi^* = \gamma + \gamma \frac{(k-1)^2 y_n^2}{\sigma_u^2}\left(1 + \frac{\alpha^2 \gamma \phi}{\xi^*}\right)^3. \tag{7.19}$$

As in Rogoff (1985), ξ^* increases when γ, α, ϕ and k *all* increase but decreases with σ_u.

The implication of this exercise is that there is no preferred level of conservativeness, should we be able to choose an optimal disincentive, ψ, for central bankers. Otherwise, a conservative central banker will always be desired and the optimal degree of conservativeness critically depends on whether the central banker's penalty disincentive on inflation is too large or too small.

THE DIVERGENCE BETWEEN UM_t AND UP_t

In our model the private sector also cares about unemployment and it can influence the monetary authorities' policy conduct in three different ways: through political pressure, by selecting a conservative central banker and by offering the central banker an incentive contract. The private sector's utility function, although not identical to that of the monetary authorities, becomes an integral part of that of the monetary authorities. An interesting exercise is to examine the divergence between the two utility functions.

We can examine the divergence between UM_t and UP_t at $\xi = \xi^*$. Substituting $\xi = \xi^*$ into the monetary authorities' utility function (7.2), we have

$$\begin{aligned} UM_t &= -\gamma\phi\left(y_t - y^*\right)^2 - \left\{\gamma + \frac{\left[\alpha\gamma\phi(k-1)y_n - \psi\right]^2}{\alpha^2\gamma\phi^2\sigma_u^2}\left(1 + \frac{\alpha^2\gamma\phi^2}{\xi^*}\right)^3\right\}\left(\pi_t - \pi^*\right)^2 - 2\psi\pi_t \\ &= -\gamma\left[\phi\left(y_t - y^*\right)^2 - \left(\pi_t - \pi^*\right)^2\right] - \frac{\left[\alpha\gamma\phi(k-1)y_n - \psi\right]^2}{\alpha^2\gamma\phi^2\sigma_u^2}\left(1 + \frac{\alpha^2\gamma\phi^2}{\xi^*}\right)^3\left(\pi_t - \pi^*\right)^2 - 2\psi\pi_t. \end{aligned}$$

Hence, the divergence between UP_t and UM_t is:

$$UM_t - \gamma UP_t = -\frac{\left[\alpha\gamma\phi(k-1)y_n - \psi\right]^2}{\alpha^2\gamma\phi^2\sigma_u^2}\left(1 + \frac{\alpha^2\gamma\phi^2}{\xi^*}\right)^3\left(\pi_t - \pi^*\right)^2 - 2\psi\pi_t. \tag{7.20}$$

The first case is $\psi = \psi^*$, hence, $\xi^* = \gamma$. The expected divergence between UP_t and UM_t in this case is:

$$E[UM_t - \gamma UP_t] = -\,2\gamma\alpha\phi(k-1)y_n\pi^*.$$

Obviously, the absolute value of this expected divergence increases, if ϕ increases; that is, the private sector cares more deeply about unemployment; if γ increases; that is, the private sector puts more political pressure on the central banker on unemployment; if α increases; that is, the monetary policy has more effect on unemployment; if k or y^* increases; that is, the output/employment target is set higher; and if π^* increases; that is the inflation target increases.[9] The absolute value of this expected divergence is irrelevant to σ_u^2, the variance of the stochastic supply shock.

This condition, that $\psi = \psi^*$ and $\xi^* = \gamma$, is the first best possible for the private sector because it cannot improve on that institutional arrangement. Consequently, the expected divergence between the absolute value of the expected divergence reaches its unique minimum point at $\psi = \psi^*$ and $\xi = \xi^*$. Intuitively, this is because, at $\psi = \psi^*$ and $\xi = \xi^*$, $|\,E[UM_t - \gamma UP_t]\,| = 2\gamma E\pi_t$; and $E\pi_t$ reaches its minimum value π^*, since at $\psi = \psi^*$ there is no inflationary bias.

The second case is $\psi, = 0$, but $\xi = \xi^*$. The (expected) divergence between UP_t and UM_t in this case is:

$$E\left[UM_t - \gamma UP_t\right] = -\alpha^2\gamma^3\phi^2(k-1)^2 y_n^2\left(1+\frac{\alpha^2\gamma\phi}{\xi^*}\right)^3\left[\frac{(k-1)^2 y_n^2}{\xi^{*2}\sigma_u^2}+\frac{1}{\left(\alpha^2\gamma\phi+\xi^*\right)^2}\right].$$

The absolute value of this divergence increases, as before when ϕ, γ, α, k and y^* are larger. But now the absolute value of this divergence decreases, if σ_u^2 is large, that is the variance of the stochastic supply shock is big, and it is not affected by π^*, the inflation target.[10]

Basically the expected divergence between UM_t and UP_t is caused by two sources. The first is that the authorities get an extra penalty, $\psi\pi$, from the Walsh-type contract even if $\psi - \psi^*$. The second is that the authorities get a (one period) benefit from either surprise in inflation if $\psi < \psi^*$, or surprise in deflation if $\psi > \psi^*$, while neither surprise helps the private sector. So those factors which raise the penalty on, and the benefit of, such surprise inflation/deflation, a higher ϕ, γ, α, k and y^*, cause a bigger divergence. When $\psi \neq \psi^*$, the monetary authorities do not have an optimal incentive to stabilize supply shocks, so the divergence falls as σ_u^2 rises.

Note, however, that the divergence, $UM_t - \gamma UP_t$, is a function of institutional conditions, the level of ψ and ξ. If the divergence becomes too large, so that average expected inflation becomes too high, one would expect institutional changes, that is, raising ψ and ξ towards ψ^* and ξ^*, that would restrain such behaviour. Put another way, if this time inconsistency model is correct, why have rational private agents not already insisted on institutional changes that would mitigate the problem? Or perhaps the current enthusiasm for independent central banks is an indication of such a response.

What we are doing here is to regard the institutional settings, notably ψ and ξ, as also partly endogenous within the model, rather than exogenously assumed.

THE OPTIMAL STRENGTH OF POLITICAL PRESSURE

Within the same framework we can examine what the private sector would consider to be the optimal degree of direct concern among the monetary authorities for employment, by maximizing EUP_t with respect to γ; that is, $\partial EUP_t / \partial\gamma = 0$. This requires

$$\frac{\alpha^2\phi^2\xi\sigma_u^2(\gamma-\xi)}{\left(\alpha^2\phi\gamma+\xi\right)^3} = \frac{\alpha\phi(k-1)y_n\left[\psi-\alpha\phi(k-1)y_n\gamma\right]}{\xi^2}. \tag{7.21}$$

If $\psi = \psi^*$, then $\gamma^* = \xi$, so γ^* increases if ξ increases. This implies that the private sector wants the authorities to have the same preference as they do, that is, no more or less conservative than the private sector if it is subject to an optimal compensation contract. This result is not only consistent with the above result shown in (7.17) but is also a symmetric reflection of conservativeness in the new context of political pressure. Otherwise, when $\psi \neq \psi^*$, we have

$$\gamma^* = \xi + \frac{(k-1)y_n\left[\psi-\alpha\phi(k-1)y_n\gamma^*\right]}{\alpha\phi\sigma_u^2}\left(1+\frac{\alpha^2\phi\gamma^*}{\xi}\right)^3.$$

Hence γ^* and ψ are moving in the same direction. That is, $\gamma^* > \xi$ if and only if $\psi > \psi^*$ and vice versa.

Intuitively, this is because the political pressure (to increase output/employment) coming out of the private sector is a counterbalance to the central banker's incentive for disinflation caused by the penalty contract, ψ. Since a high output/employment comes at the cost of high inflation according to the Lucas supply function, and the private sector cares about both output/employment and inflation, in equilibrium the optimal strength of political pressure, γ, should endogenously increase with the central banker's disincentive for inflation, ψ.

CONCLUSIONS

This chapter is concerned with the fact that the utility functions of both the monetary authorities and the private sector in the present structure of the game-theoretic models for monetary analysis since Barro and Gordon (1983) are not motivated with sufficient realism. The private sector's sole function in most of the current games in the literature is assumed to be to select a level of nominal wages and prices, conditioned on its expectations of future inflation. Even when the private sector cares about unemployment, such concern is immaterial for the game. In contrast, the monetary authority is supposed to wish to achieve a level of employment above the equilibrium natural rate. But since the private sector either does not care about unemployment, or cannot punish the authorities for high unemployment, the motivation for this preference is rarely clear.

Our objective in this chapter is to provide a more realistic motivational basis for the actions of the monetary authorities and the private sector while remaining within the context of the standard game-theoretic analysis. We argue that there are several reasons for the private sector to be very much concerned with unemployment as well. The private sector's utility is not only related to that of the monetary authorities, it should enter the utility function of the political authorities since in a democracy, in particular through election, the politicians will be removed from power if the electorate becomes unhappy. Thus, if the monetary authorities are dominated by the decisions of the political authorities, their utility function will incorporate the utility function of the private sector, although they will probably place a differing weighting on employment and inflation, depending on differences in position, information and tastes. In our model there remain several routes through which the feeling of the general public will influence central bankers.

This more realistic game-theoretical framework, with the additional feature of a Walsh-type inflation penalty imposed on the authorities, is close to the standard format of the Barro–Gordon, or Cukierman, game structure; hence it keeps the good features of the Barro–Gordon or Cukierman game structure such as its simplicity and tractability. Our model is general and convenient for addressing such important policy issues as granting the central bank independence, with a mandate to achieve price stability, appointing a conservative central bank governor, and/or penalizing the monetary authorities for inflationary outcomes through an incentive contract. Constitutional changes to the status of the central bank may well, and are so intended to, change the coefficients in the monetary authority's utility function, but do not change its functional form.

As we have shown in this chapter, the basic results of this game include an inflationary bias, unless the weight on the central bank's disutility from inflation is raised sufficiently to offset the inflationary bias, which is consistent with the work by Walsh (1995) and by Persson and Tabellini (1993). However, the inflationary bias here arises, not because the authorities want to fool the people for their own good into working harder, but because the general public wants a boom, an expanding economy, and the politicians do not have the strength to resist what the public wants. This result throws a somewhat different light on the contrainflationary success of the Bundesbank, since it may reflect the German public's preference as mush as, or rather than, the Bundesbank's own particular constitutional and operational characteristics; this implies that constitutional change towards central bank independence may be more difficult than is sometimes suggested by the more standard exercises.

We also find that, if the central banker is subject to an optimal compensation contract, it should be no more or less conservative than the private sector. In this case, although its utility increases proportionally with the relative weight the private sector places on employment through political pressure, this political pressure factor is actually irrelevant to its decision on monetary policy. However, without an optimal compensation contract, the central banker should always be more conservative than the private sector, regardless of whether the inflationary penalty on the central banker is too strong or too weak. In this case the divergence between the private sector's and the central banker's objectives increases if the private sector cares deeply about unemployment, and/or puts more political pressure on the central banker to counter unemployment, or if monetary policy has more effect on unemployment, or if the output/employment and inflationary targets are very high. Furthermore, the political pressure to increase output/employment coming out of the private sector is a counterbalance to the central banker's incentive for disinflation caused by the penalty contract, and in equilibrium the optimal strength of political pressure should endogenously increase with the central banker's disincentive for inflation.

We have other concerns on the structure of these models, in particular, that the structure of the models does not incorporate persistence or lag effects. Persistence is not incorporated into the structure of the models because the Lucas-type supply functions perfectly clear markets; hence in most cases each game lasts for one period only. It would seem more sensible to incorporate such persistence, autocorrelation, which is observed in fluctuations of output and employment around their trend levels, directly into the model. More importantly, virtually all these models assume that monetary policy measures affect the economy instantaneously, albeit sometimes with imperfect precision. This abstracts entirely from a major, probably the main, problem that the monetary authorities face in reality. This is that there are long and variable lags between adjusting the instrument of monetary policy, in practice short-term interest rates (not the monetary base), and that having its full effect on the economy. Consequently, the monetary authorities have to predict the likely future state of the economy, and to do so in a world which, because of persistence, cannot be expected to have real variables in equilibrium subject only to some purely stochastic shock. The more realistic game-theoretical framework developed here can also be useful in analysing these two important issues, as we have shown in Goodhart and Huang (1995).

NOTES

1. There are, of course, other possible reasons for an inflationary bias to monetary policy, besides the attempt to raise real output above its equilibrium level. These reasons could be either a revenue motive (Alesina and Tabellini, 1987; Cukierman, 1992, ch. 4; Rovelli, 1994) or a mercantilist or balance of payment motive (Alesina and Tabellini, 1987; Cukierman, 1992, ch. 5) or a financial stability motive (Cukierman, 1992, ch. 7). But the primary focus of the game-theoretic models of monetary analysis is on the inflation bias generated through the interaction between the private sector's expectation and the monetary authority's incentive to expand output.
2. Our two other main concerns regarding the structure of the models are that they do not incorporate persistence or lag effects. We deal with these two concerns elsewhere (Goodhart and Huang, 1995). In the concluding section we will discuss these other two concerns in the light of our purpose in this chapter.
3. Other economists, such as Tabellini (1988) and Persson and Tabellini (1990), however, have argued that the structure of the labour market, for example with a monopolistic trade union and intensive insider power, can provide a sufficient basis for this argument.
4. An alternative, and possibly preferable, way of setting up this utility function would be to express the costs of inflation in two parts. The first would relate to the deviation of actual from *expected*, rather than desired, inflation, and would relate to unanticipated inflation. The second term, perhaps linear in inflation, could then account for the costs of anticipated inflation. We did not attempt this in this exercise, because it would have both involved extra complications and taken our formulation of the model further from the mainstream of the existing literature in this field. We leave this for future work.
5. The effect of the instrument on inflation, equation (7.4), can be derived from the quantity equation, $E\Delta m_t = E\pi_t + E\Delta y_t$. Without persistence $E\Delta y_t = 0$, hence, $i_t = \Delta m_t = \pi_t$. We could have included an error term (lack of precision) in this equation, but we felt that this was unnecessary for the purposes of this exercise. Also the equilibrium real interest rate is positive, not zero as here; but the addition of a constant term in this equation makes no difference to the basic results, and is omitted for simplicity.
6. In a repeated game, as set out in Barro and Gordon (1983), the inflationary bias can also be eliminated if the private sector can employ strategies, such as trigger strategies, that penalize the authorities for any such bias.
7. See al-Nowaihi and Levine (1996) for a critical theoretical assessment of the Walsh contract on the ground of non-renegotiation-proofness, and Walsh (1994) and Forder (1996) for analyses of the Reserve Bank of New Zealand in the light of the Walsh contract.
8. This graphic method is adopted from Eijffinger and Schaling (1995).
9. If the desired rate of inflation, π^*, is zero or very low, as is the normal case, there will be little divergence in any case. We assume π^* to be non-negative for a variety of reasons, including

the need for a positive real interest rate, known potential measurement biases and, perhaps, some residual downward wage stickiness (Akerlof *et al.*, 1996).

10. In the general case of $\xi = \xi^*$ but $\psi \neq \psi^*$ and $\psi \neq 0$, the expected divergence between UP_t and UM_t is:

$$E[UM_t - \gamma UP_t] = -\frac{[\alpha\gamma\phi(k-1)y_n - \psi]^2}{\alpha^2\gamma\phi^2\sigma_u^2}\left(1+\frac{\alpha^2\gamma\phi^2}{\xi^*}\right)^3(\pi_t - \pi^*)^2 - 2\psi E\pi_t$$

$$= -\frac{[\alpha\gamma\phi(k-1)y_n - \psi]^2}{\alpha^2\gamma\phi^2}\left(1+\frac{\alpha^2\gamma\phi^2}{\xi^*}\right)^3\left[\frac{[\alpha\gamma\phi(k-1)^2 y_n^2 - \psi]^2}{\xi^{*2}\sigma_u^2} + \frac{\alpha^2\gamma^2\phi^2}{(\alpha^2\gamma\phi+\xi^*)^2}\right] - 2\psi\left[\pi^* + \frac{\alpha\gamma\phi(k-1)y_n - \psi}{\xi^*}\right].$$

Once again this is increasing in ϕ, γ, α, k and y^* and decreasing in σ_u^2. Unlike the case when $\psi = 0$, it is also increasing in π^*, that is, when the inflation target is higher.

REFERENCES

Akerlof, George A., Dickens, William T. and Perry, George L. (1996) 'The Macroeconomics of Low Inflation', *Brookings Papers on Economic Activity (Macroeconomics 1 :96)*.

Alesina, Alberto (1989) 'Politics and Business Cycles in Industrial Democracies', *Economic Policy*, **8**, 57–98.

Alesina, Alberto and Tabellini, Guido (1987), 'Rules and Discretion with Noncoordinated Monetary and Fiscal Policies,' *Economic Inquiry*, 25: 619–30.

al-Nowaihi, Ali and Levine, Paul (1996) 'Independent but Accountable: Walsh Contracts and the Credibility Problem', mimeo.

Barro, Robert and Gordon, David (1983) 'Rules, Discretion and Reputation in a Model of a Monetary Game', *Journal of Monetary Economics*, **12**, 101–22.

Cukierman, Alex (1992) *Central Bank Strategy, Credibility, and Independence*, Cambridge, Mass.: MIT Press.

Eijffinger, Sylvester and Schaling, Eric (1995) 'The Ultimate Determinants of Central Bank Independence', Discussion Paper, Center for Economic Research, No. 9505 Tilburg University, Tilburg, Netherlands.

Fischer, Stanley (1994) 'Modern Central Banking', in Forrest Capie, Charles Goodhart, Stanley Fischer and Norbert Schnadt, *The Future of Central Banking*, Cambridge: Cambridge University Press.

Forder, James (1996) 'The New Zealand Experience', mimeo, St Peter's College, Oxford University.

Goodhart, Charles A.E. (1994) 'What Should Central Bankers Do? What Should Be Their Macroeconomic Objectives and Operations?', *Economic Journal*, **104**, 1424–36.

Goodhart, Charles A.E. and Huang, Haizhou (1995) 'What is the Central Bank's Game?', Financial Markets Group Discussion Paper No. 222, London School of Economics.

Kydland, Finn E. and Prescott, Edward C. (1977) 'Rules Rather Than Discretion: the Inconsistency of Optimal Plans', *Journal of Political Economy*, **85**, 473–90.

Minford, Patrick (1995) 'Time-Inconsistency, Democracy and Optimal Contingent Rules', *Oxford Economic Papers*, **47**(2), 195–210.

Persson, Torsten and Tabellini, Guido (1990) *Macroeconomic Policy, Credibility and Politics*, Chur, Switzerland: Harwood Academic Publishers.

Persson, Torsten and Tabellini, Guido (1993) 'Designing Institutions for Monetary Stability', *Carnegie-Rochester Conference Series on Public Policy*, **39**, 53–84.

Posen, Adam (1995) 'Declarations Are Not Enough: Financial Sector Sources of Central Bank Independence', in B. Bernanke and J. Rotemberg (eds), *NBER Macroeconomics Annual 1995*, Cambridge: MIT Press.

Rogoff, Kenneth (1985) 'The Optimal Degree of Commitment to an Intermediate Monetary Target', *Quarterly Journal of Economics*, **100**, 1169–90.

Rovelli, Riccardo (1994) 'Central Banking, Seigniorage and the Financing of the Government', Centro di Economia Monetaria e Finanziaria 'Paolo Baffi', Discussion Paper No. 85, Universita Boccoli.

Tabellini, Guido (1988) 'Centralized Wage Setting and Monetary Policy in a Reputational Equilibrium', *Journal of Money, Credit and Banking*, **20**, 102–18.

von Hagen, Jürgen (1995) 'Germany', in Leonardo Leiderman and Lars Svensson (eds), *Inflation Targets*, Centre for Economic Policy Research, London.

Walsh, Carl E. (1994) 'Is New Zealand's Reserve Bank Act of 1989 an Optimal Central Bank Contract?', mimeo, University of California, Santa Cruz, January.

Walsh, Carl E. (1995) 'Optimal Contract for Central Bankers', *American Economic Review*, **85**(1), 150–67.

PART III

Emerging Problems in Macroeconomic Policy

8. The economics and politics of European Monetary Union: Labour and the Euro

David Currie

INTRODUCTION

It is a great pleasure and honour to contribute to this set of essays in honour of Bernard Corry and Maurice Peston. Like many of the other contributors, as well as many generations of students working in business, government and academia, I owe an enormous debt to them both.

Bernard and Maurice built a highly successful centre for teaching and research in economics at Queen Mary College (as we then called it, prior to its expansion in the past decade), with a particularly strong postgraduate school. They shared a passionate belief in the key role of education, in the importance of ideas, however unpopular, and in the capacity of the young to reshape the future for themselves. Together with their infectious enthusiasm and their energy, these were the foundations on which they built a first-rate department.

In a formal sense, I was a student of neither Maurice nor Bernard, yet I learned almost all my economics under their guidance. I well remember my interview with the two of them. I had walked down the Mile End Road to the main college (they wisely chose not to interview in the old dog food factory which was the Economics Department in the early days!) and, despite coming from the industrial wasteland of the Durham mining area, vowed to myself that I would not work in the physical desolation that surrounded the college. (Tower Hamlets has since done much to improve the neighbourhood.) But a few minutes of interview quickly changed my mind, beguiled by the combination of charm and intellectual challenge. I had applied to teach monetary economics, and when Bernard asked me whether I was familiar with the work of a number of leading monetary theorists, reeling off a list, I had to confess ignorance and felt my chances of success recede. But it was the height of the Barber boom, when only the misguided, mentally ill or the motivated applied to academia from the world of the City and consultancy, so it was Hobson's choice and I got the job. In these more litigious days, they and I might have been treated differently by the first group of graduate students that I supposedly taught, but they treated me kindly and I learnt an enormous amount with them. I have always been grateful to Maurice and Bernard for that first step-up in the academic world.

An especial strength of Queen Mary College in the first two decades was macroeconomic policy, shamefully neglected elsewhere at the LSE, Oxford and Cambridge, and so I found myself working on the issues of macroeconomic policy design, a subject which Maurice had made very much his own. It was a particularly exciting period, with the start of the rational expectations revolution and the rethinking of conventional Keynesian economics, and to be able to debate these issues with Bernard and Maurice was a rare privilege. I well remember the course that Maurice taught one year, with which I helped, with the central proposition that all advances in macroeconomics over the past 50 years were prefigured in the sole text for the course, *The General Theory*. That course highlighted for me one of the major strengths of both Bernard and Maurice: their ability to combine microeconomics and macroeconomics, rather than treat them as separate domains, as our more specialized approach to economics all too often does.

With his characteristic generosity, Maurice also brought me into the world of practical policy making, introducing me to a small group of advisers around Roy Hattersley, the shadow Labour chancellor after the disastrous Labour defeat of 1983. It was fascinating to watch Maurice in that context, demonstrating his shrewd combination of economic creativity and political realism. It was a real privilege to have the opportunity to see policy making in practice, and to help inject realism into Labour's economic agenda, a process that continued with supreme success under John Smith, Tony Blair and Gordon Brown. It was that early introduction to Labour at a high level that led to my nomination in 1996 by Tony Blair for the House of Lords. Without Maurice, that would not have been. It has given me the opportunity to see Maurice in action in yet another sphere, and a great pleasure it was. The only regret has been that Maurice was passed over for a position in government, and I have no doubt that the government is the poorer for that.

The work of both Maurice and Bernard demonstrates a keen interest in the key economic issues that dominate the policy agenda. For that reason, it seemed appropriate to choose for the subject of this chapter a subject of key historic importance to the UK and Europe, that of European Monetary Union (EMU). This is an issue where economics and politics are inextricably intertwined. The economic policy adviser has no choice but to take account of both. I suspect also that it is one of the key issues on which history will judge this Labour government. As they have been long-standing, though not uncritical, supporters of Labour over many years, it is therefore an issue close to the hearts of both Bernard and Maurice. They may not agree with all that I say, but I think that they will agree with its centrality.

THE BACKGROUND

Surprising though it seemed to some UK commentators, EMU is going to happen on time with a wide participation. This will be a remarkable historical venture: the formation of a major currency area between a group of advanced industrial countries that have traditionally guarded their independence jealously and, within living memory, by force of arms. This venture is not without risk, and if it goes wrong the economic, social and political costs to Europe and the rest of the world could be very high indeed. The challenge for the members of the European Union is to make the Euro work well. This will require some hard policy choices for all countries involved, not least in securing sufficient flexibility of European labour and product markets to ensure that major structural imbalances do not arise within the EMU zone.

The Labour government's initiative on *Getting Europe Back To Work*, discussed at the European Jobs Summit in November 1997, was therefore both timely and welcome. Moreover, from the British perspective, the government is in the fortunate position of having inherited from the Conservatives a flexible labour market well adapted to EMU. However, the Labour government faced other challenges. There was the challenge of the British presidency which oversaw the key negotiations and preparations for the launch of the Euro on 1 January 1999. More critically, in view of the chancellor's Commons statement of 27 October 1997 that, despite its commitment in principle to EMU and its pro-EMU sentiments, virtually ruled out both entry and a decision on entry in the lifetime of this parliament, there remain the difficult questions of whether, when and how the UK will join EMU.

In the following, we first review the background to the launch of the Euro. We then move on to consider how the Euro will work and the possible risks of instability under EMU, and what is required to make EMU work well. We also address the question of how the UK should prepare, now that entry to EMU is the stated aim of UK government policy. Finally, we address the question of British entry and ask whether the chancellor's statement in effect rules out the possibility of entry in 2002, and delays entry in practice until the middle of the next decade.

THE EURO IS READY TO START ON TIME

A number of commentators, especially in the United Kingdom, have been sceptical about the chances of the Euro being launched on time, if at all. But their analysis ignored a number of reasons against the options of delay or abort that have made some of us confident that the timetable will be met. First, a great deal of political capital has been invested in the EMU project, both at a European and a national level. Its abandonment or delay would be a major political setback for key politicians, notably Chancellor Kohl. Moreover, the timetable for the Euro's introduction is laid down in a treaty commitment, to which all member states but Denmark and the UK are signed up. Although this commitment will not force countries into EMU against their will (as the case of Sweden shows), it makes a decision to delay much more difficult.

More fundamentally, European countries made great strides in making major policy adjustments in preparation for EMU. Few would have predicted even two years ago the remarkable convergence of fiscal deficits, inflation and long-term interest rates to conform with the Maastricht convergence criteria. Greece is the odd man out, failing to conform to any of the convergence criteria. But elsewhere convergence is quite general. The most dramatic turnaround has been seen in Italy, with a move to a primary surplus of some 4–5 per cent of GDP. If allowance is made for the depressed condition of the European economy by examining cyclically adjusted fiscal deficits, the fiscal position is even sounder: all except Greece within 3 per cent, most appreciably below. Debt ratios are also falling in the high-debt countries, and will fall even faster when economic growth picks up.

This background means that the heat was taken out of the decisions on convergence, so that conformity to the Maastricht convergence criteria meant a large first wave. But this does not mean that EMU will necessarily work well; indeed, there are circumstances in which it could work rather badly. In the next sections, we consider the factors that will determine the success of EMU: first in a short-term perspective, looking at the likely evolution of monetary and fiscal policy, and hence at the implications for the Euro against the dollar, yen and other currencies; and second, the longer-term supply-side development of European economies, particularly labour market performance.

HOW WILL THE EURO WORK?

A common link is often made between a large participation in EMU and a soft Euro. The logic is that participation of countries, such as Italy, Portugal and Spain, that have suffered high inflation in the past will necessarily imply a softer stance for monetary policy, with higher inflation and a weaker Euro. This logic ignores the stern Teutonic framework within which the European Central Bank (ECB) will operate. It is true that the inclusion of countries that only marginally meet the Maastricht criteria and which have a history of inflation and fiscal ill-discipline may mean that fiscal deficits across the EMU zone are higher than with a narrower group. This will be particularly the case if the fiscal discipline of the Growth and Stability Pact is found in practice to lack teeth. But it is most unlikely that this will induce the ECB to adopt a more relaxed monetary stance. Rather, the ECB is likely to emulate the Bundesbank over many decades and the Fed under Volcker in the 1980s by offsetting fiscal laxity with higher interest rates to ensure that the ECB is successful in achieving price stability (interpreted as inflation below 2 per cent). The combination of loose fiscal/tight monetary policy could easily lead to an overvalued and volatile Euro, as the experience of the dollar in the early 1980s illustrates. Since overvaluation and volatility would exacerbate problems of European competitiveness, this highlights the need for continued fiscal discipline under EMU.

But such discipline may not be easy to achieve. It is possible to paint a scenario in which unemployment remains high and political pressures build for a relaxation of fiscal policy once the Euro has been launched.[1] In this situation, conflict could arise between Ecofin (the Council of Ministers meeting to consider financial matters) and the ECB. In particular, the finance ministers might question the authority of the ECB, particularly if a change of government means that they had no say in their appointment. It is unlikely that the authority of the ECB will be undermined. But the Euro/dollar and Euro/yen rates may respond in a volatile way to signs of conflict between the ECB and Ecofin that signal potential shifts in the monetary/fiscal mix that have important implications for the value of the Euro against the dollar and yen. Such volatility may be exacerbated by any technical errors the ECB makes in the setting of interest rates: although not inevitable, such errors could well arise because of the difficulties of conducting policy across a monetary regime change of the kind that the introduction of the Euro will represent.

This discussion suggests that three things are required to avoid a bumpy debut for EMU, with an overvalued and possibly volatile Euro against other currencies. The first is for the ECB to overcome the early difficulties of conducting monetary policy and thereby avoid erratic movements in interest rates. The second is that the commitment to sound fiscal policy seen in the run-up to the launch of the Euro should continue once it is up and running. This should go beyond the commitment to remain within the 3 per cent Maastricht budget ceiling, but also to aim for the 0–1 per cent average deficit level implied in the Growth and Stability Pact, leaving scope for automatic fiscal stabilizers to operate over the economic cycle without resulting in excessive deficits. The third is the avoidance of conflict between the ECB and Ecofin. One way to accomplish this would be for the ECB to set out broad guidelines as to how to interpret its brief under the Maastricht Treaty: in particular, how it will interpret price stability and, subject to that, its requirement to support the general economic policy of the EU. It could then ask the finance ministers to comment publicly on these guidelines. It will be hard for the finance ministers not to endorse sensibly drafted guidelines, but public concurrence will then make it hard for them subsequently to take issue with the ECB. Such an exchange does nothing to weaken the formal independence of the ECB under the Maastricht Treaty, but it will make it easier for the ECB to operate with authority and free from populist challenge.

MAKING EMU WORK WELL

But the success of EMU requires more than just the effective conduct of monetary and fiscal policy within the EMU zone. Supply-side measures must also be adopted to ensure that EMU works well in the longer run. The single currency rules out the flexibility that exchange rates provided, a flexibility that was often abused but sometimes proved useful. European policy makers must take action to induce greater flexibility in their labour and product markets.

This flexibility agenda is often linked to the Anglo-Saxon deregulation agenda pursued by Thatcher and Reagan in the 1980s. This is certainly part of the agenda. Continental European countries do have appreciable constraints on the freedom of companies to shed labour, with the inevitable consequence that they are reluctant to hire labour, resulting in high unemployment. EMU does require a greater willingness to allow markets to work, even in an area as sensitive as that of people's jobs.

But deregulation is only one blade of the flexibility agenda, as Labour's Employment Action Plan emphasizes. The Netherlands illustrates the point that low unemployment and a well-functioning labour market can be achieved *without* a number of the features of the Anglo-Saxon model (downsizing, low wages, marginal jobs) that continental Europeans find so objectionable. Crucially for the United Kingdom, flexibility must be accompanied by effective education, training and skills, to ensure that people have the capacity to take advantage of market opportunities. Otherwise, flexibility will mean a flexible slide into unemployment: this was the weakness of the Thatcher labour market model, which has left so many ill-trained and marginalized in the labour market through restructuring. But labour market flexibility must also be associated with dynamism elsewhere, not just in labour markets. Promoting new start-ups, entrepreneurship and risk taking, ensuring fair and effective competition and creating an environment in which businesses can start and thrive is just as crucial to labour market performance and unemployment.

This is the agenda that the European Union must address, and that Labour must advance as part of its presidency, alongside the important issues of getting EMU up and running. The new Labour government is distinguished in Europe by its clear mandate and authority, which contrasts with the political scene in the other major countries of Europe, notably France, Germany and Italy. It has a major opportunity to shape the European policy agenda for the next five years to ensure that EMU works well in the longer run. But its capacity to achieve this depends critically on how the Labour government is perceived in Europe, and that in turn depends on its position on EMU and sterling.

BRITAIN AND EMU: PREPARING FOR ENTRY

In September and the first half of October 1997, the press and markets speculated furiously about the possibility that the Labour government would decide on early entry into EMU. This resulted in declining long-term rates of interest and a surging stock market. The chancellor's *Times* interview on 18 October appeared to rule out entry before the next election, and led to a significant market correction and an appreciation of sterling. This episode illustrates the capricious, speculative and unpredictable nature of markets and of associated press speculation. For there was never any serious possibility that Britain would enter EMU before 2001/2, around the time of the next election. If markets thought to the contrary, they failed to understand the economic and political realities surrounding UK entry.

The principal *economic* obstacle to an early UK entry is the fact that the British economy is out of kilter with the continental cycle, so that interest rates are out of line. Early entry would bring convergence of interest rates, and inevitably appreciably lower rates for the United Kingdom. This would add to the strength of demand in the British economy, leading to overheating and an inevitable bust, with all the costs of uncertainty and unemployment that have resulted from past booms and busts in the British economy. There is no intrinsic reason why the UK and continental European cycles need be out of kilter as the 1970s illustrate, and a single currency will do much to align them; but the issue of transition remains.

The principal *political* obstacle is the fact that EMU is currently deeply unpopular with ordinary people, recent polls showing a rough 2:1 view against. This unpopularity led the prime minister, when in opposition, to commit himself to a referendum on the issue before joining. This was wholly appropriate in view of the importance of the issue, but erected a significant hurdle to be cleared before entry. Public opinion could well have changed quite quickly on this issue, particularly if the government had taken a clear position for entry: the precedent of the 1975 referendum is relevant here, when public opinion moved from 2:1 against to 2:1 in favour, despite a divided cabinet. But an early referendum on the Euro was clearly risky. It is understandable that the prime minister and chancellor were reluctant to gamble the unprecedented high standing of the new government on an early rush at this hurdle, particularly with other pressing and important domestic reform agendas, in the economic, social and constitutional areas.

The chancellor has set five British tests for entry: that it should be good for (a) jobs, (b) investment and (c) the City; that the problem of desynchronization of the British and continental cycle is tackled; and that Europe addresses the need for greater flexibility in its economies for EMU to work well. Once EMU is up and running, and if European governments are tackling the flexibility agenda, the British government could well decide that these British conditions for entry are satisfied and that entry is desirable. Longer-term exclusion from EMU could have major costs in terms of inward investment, and hence jobs. It could also damage the prospects of the City. Provided that the new Monetary Policy Committee of the Bank of England avoids undue overheating of the British economy and any consequent downturn, and particularly if the chancellor lowers the inflation target to align better with average European performance, UK interest rates could be converging with continental rates. Locking into the Euro at that point could well have the major advantage of sustaining the UK non-inflationary growth phase. If partner countries are tackling the issue of flexibility, helped by the more propitious labour market conditions with the economic upturn, the way could be clear for the British government to declare that the conditions are met and to seek the approval of the country for entry. Entry at that time, with appropriate notice, also gives time to mortgage lenders and borrowers to move to a longer maturity structure more appropriate for a low inflation environment.

The costs of remaining out in the longer term are political as well as economic. With EMU, we are starting to see for the first time the growth of EU institutions over which only a subset of EU members have control. The ECB is the first such institution, governing monetary policy. The proposed E10/11 Council, agreed between the German and French governments and coordinating fiscal policy among the EMU members, will be the second. This Council will meet ahead of Ecofin, and is likely to gradually undermine the influence of Ecofin itself. What this could well represent is the gradual separation of EU members into an inner core, committed to a table d'hôte acceptance of the whole integration agenda, and an outer group, adopting an à-la-carte selective adoption of integration. If the United Kingdom stands aside in the longer term, her influence as part of the outer group will be appreciably diminished.

Many realistic British supporters of EMU, including those in business, accepted that early entry in 1999 or 2000 was out of the question, but that a referendum in this parliament would allow British entry in 2001/2, around the time when Euro notes and coin start to circulate. A favoured timing was a referendum in 1999, around the time of the European elections, by which time EMU would have been up and running for a number of months and UK public opinion might have been moving in favour of entry. A possible objection to this timing was that 1999 would have been too early to judge the issue of convergence; but the referendum could have been on the principle of entry, arguably the issue on which public opinion is best consulted, and not on the timing.

This position has clearly been overtaken by the chancellor's Commons statement of 27 October 1997. This stated for the first time the government's commitment in principle to entry, to be welcomed by those in favour of UK entry. The key question now is when economic and political conditions will allow UK entry in practice. The statement all but ruled out a decision to enter in the present parliament. If the decision is delayed until the next parliament, what does this imply for the possible timing of UK entry, if it happens? Is there the possibility that entry will then be delayed beyond 2002 until 2004 or 2005? We consider three possible sources of such delay: the EU administrative process for approving entry, the time needed for business to be prepared, and the political preconditions.

Suppose there is a Labour victory in the next election and the question of EMU entry is put to an early referendum which votes in favour. The UK government will then have to apply quickly for approval of UK membership of EMU by our European partners. That is likely to be forthcoming quite quickly, provided that the United Kingdom continues to satisfy the convergence criteria. Some member states might wish to insist on the United Kingdom satisfying the ERM criterion of participation for two years (or the 16 or 17 months that Italy and Finland will have observed, if they are admitted). But since Denmark and Sweden may well be following behind the United Kingdom, it is probable that the prize of having near complete EMU membership may well overcome insistence on this point. With agreement to entry secured, there is no reason then why the United Kingdom could not enter EMU within a few months, with sterling continuing to circulate but tied irrevocably and unalterably to the Euro, and with the powers of the Bank of England passing to the ECB. The transition to Euro notes and coin could then follow within two years, when the necessary retail preparations have been made.

To give illustrative timings, on this timetable, an election in the spring of 2002 (the latest being May of that year) would allow a bill authorizing the Euro referendum to be passed before the summer, with a view to a referendum in the early autumn and entry to EMU on 1 January 2003. Euro notes and coin would replace pounds in 2005. An earlier election would bring forward these dates.

But is such a rapid entry to EMU feasible from the business perspective, given the great emphasis currently put on the need for preparation? The answer is probably yes, since rather little preparation is needed for the transition to the first stage of membership, in which pounds continue to circulate but in a fixed relationship to the Euro. Thus banks and other financial companies operating in wholesale markets should have prepared for 1 January 1999, whatever the United Kingdom's position, in order to remain competitive at a European level. Retail companies must prepare for Euro notes and coin by 2005, but will have plenty of time for that. Ensuring continuity of contracts, especially ECU-denominated ones, is an issue that must be addressed by 1 January 1999, irrespective of UK participation. The preparation of Euro accounts, transfer of debt and equity and other preparations can all wait until after the initial entry. And the strategic issues that will concern companies most should be a matter of immediate concern and continuing review beyond the date of entry.

If these obstacles are absent, what of the political? The decision to rule out a decision in this parliament was motivated by the wish to create a period of stability free from speculation on the issue of EMU entry. It remains to be seen whether it will achieve this. Uncertainty about the timing of entry remains, and one of its effects will be that, as the term of this parliament approaches its end, so the EMU issue will come to the fore. Politically, this runs the risk that the next election will be fought on the EMU question, even if a referendum immediately after the election is on offer.

If public opinion has moved more in favour, then EMU could be managed politically rather like the issue of Scottish devolution: a manifesto commitment to be approved by the people after the election and dealt with expeditiously. In these conditions, UK entry will be easy to engineer. But if, as is possible with continued press opposition, public opinion remains divided, the Labour government will face another difficult choice: whether to argue vigorously for EMU at the time of the election or, in effect, to replay the last election by adopting a guarded position. The latter strategy will have two consequences. First, it will weaken the chances of the government being able to lead in Europe. Second, it will delay further the date of British entry, probably to 2005 or beyond, since a neutral election campaign will be a poor basis for a referendum campaign in favour of British entry.

Bifurcated possibilities, in this case decision on entry around or much later, are always the stuff of market speculation. The danger is that, without a clear lead on timing by Government, small shifts of public opinion will be fanned by the press into perceived big differences in the probabilities of entry, especially as the next election approaches. The chancellor's aim in making the welcome statement of principle in favour of UK entry, but putting off a decision in practice until the next parliament, was carefully to defuse the EMU issue to allow the United Kingdom's march towards EMU to begin. The intriguing question is whether it has instead merely delayed the explosion until the heart of the next election campaign. History may well judge this Labour government on the answer to that conundrum. The key point is that the answer is not yet determined, and much will depend on government leadership, with the support of business, on this issue over the next few years.

NOTE

1. For details of such a scenario, together with an optimistic EMU scenario in which the Euro works well, see Currie (1997). For what it is worth, we consider the optimistic scenario to be more likely, but the pessimistic scenario is possible and highlights some of the risks of EMU.

REFERENCES

Currie, David (1997) *The Pros and Cons of EMU*, London: Economist Intelligence Unit, published in summary form by HM Treasury, July 1997, and accessible on the EIU web site eiu.com.

Currie, David (1998): *Will the Euro Work? The Ins and Outs of EMU*, London: Economist Intelligence Unit.

H.M. Treasury (1997) *UK Membership of the Single Currency: An Assessment of the Five Economic Tests*, London.

9. Convergence in European bond markets

Joe A. Ganley[1]

I went to the Economics Department at Queen Mary College in September 1984 to begin a master's degree. I had no intention of staying longer than a year before finding a job. Yet a few months later Maurice Peston asked me to stay and do a PhD on the growth and efficiency of the public sector. This was very much in the spirit of academic and popular thinking at that time. But Maurice had been interested in public goods and public policy since the 1950s. This enduring attraction reflects the intractable nature of some of the issues involved: just how would *you* measure the output of the public sector?

The issue of measurement concerns me in this chapter. In particular, I want to ask how far the yields on sovereign debt issued by EU economies reflect the economic convergence of these economies. It is hard to think of something of greater practical importance to policy makers at the current time – as is now recognized in the literature.[2] If a single currency is introduced across the whole of the EU area, 15 monetary policies will be replaced by one. Without close cyclical and structural convergence of the real economies concerned, a single monetary policy could become inappropriate in some parts of the EU. German unification gave a good example of the problems that the coincidence of boom conditions and recession in different parts of Europe can cause.

In 1992, the Maastricht Treaty suggested a number of measures of economic convergence, based on target levels of sovereign debt, deficits, inflation and long-bond yields. The advantage of looking to measures such as bond yields is that they are determined independently by financial markets and are updated on a daily basis. Most of the analysis and comment produced so far has trumpeted the narrowing of spreads in bond yields relative to Germany. But as yet there has not been much work done in dissecting these changes. Are these changes part of some broader cyclical movement, wholly or partly unrelated to the approach of EMU? If EMU is the principal factor driving bond yield convergence, at what point would this become sufficient to indicate that 'real' convergence – in the labour market and in corporate behaviour for example – is great enough to justify joining a single currency?

With this motivation, I will now go on to look at changes in EU bond yields since 1992 when the Maastricht Treaty was signed. This leads on to a discussion of the disappearance of currency risk and later to consideration of what econometric evidence there might be for bond market convergence. Finally, I discuss Canada as an analogy to an EU bond market without currency risk.

BOND MARKETS SINCE MAASTRICHT

Prices in bond markets are usually quoted in yield terms as a spread over some benchmark – very often Germany. Convergence in the government bond markets is most readily defined in the same way. In the United Kingdom this suggests a comparison of the level of gilt yields at, say, a maturity of ten years with the yield on German bunds at the same maturity. (Ten year bonds, incidentally, are often used as a proxy for the 'long end' of the yield curve.) 'Convergence' in this sense is the elimination of the spread between the yields on UK debt and those in the benchmark country.

After the suspension of sterling's membership of the ERM in September 1992, the UK spread over Germany began to fall and soon got caught up in the worldwide bond market rally the following year. This saw the spread of gilts over bunds decline from 200 basis points prior to the United Kingdom's departure from the ERM to under 50 by the end of 1993. But there is little doubt that this improvement was a cyclical rather than a structural change, with measures of both expected inflation and bond market risk premia declining significantly through 1993. In February 1994, the American Federal Reserve began to tighten monetary policy. This was interpreted as a signal of new inflationary pressure and led to a long reversal in yields during 1994 and a widening in spreads the world over. By the end of 1994 the gilt/bund spread was close to 150 basis points and it has drifted upwards since then.[3]

Although the UK experience is unusual, Denmark has seen spreads behave in a similar way since 1992. Like the United Kingdom, it saw the cyclical convergence of spreads in 1993 and later divergence in 1994. Thereafter spreads of Danish debt have declined to around 80 basis points, but through 1996 they got stuck at this level and they show no immediate sign of converging further on Germany. This presumably reflects the Danish ambivalence about European integration and, more specifically, Denmark's possible opt-out from a single currency. The lack of convergence in both UK and Danish government bond yields is apparent from Figure 9.1 which shows daily spreads against Germany through 1996.

Elsewhere in Europe the story is very different. Perhaps the best example is that of France. The long bond market correction in 1994 drove spreads with Germany from around zero to 100 basis points at the end of 1995. The turnaround that occurred in the first quarter of 1996 is, however, little short of startling. From a peak in October 1995, French yields relative to Germany had all but converged by April 1996 – and they have stayed there since (Figure 9.2).

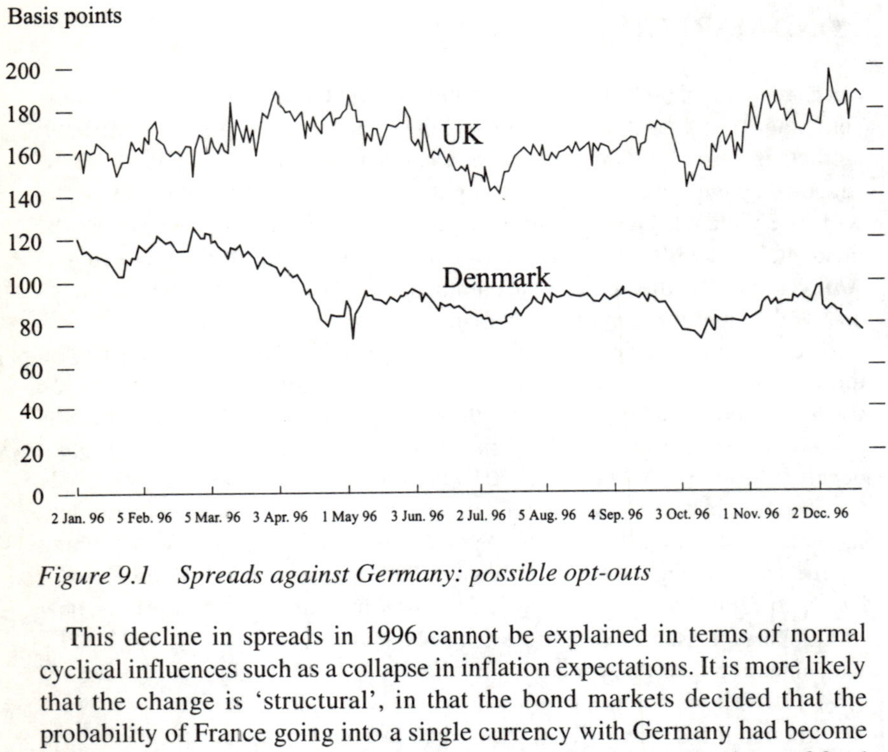

Figure 9.1 Spreads against Germany: possible opt-outs

This decline in spreads in 1996 cannot be explained in terms of normal cyclical influences such as a collapse in inflation expectations. It is more likely that the change is 'structural', in that the bond markets decided that the probability of France going into a single currency with Germany had become a virtual certainty. This is borne out in survey evidence on the views of fund managers. In Figure 9.3 the balance of fund managers expecting a monetary union including France and Germany to begin on time in January 1999 rose sharply through 1996 to something approaching unanimity by the end of the year.

Like France, a number of countries have for several years been considered very likely to join a single currency, if it goes ahead. These would include, in addition to France and Germany, the Benelux countries and possibly Ireland. These countries have often been referred to loosely as the 'core'. The Netherlands is perhaps the best example. For several years now it has closely replicated changes in German monetary policy. This reflects not merely a commitment to EMU-style integration, but the reality that its economic cycle is closely synchronized with that of Germany. These factors have ensured that Dutch bond

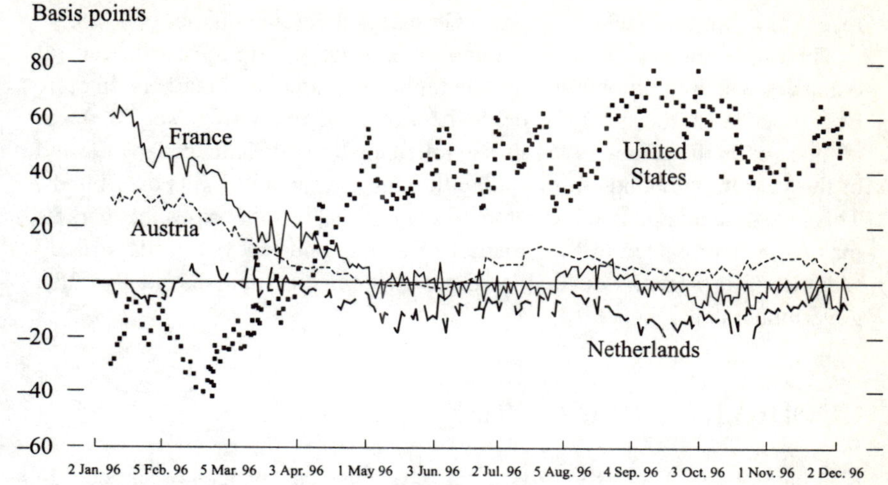

Figure 9.2 Spreads against Germany: core Europe and United States

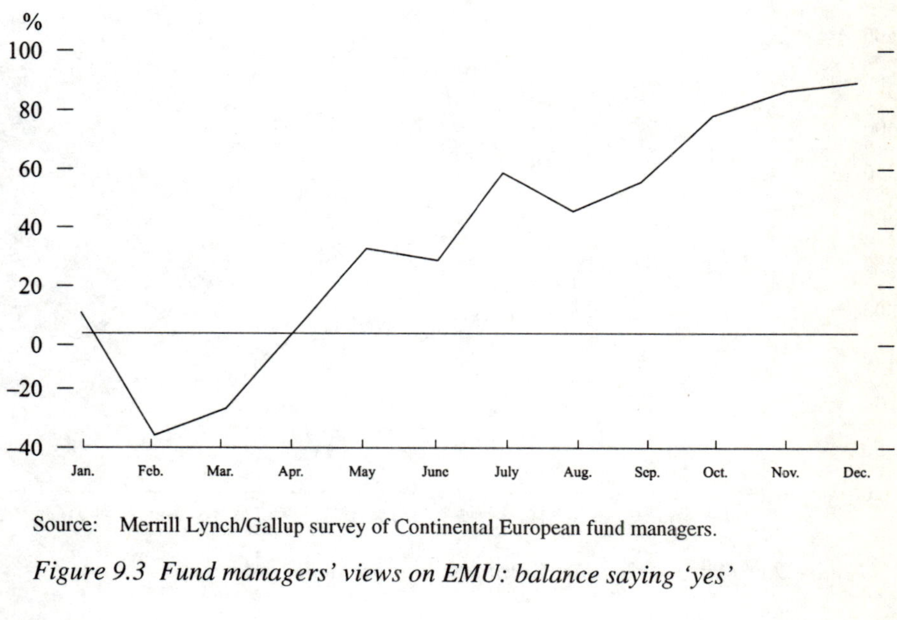

Source: Merrill Lynch/Gallup survey of Continental European fund managers.

Figure 9.3 Fund managers' views on EMU: balance saying 'yes'

yields traded close to German bunds (within 20 basis points) for the past three or four years. So Dutch yields show no sudden convergence effect in 1996. Other so-called core countries, Austria for example, saw a marked, but much more recent, downturn in yields relative to Germany in the first quarter of 1996.

The implications of this turnaround in expectations are apparent even for countries which traditionally have had higher-yielding bond markets. In early December 1995, the spread of Italian debt over Germany was over 500 basis points; yet by the end of 1996 this had fallen to almost 150. Indeed, by the end of the year Italian bonds were trading through the spread of gilts over bunds. This led some market commentators to suggest that in some cases the markets may have overreacted to the prospect of a single currency. Similar striking reductions in spreads during 1996 are evident on Spanish and Swedish government debt (Figure 9.4).

GOODBYE CURRENCY RISK

It is natural to ask what is driving these spectacular changes in spreads. In particular, how much is driven by the approach of EMU? And how much is

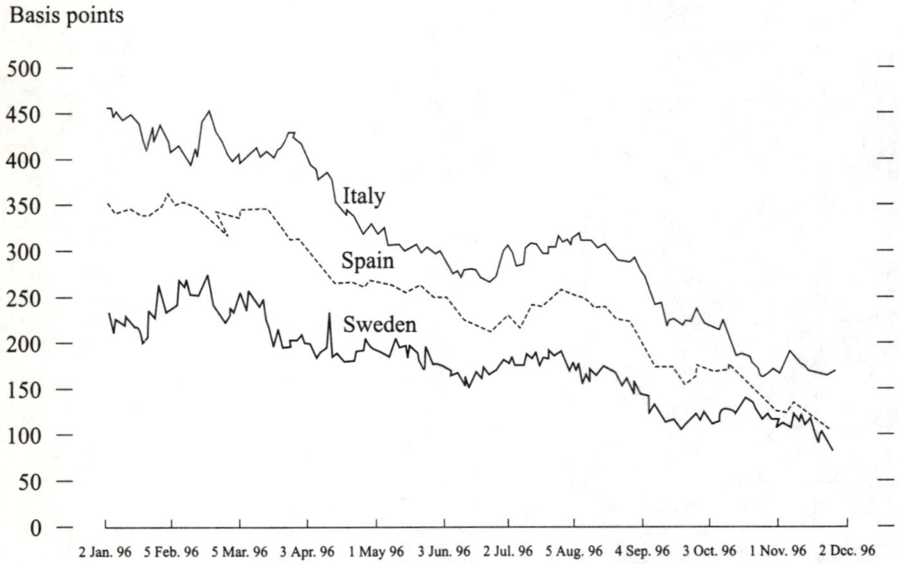

Figure 9.4 Spreads against Germany: high yielders

merely a cyclical and reversible change? The Maastricht Treaty was signed in February 1992. This contained the so-called 'convergence criteria' on debt and inflation. Later, Stage 2 of EMU began in November 1993. At this point the Maastricht Treaty came into force and the European Monetary Institute was established in Frankfurt. But this had little impact on the markets at the time, as the long, cyclically-driven divergence in yields through 1994 demonstrated. In December 1995, the European Council summit in Madrid agreed the name of the putative single currency as the 'Euro'. But there was still little decisive evidence of convergence in European bond yields. Nevertheless, a sea change in sentiment appears to have taken hold in the first quarter of 1996, driving yields across Europe towards Germany, with only one or two exceptions. This change suggested not only that a single currency was expected to come into existence on the planned date of 1 January 1999, but also that the participating club might now be quite broad. The pervasiveness of the decline in yields indicated that countries with a less credible monetary and fiscal tradition would be admitted. Prior to 1996, the most common expectation in the markets had been for a much smaller core group of perhaps six countries going in on time in January 1999.

So, if EMU goes ahead on time, why should bond yields fall? This is analogous to asking about the components of a bond yield. Most obviously, it is possible to say that this will contain an expected real interest rate and an inflation expectation. But beyond this it may be possible to identify a substantial bundle of risk premia. Frank Fabozzi quotes a catalogue of possibilities ranging from market risk through call risk, default risk, inflation risk and even 'risk risk', which is really the risk of the unknown.[4] Of course, EMU convergence is the result of the gradual elimination of currency risk. In principle, the return on an overseas bond in an investor's home currency can be wiped out by adverse fluctuations in exchange rates. For investors resident in single currency nations this risk will disappear when they buy Euro-denominated debt. It is now widely accepted that the yield which remains should be a better indicator of sovereign credit risk, because EMU countries will remain individually responsible for their debt obligations.

There are reasons for believing that the persistence of national credit risks will limit, or at least delay, the emergence of a single, composite yield curve in the Euro area. The fiscal traditions of the likely members are very different and large stocks of national debt will not disappear overnight, even if current policies augur better management of the public finances. This suggests that the probability of national default will not converge for a long time. In this context, any perception of a fiscal guarantee would probably be reflected in higher credit risks for possible 'free-rider' countries. The recently announced fiscal stability pact is clearly intended to make best practice in European fiscal policy the norm. It nevertheless appears likely that the emergence of a single, homogeneous bond market in 1999 is unlikely, despite the disappearance of currency risk. In a recent article, Doug Jones suggested there are already signs of 'austerity fatigue' in Europe.[5] He argues that, once countries have entered the single currency, these pressures could make it difficult to enforce the stability pact, leading to long-run divergences in yields on Euro-denominated debt. An analogous situation, that of the markets for debt issued by the Canadian provinces, will be considered later.

ECONOMETRIC EVIDENCE FOR CONVERGENCE?

If currency risk is being eliminated by the prospect of EMU, can it be said that the yields on likely member countries' debt have now fully converged? Prima facie, this would look to be the case in some countries, such as France. But others, notably the United Kingdom, Italy and Denmark, continue to trade well over Germany. It is helpful to explore this question of bond yield convergence with some simple econometric analysis. Specifically, the methodology used by Pier Giogio Ardeni can be brought to bear here.[6] He tests for the absence of EU country differentials in monthly data on nominal exchange rates, short-term interest rates, consumer price indices, wage rates, industrial production and money supplies. The definition of convergence amounts to a test on the form of the long-run cointegrating vector between, for example, French and German short-term interest rates. These tests are easily accomplished using the well-known maximum likelihood procedure developed by Søren Johansen.[7] Ardeni's results show that, while cointegration is present among the relevant variables, there is little evidence of convergence, excepting in nominal wage rates.

The lack of convergence in short-term interest rates in Ardeni's results is interesting, if unsurprising, given the differences in existing monetary policy regimes around Europe. Convergence in bond yields, for which Ardeni did not test, would tell us that participants in financial markets believe that in the longer run these differences in national monetary policies will have disappeared; that is, that the countries concerned are expected to enter a single currency.[8]

As a preliminary to the question of cointegration, it is sensible to look at the simple time series properties of government bond yields since the beginning of 1992 when the Maastricht Treaty was signed. Convergence implies some form of deep-seated or 'structural' change in the underlying processes that generate yields. This should manifest itself in the mean and variance of yields which will have been changing over time if national bond markets are converging on those of Germany. So I have tested for stationarity in yields in nine of the 15 EU countries and in Switzerland. I have done this in only nine EU countries simply to save time and because the nine EU economies I have chosen represent different strands of EMU possibility. So we can choose Germany, the Netherlands, Belgium and France as a proxy, but not a definition, for the core group most likely to enter a single currency. Italy and Spain should be included as examples of countries whose debt would usually be thought of as 'high yielding' in European terms and, in this sense, less suitable for early inclusion within the single currency. Denmark, Sweden and the United Kingdom could qualify on some of the Maastricht criteria in pure accounting terms, but might choose not to join (in the first wave). Switzerland is worth including as a non-EU counterfactual.

The daily data set I have collected starts in January 1992 to correspond (roughly) with the signing of the Maastricht Treaty. I have tested over the whole sample period (1992–6 inclusive) and two subsamples: 1992–5 inclusive and 1996, when the convergence effect may have been most marked. Standard augmented Dickey–Fuller tests show that in every case bond yields are non-stationary – over the full period and both subsample periods and for each of the nine EU countries.[9] If the mean and variance of national bond yields are moving systematically over time, this is consistent, inter alia, with the *approach* of convergence. In achieving convergence it may be that, while yields in most countries will fall steadily towards those in Germany, there will be some gradual upward drift in German yields: convergence is not inevitably a process of decline in yields towards those of the strongest economy. The eventual benchmark may turn out to be some composite of the yields in all likely member countries, albeit heavily weighted towards the level of German yields.

We can interpret the Ardeni methodology as a test of whether, in the long run, the difference between, say, French and German yields is equal to zero. In order to establish this we first test for whether country yields are cointegrated with the benchmark country. That is, assume that the convergence hypothesis suggests an equilibrium relationship between yields in country i and the benchmark country j:

$$Y_{i,t} = b.Y_{j,t}.$$

If yields in both countries are (approximately) equal in every period t, then:

$$Y_{i,t} - b.Y_{j,t} = 0.$$

For this condition to hold, we need simply to test the restriction that the coefficient $b = 1$. This is what might be called 'strong convergence', since it implies that national bond yields are equal in all respects, including credit risk.

The Annex reports results of cointegration tests between German bond yields, eight EU countries and Switzerland using daily data for 1996 and the standard Johansen methodology. As the results show, in none of the eight EU countries tested is there an identifiable cointegrating vector with Germany.

Ironically, only in the case of Swiss yields is a cointegrating vector found. But even in this case the convergence test that $b = 1$ is not passed![10]

So it appears that, using this methodology, there is little decisive evidence yet for convergence in EU government bond yields. A number of important caveats can be made to this conclusion, however. The markets may be in the process of converging, but until this has been achieved fully, it may not be identifiable econometrically: the road to Damascus may not be well signposted! So similar work in a year or two may yield different conclusions. Further, while sovereign credit risks persist, a weaker definition of convergence might be appropriate. In this case the spread in 'converged' country bond yields could be persistently non-zero suggesting a different restriction on the cointegrating vector.

A CANADIAN ANALOGY

Several countries around the world with a federal structure allow provinces or states to issue their own debt. Countries like the United States, Australia and Canada are all examples of this. The commonality with these countries and a Europe with a single currency is the absence of currency risk. Yields on debt issued by, say, the Canadian provinces should be distinguishable primarily as a result of different provincial credit risks. This credit risk will reflect many factors such as local political stability, in addition to more obvious economic determinants such as the growth rate of the regional economy relative to the real interest rate it must pay to service its debt.

In Canada there are ten provincial issuers. Of these, Ontario, Quebec, British Columbia and Alberta are reasonably large. As a proxy for their credit risk, we can compare ten-year provincial yields with the Canadian national curve as a risk-free benchmark. Figure 9.5 contains weekly observations on spreads in Ontario (the largest market), Quebec (a large market possibly with a high political risk premium) and Prince Edward Island (one of the smallest markets). It is interesting to observe that the movements in these spreads are quite large over relatively short periods. Prima facie, credit risk ought to be quite stable over short periods unless there are significant structural changes such as a new government. The chart also shows that the ranking of spreads changes quite often: notice, for example, that Prince Edward Island trades above and below Quebec. This is quite surprising. Intuitively, one might expect that the ordering of credit risks would be unlikely to change, at least in the short run.

So in several ways the Canadian analogy is instructive. It suggests that spreads will persist and that the disappearance of currency risk will not necessarily make spreads more predictable. This means that, while the debt stocks of the 'in-countries' will be redenominated in a single currency, this may not

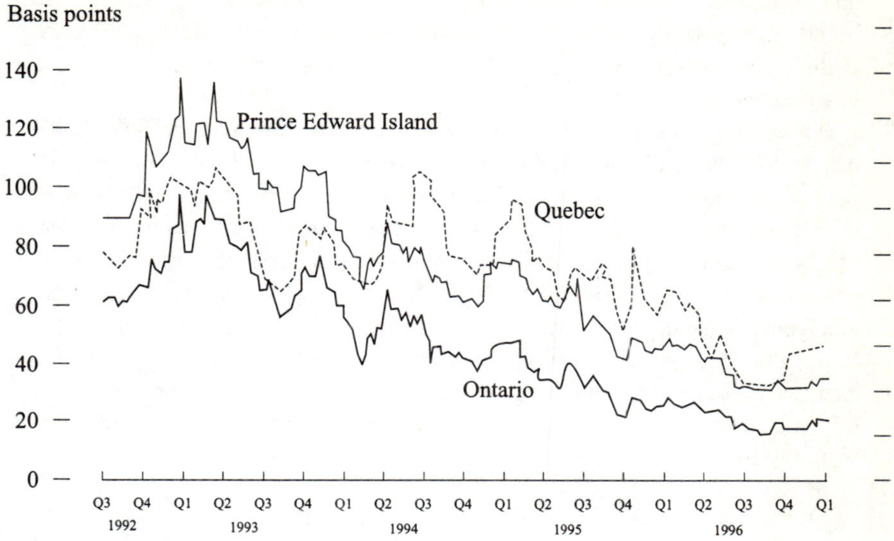

Figure 9.5 Spreads against Canada

in itself lead to the creation of a large, homogeneous bond market. There will still be national factors left to trade: sovereign differences, of one sort or another, will persist.

REFLECTIONS

The theory of optimal currency areas (OCAs) gives reasonably clear guidance on the requirements for currency integration. These are really 'homogeneity' provisos, which suggest that economic fundamentals in all areas of a potential currency union ought to be broadly the same. Goods and services need to be tradeable throughout the union, and capital and labour should also be fully mobile.[11] This will help to create an environment in which shocks to the union as a whole will have a pervasive but similar impact everywhere. In this context it would be more likely for an aggregate monetary policy response to shocks to be appropriate in all parts of the union.

Melitz has argued that 'achieving an optimal zone of fixed exchange rates or an OCA is not an optimisation exercise in the usual sense, but requires concerted action. Furthermore, when the issue of an OCA does arise, membership will usually be determined from the start largely by non-monetary considerations'.[12] This suggests that the creation of a Euro without the goods and factor market mobility suggested by theory might be enough in itself to drive together the yields of likely member countries. But bond market convergence in these circumstances need not be a signal that a broader economic convergence has also been achieved.

It is also plain that some of the observed bond market convergence in the 1990s has been cyclical. This is quite normal and we should expect some convergence (and divergence) in yields to come and go over time, just like the tides. The main recent influence in this respect has been the coming of a low(er) inflation world through greater consensus among policy makers about the inflation objective. This has had a moderating influence on yield levels and led to the emergence of a more 'bond-friendly' environment. Richard Benzie has also noted important changes in institutional forces for bond market integration, for example in the reform or abolition of withholding tax regimes.[13] Even if the goal of a single currency disappeared, it is likely that these other forces for convergence would remain.

NOTES

1. I am grateful to Matt Davies for research assistance and to Allison Holland and Ian Bond for many helpful comments. However, the contents of this essay are entirely my own work and I alone am responsible for errors and omissions. The views expressed do not necessarily reflect the views of the Bank of England. This chapter was written in January 1997 and reflects developments up to that point.
2. See, for example, Koos Alders *et al.* (eds), *Monetary policy in a converging Europe*, Dordrecht Kluwer Academic Publishers, 1996.
3. These large cyclical swings in bond markets are discussed more fully in Joe Ganley and Gilles Noblet, 'Bond yield changes in 1993 and 1994: an interpretation', *Bank of England Quarterly Bulletin*, **35**, 1995, 154–9.
4. See chapter 1 of Frank J. Fabozzi, *Bond markets, analysis and strategies*, Englewood Cliffs, NJ: Prentice-Hall International, 1996.
5. *The Times*, 13 January 1997, p. 41.
6. See his 'On the way to EMU: Testing convergence of the European economies', *Economic Notes*, **21**, 1992, 238–57.
7. 'Statistical analysis of cointegration vectors', *Journal of Economic Dynamics and Control*, **12**, 1988, 231–54.
8. In principle, bond market convergence should be measured as the spread between *implied forward interest rates*, rather than in redemption yields, as I have done here. Derived from the zero-coupon yield curve, implied forward rates are the one-period interest rates expected to prevail in future years. However, estimates of implied forward rates for most EU economies are not widely available and so market convention has been to compare spreads in redemption yields.
9. Full details of these test results are available from the author on request.
10. The estimated cointegrating vector in the Swiss case is $(Y_{i,t} - 0.98429Y_{j,t})$. Testing the null hypothesis that $b = 1$ gives a calculated chi-squared value of 8.9363, in which case we reject the null at the 5 per cent level. The cointegration tests in the Annex are based on the trace of the long-run cointegrating vector where, using standard notation, 'r' is the rank of this matrix.

11. The original thinking on OCA theory is due to Robert Mundell, 'A theory of optimum currency areas', *American Economic Review*, **51**, 1961, 657–65.
12. J. Melitz, 'A suggested reformulation of the theory of optimum currency areas', *CEPR Discussion Paper*, no. 590, October 1991.
13. See his *The development of the international bond market*, BIS Economic Papers, no. 32, January 1992.

ANNEX

Tests for number of cointegrating vectors with Germany, 2 January to 18 December 1996

Lags[1]	Null	Alternative	λ_{trace}	$\lambda_{crit,\,95\%}$
Belgium				
1	r = 0	r ≥ 1	9.37	15.41
	r ≤ 1	r = 2	0.27	3.76
Denmark				
2	r = 0	r ≥ 1	6.04	15.41
	r ≤ 1	r = 2	0.83	3.76
France				
2	r = 0	r ≥ 1	6.88	15.41
	r ≤ 1	r = 2	0.30	3.76
Italy				
1	r = 0	r ≥ 1	4.59	15.41
	r ≤ 1	r = 2	0.00	3.76
Netherlands				
4	r = 0	r ≥ 1	12.97	15.41
	r ≤ 1	r = 2	1.57	3.76
Spain				
4	r = 0	r ≥ 1	5.46	15.41
	r ≤ 1	r = 2	0.11	3.76
Sweden				
1	r = 0	r ≥ 1	9.77	15.41
	r ≤ 1	r = 2	0.22	3.76
Switzerland				
1	r = 0	r ≥ 1	15.83	15.41
	r ≤ 1	r = 2	3.10	3.76
UK				
2	r = 0	r ≥ 1	11.12	15.41
	r ≤ 1	r = 2	0.97	3.76

Note: 1. The maximum number of lags in the VAR.

10. Severe fiscal contractions and expansions: a further tale of a European economy[1]

Brian Henry and James Nixon

INTRODUCTION

The issue we address in this chapter on Keynesian versus non-Keynesian effects of fiscal policy is, we believe, highly appropriate in a volume commemorating the work of Maurice Peston and Bernard Corry. Throughout their academic careers, both have had the closest interest in the analysis of public policy. Maurice Peston has long been recognized as an authority on the macro analysis of fiscal policy. Moreover, and this touches on the methodological aspect of our work here, he has had a long and distinguished involvement in the application of optimal control methods to macro policy design, being a founding member of the PREM (Programme of Research in Economic Modelling). This began in the early 1970s, at Queen Mary College in London, before, with changes in personnel, location, and name (PROPE: Programme of Research in Optimal Policy in Economics), moving to Imperial College, and made many important contributions to the public policy debate. Bernard Corry has throughout his career been involved in macro policy matters, making a number of contributions to the Phillips curve literature. From his earliest days as a lecturer at the London School of Economics he has continued to be a serious student of 'Keynesian' economics, an interest dating from one of his earliest contributions which argued against the fairly widespread view that there are Keynesian aspects to be found in that most pessimistic of classical economists, Malthus (see Corry, 1959).

A conviction which both Maurice Peston and Bernard Corry have retained is that of the value of empirical and econometric research in economics. They played a leading role in the creation of the research environment in the LSE of the 1960s dedicated to promoting the 'positive' approach to applied economic questions. This approach aimed to evaluate rival policies and their underlying models, using quantified approaches. Testing alternative models was seen as a positive way for applied economics to develop. Even in today's more sophisticated (and sceptical?) times, such a positive methodology has a central role to play. We hope in all modesty that this is reflected in the present offering.

This chapter considers an issue which has resonances in the interests of Maurice and Bernard, since we evaluate the likely macroeconomic consequences of a substantial fiscal consolidation. It is an empirical study, and we take the case of the United Kingdom in the 1980s as the subject. More specifically, we take issue with recent 'non-Keynesian' literature which argues that the fiscal multiplier may be negative even in the short run. Although there is a substantial literature on this subject, we concentrate on two particular studies by Giavazzi and Pagano, since these are empirical and econometric, and we want to focus on matters of empirical evidence for the non-Keynesian proposition.

In Giavazzi and Pagano (1990) and (1995) (hereafter GP (1990) and (1995)) the possibility that a drastic fiscal consolidation is followed by (for which read 'causes') a vigorous expansion is advanced. In their 1990 paper, the cases of the 1983–6 Danish and the 1987–9 Irish fiscal stabilization were analysed in support of this contention. Their later paper applied a similar methodology to the case of falling taxes: they argued that the decrease in net taxes in Sweden in the early 1990s was associated with a *fall* in private demand. In other words, these cases suggested that the fiscal multiplier is negative. Of course, the argument that the fiscal multiplier can be negative is not new, but much earlier literature had taken the view that it was in the long run that the fiscal multiplier became negative, after being 'Keynesian' (that is, positive) in the short run, turning negative in the long run through a variety of crowding out mechanisms. The argument advanced in GP is that the multiplier may be negative in the short run also, mainly because of the effect of tax changes on forward-looking informed consumers.

An obvious additional candidate country to add to the cases of Denmark, Ireland and Sweden is the United Kingdom following its experience with a drastic fiscal consolidation in the period 1980–81. As in the other countries, private consumption in the United Kingdom appeared to respond following the consolidation, rising sharply, and by the mid-1980s its rate of growth and that of output were rapid by historical standards, with GDP growing above 4.5 per cent between 1986 and the start of 1989. So the question arises, does the UK experience provide further confirmation of 'non-Keynesian' effects from fiscal consolidation to which GP draw attention? We present an analysis of the UK experience over the 1980s, using a somewhat different methodology from GP. The GP argument is largely based on an econometric model of consumption (see the fourth section, below). Our methods use econometric evidence, but also report on complete macro model simulations using an economy-wide econometric macro model (the LBS Model; see Allen and Hall, 1997). Alternative methods of generating expectations figure in this in a very important way. Amongst other things, the model includes a recently developed econometric model of consumption based on representative agents with forward-looking expectations (see Caporale and Williams, 1997).

We begin by reviewing the general argument of fiscal consolidation with rational expectations. The third section comments on UK macro experience in the first half of the 1980s, including developments in its public finances. This is followed by a description of the role which consumption might play in fiscal consolidation. Our complete model analysis with policy simulations is reported in the fifth section and the final section offers conclusions and proposals for future work.

THE ANALYSIS OF THE EFFECTS OF FISCAL CONSOLIDATION

The view that fiscal consolidation will positively encourage growth and possibly reduce inflation at the same time is not new, of course. Recommendations to cut fiscal deficits are a staple (perhaps the only staple) ingredient at the end of IMF surveillance missions for developed countries, and in conditionalities for programmes for countries in transition and other, less developed countries. The analytical basis for these supposed beneficial effects has changed over time. Early versions of the 'crowding-out' literature concentrated on long-run effects of interest rate and induced exchange rate effects of changes in fiscal deficits. They concluded that the Keynesian multiplier would eventually turn negative if these were sufficiently strong. These beliefs tended to founder on findings of weak interest rate effects on domestic expenditures. More recently, attention has switched to expectations and risk premia effects on exchange rates. In an open economy, with highly integrated capital markets, the latter offer the possibility that fiscal consolidation may actually be growth-enhancing even in the short run. This could happen with a credible commitment by a high-deficit country to follow a deficit reduction programme. With long term real interest rates between countries decoupled by risk premia, where these premia in turn depend on their relative deficit position, a consolidation could result in a fall in real long-term interest rates in the high deficit country (IMF, *World Economic Outlook*, May 1995, pp. 24–5). The fiscal multiplier in these circumstances could be negative. This view – arising from 'credibility' effects and risk premia in foreign exchange markets – is somewhat at odds with the transmission mechanism discussed in GP (1990), which attributes increased growth to the neo-Ricardian effect of the change in the deficit on the expected incomes of (rationally) forward-looking consumers, who raise their consumption in the short run.

We consider the GP argument more carefully, before commenting on the evidence. Although the GP contention is related to the notion of neo-Ricardian equivalence, it is of course different in an important way. In the original analysis of budget deficits, the neo-Ricardian view was that, given public expenditure, the mix between tax and bond finance was neutral in the long run. In a closed economy, with rational forward-looking agents, the present value of future tax payments exactly balances the value of the change in the stock of bonds. In this case bonds, which simply represent a network of claims within a closed system, are not net wealth (see Allsop and Vines, 1996). There are stringent assumptions which need to be met for this result to hold, including perfect capital markets, no liquidity constraints, agents who act as if they live forever and, lastly, fully rational expectations formation. Apart from anything else, these special conditions warn us that ex post explanations of the effects of fiscal consolidation on consumption need to be carefully separated from possible effects of financial liberalization if, as happened in the United Kingdom, these took place at roughly similar times (see further on this in the fourth section, below).

In the GP analysis the transmission mechanism is the effects of government spending on consumption working through their effect on expected income. This is the centrepiece of their argument that fiscal consolidation may have non-Keynesian effects on output. We should emphasize at this point that in both GP (1990) and GP (1995) a wide-ranging analysis of the events in Ireland, Denmark and Sweden is presented, including changes in monetary policy and real interest rates. We concentrate on the consumption link only here, because GP attach great significance to it in their overall account, and because of the intrinsic importance of the argument for the analysis of fiscal policy. On the question of consumption, they advance two arguments: one empirical and econometric, the other analytical. The empirical argument concerns consumption and government expenditure cross correlations, which we discuss more fully in the fourth section. The analytical argument then concerns the possibility that expectations of future policy – specifically, expectations of future tax cuts due to a credible commitment by government of *permanent* cuts in spending today – play an important role in explaining consumption. This argument is outlined more fully now.

The argument is, in turn, based on the Blanchard (1985) model, where consumption depends on human wealth (H), private sector wealth net of government debt (K), and the real value of the market value of debt (D). Thus the consumption function is

$$C(t) = (p + \theta)\,[H(t) + K(t) + \mathrm{D}(t)] \tag{10.1}$$

where θ is the subjective discount rate, and p the planning margin (so that if $p \to 0$, this is the infinite horizon neo-Ricardian case). We are concerned here with $D(t)$ and its effect on $C(t)$ only. The $D(t)$ variable is defined as

$$D(t) = \int_t^{\infty} [T(s) - G(s)]\, e^{-r(s-t)}\, ds. \qquad (10.2)$$

In (10.2) it is assumed there is a public debt of *B* consols, each paying £1 per period, and the discounted value of the flow of coupons on these equals the discounted value of future budget surpluses. The real value of the market value of the debt is then given as the discounted flow of coupons on the *B* consols, where *r* is the real interest rate and II the rate of inflation.

$$D(t) = \int_t^{\infty} e^{-r(s-t)} (Be^{-\Pi(s-t)})ds. \qquad (10.3)$$

Hence, according to equations (10.2) and (10.3) this discounted flow of coupons is equal to the discounted value of further real budget surpluses $(T - G)$. In equation 10.2, *G* is government spending, and permanent spending $G^p(t)$ is derived from this as the annuity value of the discounted flow of real spending; that is:

$$G^P(t) = r\int_t^{\infty} G(s)e^{-r(s-t)}ds. \qquad (10.4)$$

Finally, we state and comment on the results of relevance to what follows:

$$\frac{\partial C(t)}{\partial T(t)} = -(p+\delta)\left(1-e^{-pt}\right) \qquad (10.5)$$

$$\frac{\partial C(t)}{\partial G^P(t)} = \frac{p+\theta}{r+p} < 0. \qquad (10.6)$$

According to (10.5) with finite horizons $(p > 0)$, consumption falls when taxes rise temporarily, even if they are cut at a future date. The effect is also an increasing function of the horizon (*p*). In other words, the shorter the horizon (that is, the larger is *p*) the bigger will be the effect of a tax change on consumption. These results hold for given $G^p(t)$ (Blanchard, 1985).

Next, if actual $G(t)$ changes, but this is temporary, so $G^p(t)$ does not change, then consumption is unaltered, because this temporary change does not change the path of taxes. On the other hand, if $G(t)$ changes permanently (or is credibly expected to have changed permanently) then consumption changes, as shown in (10.6). The effect of planning horizon (l/p) is, however, ambiguous: a long horizon means that there is more time to take advantage of the expected tax decreases, but the increase in permanent income needs to be spread over a longer time period.

Nonetheless, this model provides us with an analytical reason for expecting a change in consumption following a permanent decrease in spending. Other arguments have been put forward in this general vein, each of which put the expectation of *future* tax consequences of a change in current fiscal stance (be it tax or expenditure changes) at the centre of the analysis. Sutherland (1995), for example, has a model where, with a high debt to income ratio, a tax cut may signal an increased likelihood of tax increases falling on the present generation of consumers rather than future generations. Blanchard (1990) draws attention to the effect of tax cuts today raising the probability of even further increases tomorrow, due to accrued interest payments. Under some circumstances, this can lead to a reduction in permanent income and hence consumption.

Armed with some general arguments which suggest that government spending changes and consumption may be negatively related, the obvious question is whether this holds in fact. To consider this we turn first to a review of events in the United Kingdom in the 1980s, before considering the empirical evidence that anticipation of tax changes accounts for changes in consumption.

THE UNITED KINGDOM IN THE 1980s: A BRIEF RÉSUMÉ OF CONSUMPTION AND FISCAL CHANGES

The pattern of consumption in the United Kingdom has shown remarkable changes, especially in the 1980s. Consumption growth picked up in the mid-1980s, before decelerating, and then falling in 1990, before resuming its growth rate at the end of 1992 (Figure 10.1). More revealing evidence of the possible changes in consumption behaviour is given in the marked changes in the savings ratio (S/Y), which is shown in Figure 10.2.

A remarkable fall in the savings ratio began in mid-1984, lasting until the end of 1987, followed by an equally sharp rise until well into 1992. These very substantial changes have been heavily documented, as has their dependence on the earlier period of financial liberalization, with attendant large changes in asset price inflation (particularly house prices) and huge changes in consumer borrowing and personal sector debt behaviour (debt to income rose from about 20 per cent in 1979 to over 120 per cent by 1990 for the personal sector). (See Muellbauer and Murphy, 1993; Miles, 1994; Blake and Westerway,1993, for further discussions.)

Moving to the central issue we are interested in here, we look at fiscal developments over the same period. Government borrowing (as a proportion of GDP) fell dramatically at the beginning of the 1980s, very rapidly in 1981, but more steadily over the first half of the 1980s, before actively becoming negative in 1987–90. In the 1990s, the public sector borrowing requirement (PSBR) ratio

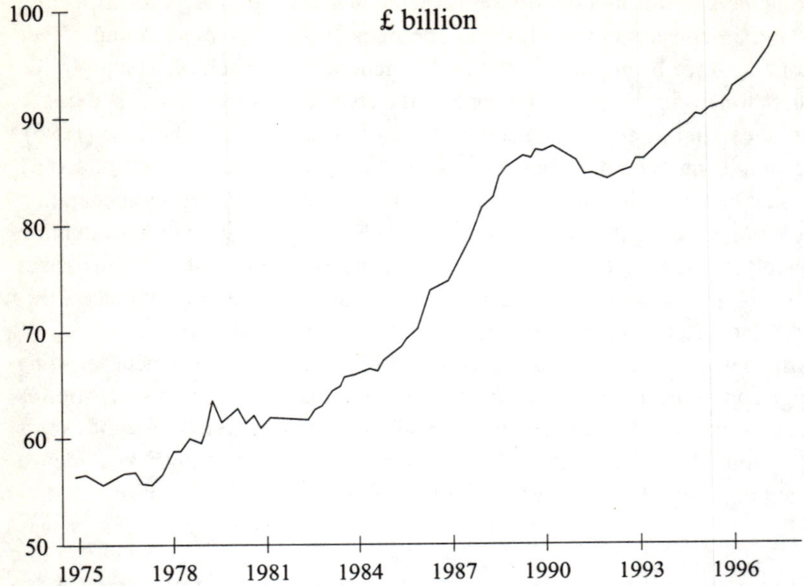

Figure 10.1 Consumers' expenditure

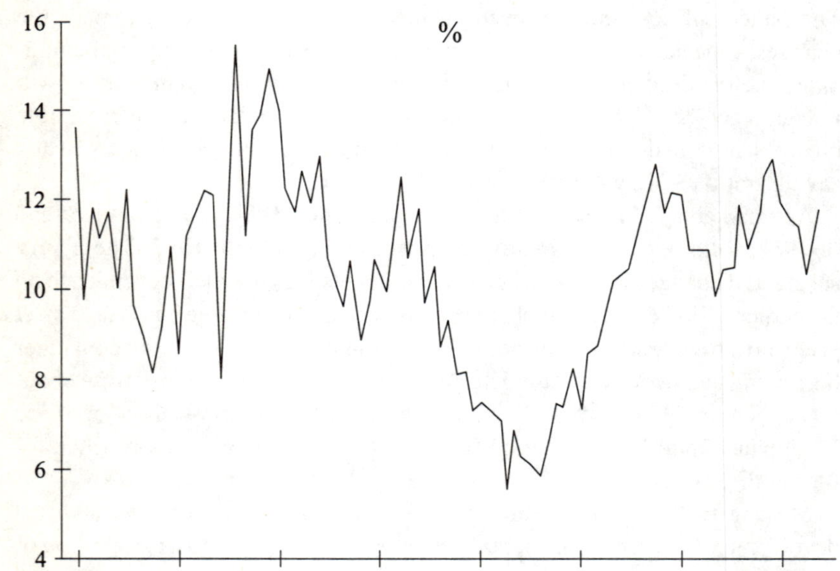

Figure 10.2 Personal sector savings ratio

then rose to about 8 per cent before falling to around 4 per cent by 1996 (Figure 10.3). Reasons for these pronounced changes are not hard to find, based on changes in the tax take in 1981 (the Howe anticyclical budget), the contribution of oil revenues over the first half of the decade, then an increasingly beneficial (for government revenues) contribution to growth of the rapid consumption increases, and these having a large tax elasticity they gave a sharp boost to government receipts (see Hall *et al.*, 1996). As Figure 10.4 shows, changes in the overall deficit have come from changes in public expenditure as well as on the revenue side.

What this short résumé shows is that, superficially at least, there appears a positive correlation between the savings ratio and the PSBR to GDP ratio over much of the 1980s and 1990s. Thus the government borrowing ratio declined over most of the 1980s when the savings ratio also fell, and when government borrowing rose at the end of the 1980s and the 1990s the savings ratio rose too (see Figures 10.2 and 10.3). Does this confirm the GP thesis? We argue that it does not, because the changes in the savings ratio appear explicable by other things which were happening at the same time, principally the changes in borrowing and lending behaviour resulting from the liberalization of the financial system in the early 1980s, and the consequent real house prices inflation–deflation cycle which this produced. We turn now to a review of the evidence for this alternative explanation.

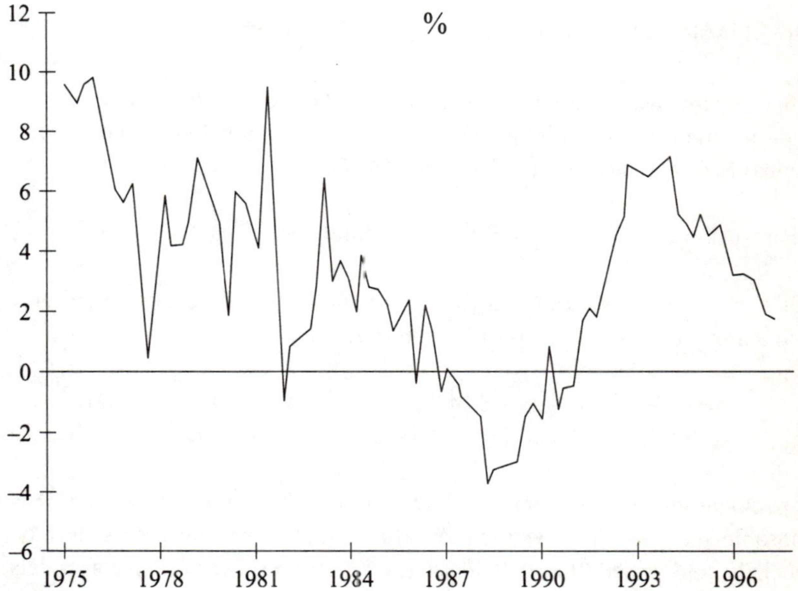

Figure 10.3 Public sector borrowing as a proportion of GDP

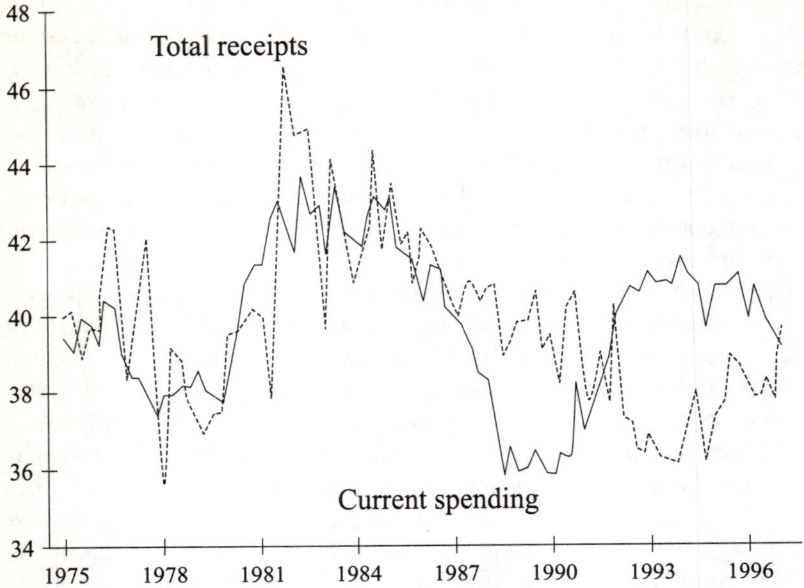

Figure 10.4 Government spending and tax revenues as a proportion of GDP

CONSUMPTION: SOME EVIDENCE

In this section we comment on the original GP results for consumption, comparing their findings with recent work on consumption done at the London Business School (Caporale and Williams,1997).

Consumption and Tax Changes: the GP Analysis

In GP (1990), the hypothesis that changes in public debt affect consumption is tested using a Hayashi-type consumption function:

$$C(t) = \alpha_0 + \alpha_1 C(t-1) + \theta [A(t) - (1+\delta)(A(t-1) + W(t-1))] + (\beta [D(t) - (1+\delta) D(t-1)] + \mu [Y(t) - (1+\delta) Y(t-1)]. \quad (10.7)$$

A is personal sector wealth net of public debt (*D*), *W* is labour income and *Y* is disposable income. The specification allows that some consumers may be financially constrained ($\mu \neq 0$). (GP also test for the presence of such constraints using excess sensitivity measures in the Euler equation for consumption.) Tests of the significance of β in (10.7) (the effect of public debt) reveal weak effects for both Ireland and (though less so) Denmark (GP, 1990 Table 3, p. 96). However, GP conduct further tests, using the *unexplained* component of consumption from (10.7) – which they interpret as consumption 'surprises' – and changes in government spending which they interpret as surprises in (permanent) public spending. They find the correlation is negative and significant (at the 10 per cent level) in Denmark, but not significant in Ireland. This is interpreted as evidence that the unexplained part of the boom in consumption spending in Denmark was related to the cuts in current government spending which signalled lower future taxes.

A Consumption Model for the United Kingdom

Part of the problem with the story advanced by GP is the weight it places upon (10.7) to account for the behaviour of consumption where there has been liberalization and consequently the importance of 'unexplained' movements in consumption and the purported correlation of these to changes in central government spending. Much work on the consumption function in the United Kingdom has adopted models which, though in keeping with the general spirit of the Hayashi model (equation (10.7)), have emphasized the possible regime change effects which the extensive financial liberalization produced there. As Figure 10.2 above shows, the changes in consumption behaviour over the second half of the 1980s appear profound. Do we have to have recourse to the changes in government spending to account for these? The short answer is negative; models reported in Muellbauer and Murphy (1993) and Darby and Ireland (1994), for example, appear broadly to account for the consumption boom using proxy measures of financial liberalization. In the present exercise we describe a consumption model which develops many of these ideas. (See Caporale and Williams, 1997, for a fuller account.)

Consumers are divided into financially constrained and unconstrained groups and the unconstrained group is forward-looking and able to use capital markets to smooth the path of consumption over time in the face of fluctuations in current income,

$$C^u_t = \beta(A^u_{t-1} + H^u_{t-1}) \tag{10.8}$$

where A^u_{t-1} is the stock of physical and financial assets held by the unconstrained group and H^u_{t-1} is the present discounted value of future post-tax labour income – the group's human capital. The parameter β is simply a function of the rate of time preference and the probability of death.

In turn, the constrained group is assumed to have small initial assets or human capital holdings and is therefore unable or unwilling to borrow, and is constrained to consume from current disposable income only,

$$C_t^c = Yd_t^c = CG_t + \lambda_t(YD_t - EC_t - IP_t) \qquad (10.9)$$

where CG_t are current grants, YD_t is post-tax disposable income.

Total consumption of the *constrained* and *unconstrained* groups is then given by

$$C_t = C_t^u + C_t^c = (1 - \lambda_t)C_t + \lambda_t C_t. \qquad (10.10)$$

The novelty in this model is to allow λ, the proportion of credit constrained consumers, to vary over time, and to be determined by the degree of liberalization in the financial sector. To make this idea operational we take proxy measures for financial liberalisation (FLIB,) and suppose that λ_t, can be expressed:

$$\lambda_t = \exp(-\alpha_0 - \alpha_1 FLIB_t). \qquad (10.11)$$

Clearly, $0 < \lambda_t < 1$, for α_0 and $\alpha_1 > 0$, and the greater is the degree of financial liberalization, the smaller is the group of credit constrained consumers.

To estimate the model, we assume that the human capital term in (10.8) is evaluated on the basis of a forward-looking expectation of future income flows discounted at a rate, ϕ_t, which is allowed to vary over time. The discount factor is measured as a mark-up, m_t on the market rate of interest, r_t. This mark-up is also assumed to vary over time with financial deregulation. As the effect of *FLIB* is picked up in λ_t we let m_t be:

$$m_t = \mu_0 + \mu_1 \lambda_t. \qquad (10.12)$$

The aggregate consumption function, based on (10.8) together with the other assumptions outlined above, is then

$$\begin{aligned} C_t = {} & \phi_t(C_{t+1} - CG_{t+1} - \lambda_{t+1}(Y_{t+1} - EC_{t+1} - IP_{t+1})) \\ & + \beta\,(A_{t+1} + \lambda_t DB_{t-1} - \phi_t(A_t + \lambda_{t+1} - (1 - \lambda)Y_t)) + CG_t \\ & + \lambda_t(Y_t - EC_t - IP_t) + e_t \end{aligned} \qquad (10.13)$$

where C_t is consumption, CG_t are current grants, Y_t is disposable labour income, EC_t is employers' contributions to pension funds (which cannot be used for current consumption), IP_t is interest payments, A_t is total assets and DB_t are total financial debts.

Caporale and Williams (1997) report on the results when measuring $FLIB_t$ in three alternative ways. These are regressions based on measures, which extend the work of Muellbauer and Murphy (1993) who perform a regression of the following form,

$$\ln(LVR) = \gamma_0 + \gamma_1 \ln(MRT) + \gamma_2 \ln(HP/Y) + \gamma_3(RMRT) + D_1 + ... + D_T \quad (10.14)$$

where *LVR* is the loan to value ratio for house buyers, *MRT* is the nominal post-tax mortgage rate, *HP/Y* is the house price to income ratio and *RMRT* is a two-year moving average of the real post-tax mortgage rate. The intangible effects of the deregulation process are picked up by the dummies D_1 ... D_T and the equation residuals. The $FLIB_t$ measure itself is then given by the residual from (10.14) plus the effects of the timing variables (D_1).

The extensions explored in Caporale and Williams first measure each of the variables using data for first-time buyers (*FLIB*1; see also Darby and Ireland, 1994). The next measure uses data on agents who are already owner occupiers, allowing for the effect of deregulation on the extent of equity withdrawal (*FLIB*2). The third measure (*FLIB*3) uses aggregate data on both groups to try to pick up their combined effect.

Figure 10.5 plots these alternatives, and each shows the clear change in trend in the 1990s, as we would expect from measures of financial liberalization. What is also noteworthy is that the effect on the measure based on first-time buyers (*FLIB*1) seems more pronounced. This is important, since in the model specification tests reported in Caporale and Williams, *FLIB*1 appears to be the

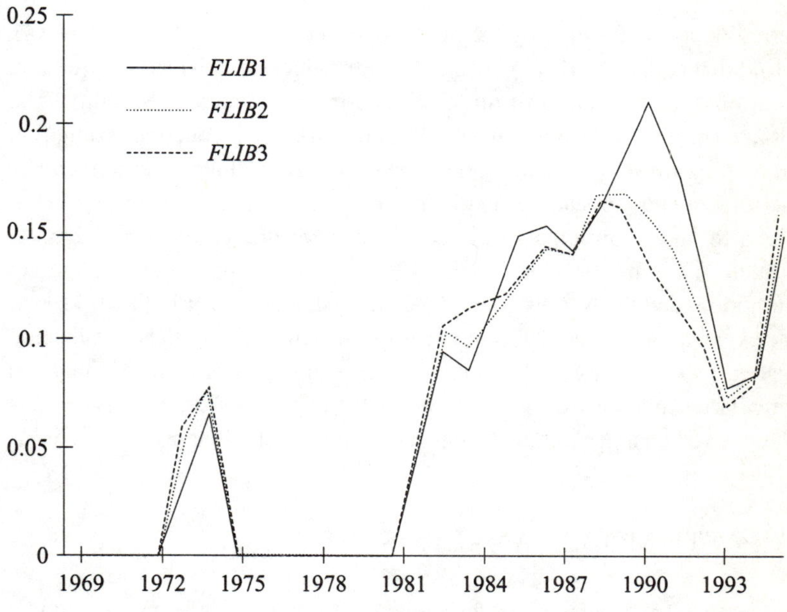

Figure 10.5 Measures of financial liberalization

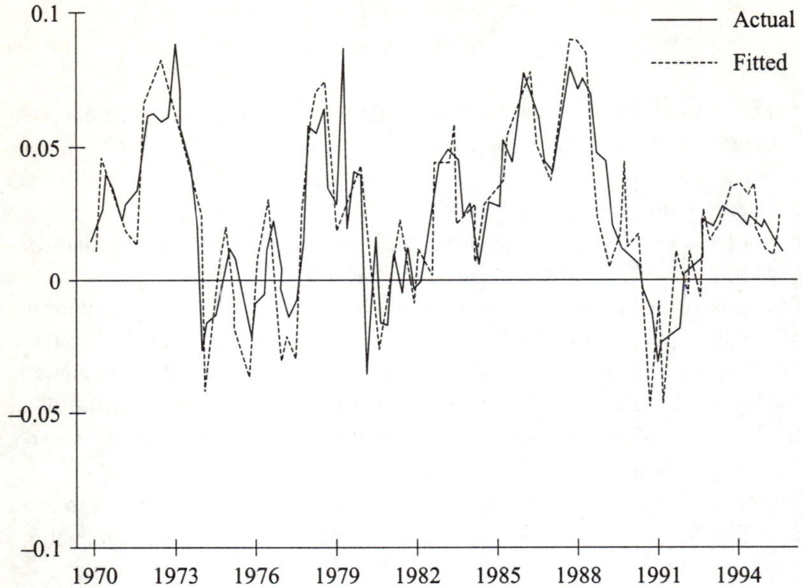

Figure 10.6 Consumption function: actual v. fitted (annual % change in consumption)

preferred measure. Estimating the model over the period 1969(1) to 1995(4), they find that equation (10.13), using *FLIB*1, produces a satisfactory equation, with no obvious indication of misspecification or parameter instability. The importance of this for the present issue is then clear. The model of consumption based on forward-looking agents, but where a time varying proportion may be credit-constrained, appears to 'explain' UK consumption experience *without* recourse to any unanticipated effects from government spending. This is illustrated in Figure 10.6, which plots the actual and predicted changes in consumption, and this shows no evidence of systematic error in the model.

The explanation offered in this model is that it is the effect of the liberalization measures, incorporating both changes in the lending behaviour of financial intermediaries and borrowing behaviour by the private sector, which accounts for the marked changes in the savings ratio we noted in the previous section.

COMPLETE MODEL ANALYSIS

We now move to the analysis of the impact of fiscal policy in complete model simulations when forward-looking behaviour in consumption is included. We do this using the London Business School model of the UK economy. This is a small structural model that is estimated econometrically. The model has a high degree of theoretical consistency and seeks to model the economy at an aggregate level, with the highest possible degree of data consistency. The model has a number of advanced features including forward-looking behaviour in equations other than consumption: principally in the exchange rate which is determined by a forward-looking uncovered interest parity (UIP) equation. Many features of the model are described in detail in Allen and Hall (1997), while its overall structure is summarized in Allen *et al.* (1994).

We use the complete model then to establish what the effect of an increase in central government current spending (*G*) will be. For this we increase *G* by 2bn per annum permanently, which is anticipated (and fully credible in the rational expectations hypothesis solution). Before describing the simulation results, we need to outline the assumption made about expectations formation and the nature of the closure rules which govern the setting of monetary policy and fiscal policy in the model solution. Both have a critical bearing on the nature of the results.

Expectations and Learning

One form of model solutions is rational expectations, and we report on model solutions using this on pp. 165–8. An alternative to this extreme assumption assumes that agents, while not having full information, are able to adapt to regime changes and in effect to 'learn' about the economic environment. A general discussion of this alternative and how it can be implemented in a large-scale macro model is given in Garratt and Hall (1997), upon which the following is based.

The assumption of learning has received increasing attention in the theoretical literature over the last decade and essentially the main approaches have depended on assumptions about the underlying knowledge which agents possess. For example, the earlier theoretical literature assumed that agents know the true structure of the model, but that some of the parameters of the system are unknown. As the true structural equations are known, the agents' learning problem is one of estimating the parameters of the system. Such learning models still make very stringent assumptions, about both agents' knowledge of the structure of the system and their processing all available information in an optimal way.

A slightly weaker form of learning is the boundedly rational learning model. Here agents are assumed to use some 'reasonable' rule of learning to form expectations where the form of the rule remains constant over time. (Usually, this rule is the reduced form of the whole system.) This form of bounded rationality entails that, even in the absence of regime changes, the reduced form of the model is a combination of the stable structural equations and the changing parameters of the expectations rule, so that it is time-varying. It is this form of learning – which we refer to as 'adaptive learning' – which is applied in the solutions we describe later. Before moving on to describe these, we first note how the assumptions about learning are applied in a large macro model like ours.

Suppose the non-linear macro model which incorporates expectations can be described by the following set of n structural equations:

$$Y_{it} = F_i(Y, X, Y^e_{t,t+1}),\ i = 1,...n;\ t = 1,...T \tag{10.15}$$

where Y is a vector of current and lagged values of the n endogenous variables, X is a vector of exogenous variables over all time periods, $Y^e_{t,t+1}$ is the expectation based on information available at time t of Y in period t+1 and Y_{it} represents the specific endogenous variable which appears only in lagged form on the right-hand side of the equations. Next we assume that agents, at time t, have the expectations rule of the following form:

$$Y^e_{t,t+1} = D_t Z + e_{1t} \text{ where } e_{1t} \text{ is} \sim N(0,\mathbf{W}) \tag{10.16}$$

which they use to form current periods' expectations of next periods' value of Y. The vector Z is the information set which can consist of a subset of the matrices Y and X over all current and lagged time periods and D is a time-varying matrix of parameters which evolves according to the following process:

$$D_t = D_{t-1} + e_{2t} \text{ where } e_{2t} \text{ is} \sim N(0,\mathbf{Q}). \tag{10.17}$$

The change in the learning parameters is therefore determined by the value of the **Q** matrix, the hyperparameters of the state equation (10.17).

In adaptive learning schemes we assume that agents utilize a standard statistical or econometric procedure for estimating the expectations rule (10.16) above. It is assumed that some elements of the rule – usually taken to be the parameters of the rule – are not known with certainty. The statistical framework we adopt for the updating of the learning parameters is the Kalman Filter. Equation (10.16), the perceived law of motion, is the measurement equation and equation (10.17) is an AR(1) representation of the states of the system. The **W** and **Q** matrices are the hyperparameters of the system. Garratt and Hall (1997) define the recursive stochastic algorithm which determines the change in the learning parameters and illustrate for the case of learning in the foreign exchange market, deriving an exchange rate model much as is also used in the applications here.

Policy Rules

Two policy rules are used in solving the model: one for fiscal policy, the other for monetary (interest rates). For the present exercise, both are crucial. Let us first consider the fiscal rule. To ensure long-run fiscal solvency in the solution, fiscal policy is set by a closed loop feedback rule which targets the debt to GDP ratio. Thus, using the average personal tax rate (T) as an instrument, we have:

$$T = T_t + \delta_1 \Delta^2(d_t - \bar{d}_t) + V_2 \Delta(d_t - \bar{d}_t) + V_3(d_t - \bar{d}_t) \qquad (10.18)$$

where d is the debt–GDP ratio and $\bar{d}_t$ the target. Rules of this general form are essential in econometric models such as the London Business School model, since they rule out non-sustainable fiscal policies in the long run (so no Ponzi-game solutions are allowed in keeping with developments in the theoretical literature). The appropriate form for the rule is an empirical issue. Bryant and Zhang (1996) have noted very powerful arguments for a debt to income target for the rule (as compared with a deficit to income rule) since this precludes possible debt instabilities. Other than that, the rule is of the 'simple' proportional, integral and derivative (PID) variety, first introduced in the seminal work of Phillips (1957). In the present case, however, the parameters are chosen optimally to minimize a separate objective function depending on deviations of the debt–GDP ratio from base.

In similar fashion, an equivalent PID rule is specified for monetary policy which targets inflation using the short-term interest rate (see Hall and Nixon, 1997, for details):

$$i = i_1 + \beta_1 \Delta^2(\Pi_t - \bar{\Pi}_t) + \beta_2 \Delta(\Pi_t - \bar{\Pi}_t) + \beta_3 (\Pi_t - \bar{\Pi}_t) \qquad (10.19)$$

where Π is inflation, and $\bar{\Pi}$ its target rate. In macro models with rational expectations, monetary rules of this type have now become standard. Their use reflects problems which other methods of setting monetary policy would produce. For example, if interest rates were fixed when solving a complete macro model with rational expectations, model indeterminacy would result. The reason is not hard to see: a positive price shock would lead to lower real interest rates, lower real and nominal exchange rates and thence higher prices, which can set off unstable price spirals leading to solution indeterminacy. On the other hand, setting monetary policy by the demand for monetary balances (say by inverting monetary targeting regimes) also introduces instabilities in solutions, since the money stock responds to interest changes with long lags. In implementing (10.19) we again select the parameters of the rule optimally, minimizing a separate objective function that penalizes deviations of inflation from target.

Before concluding this section, we should emphasize the importance of these rules in determining the outcome of the policy experiments we conduct here. Thus it is vital to model the monetary reaction to any fiscal innovations that the authorities undertake (see Hall, 1997). In common with other comparative model exercises, we find that the form of this policy reaction determines many of the properties of the model (see Church *et al.*, 1995).

Simulation Results

The figures below show the percentage deviation from base for the main macroeconomic aggregates after a permanent increase in government spending with closure rules for money and fiscal policy operating appropriately. In each figure, the results are shown for the two expectations assumptions: rational expectations (*R*) and learning (*L*).

Following the permanent increase in government spending, the level of GDP rises for both *R* and *L* cases. (Figure 10.7). It is important to note that in both cases GDP rises. Consumption falls initially, but not by enough to offset the direct stimulatory effect of the permanent increase in government spending (see Figure 10.8). The fact that consumption falls initially apparently confirms the GP thesis in part (the multiplier w.r.t consumption at this stage of the simulation

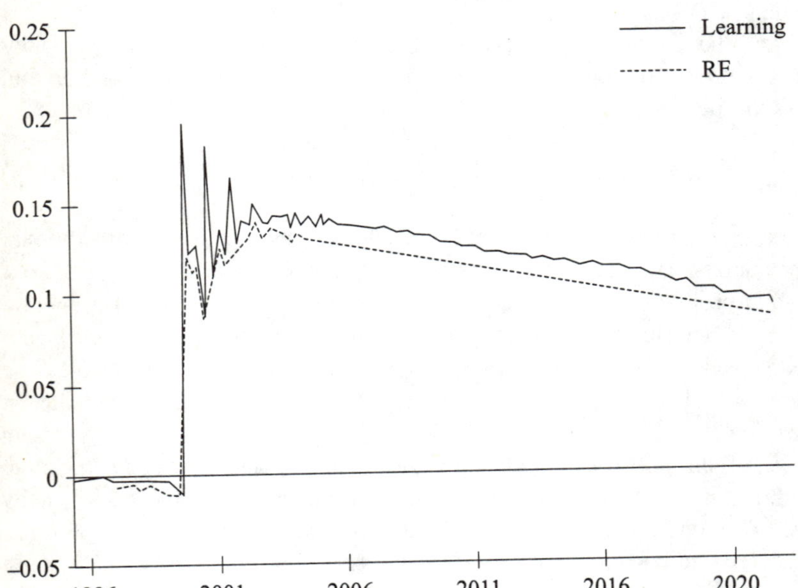

Figure 10.7 GDP

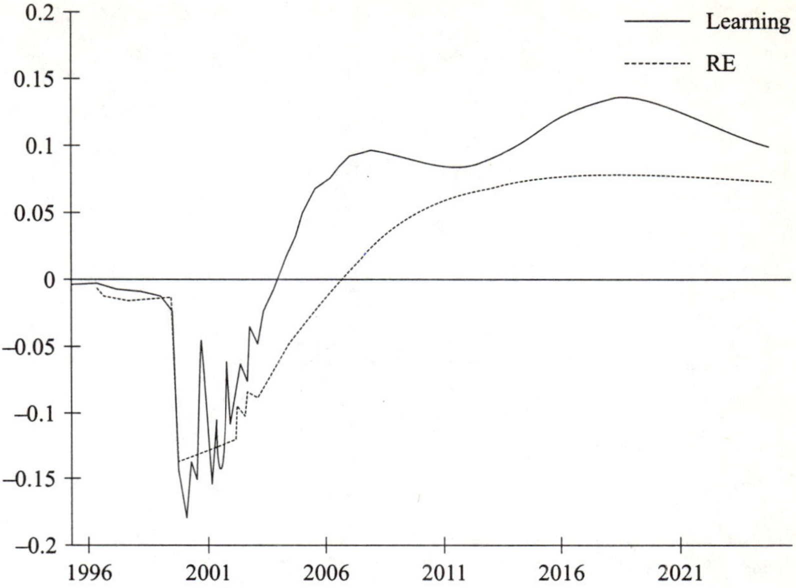

Figure 10.8 Consumption

appears negative). However, consumption falls, not because of the expectation of future tax cuts but because of the response of monetary policy. In each case, the fiscal stimulus raises inflation, which is in turn countered by the inflation control rule which raises interest rates. For the United Kingdom at least, consumption has a significant sensitivity to nominal interest rates. This reflects the high proportion of owner occupation in the housing market and the associated mortgage debt stock, most of which tends to be at short, variable, rates. In response to the increase in government expenditure, forward-looking consumers anticipate the higher mortgage interest payments that will stem from the interest rate rises needed to control inflation. This is effectively equivalent to a fall in post-tax labour income, which reduces consumption.

The success in controlling inflation is clearly different in each case, as Figure 10.9 shows. In the *R* case, inflation is restored to base within a year (in fact inflation is controlled immediately by this but it still takes 12 months to drop out of the annual inflation rate). In the *L* case, it takes some time ultimately to control inflation, and it does so only after some cycling around the target. The point, however, is that the interest rates are raised significantly in each case. That the tactic succeeds is due to the induced effects upon the nominal exchange rate, which appreciates substantially in each case. Consumption falls below base in each case for about four years, not by dint of forward-looking expectations of

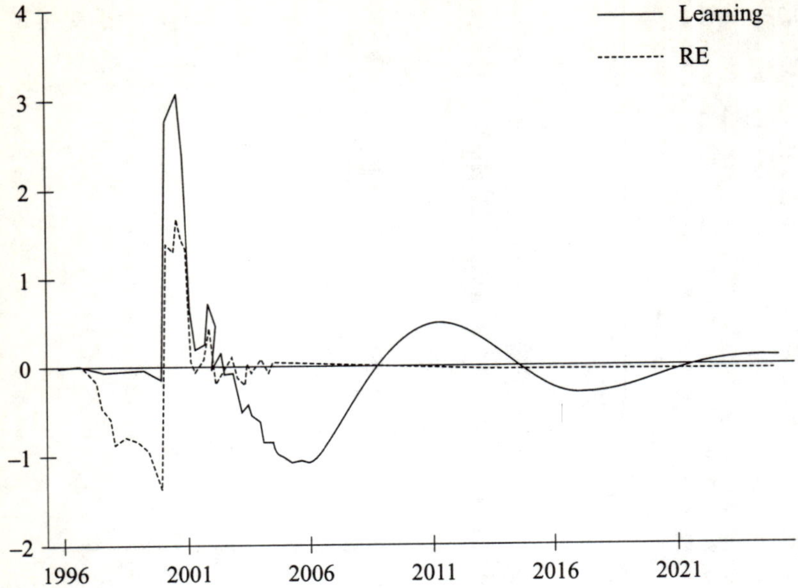

Figure 10.9 Inflation

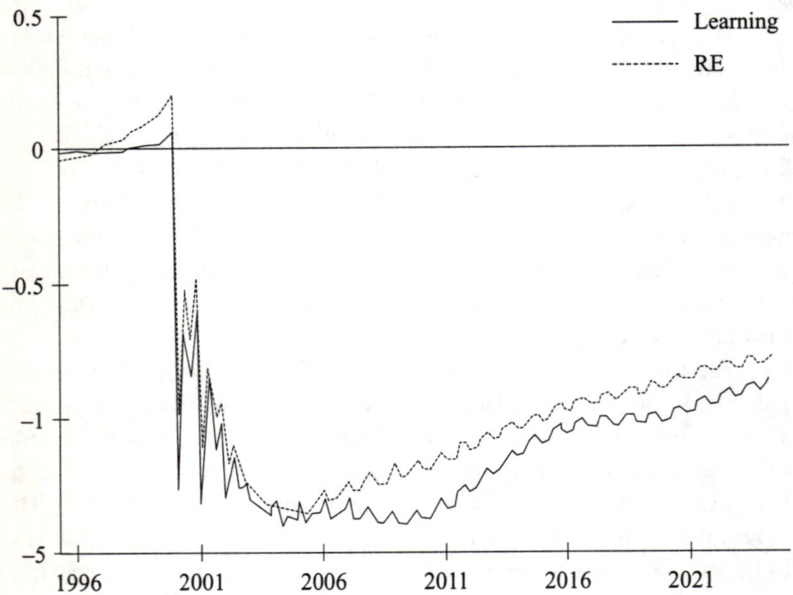

Figure 10.10 Unemployment

tax cuts but owing to the tightening of monetary policy as the authorities fight the inflationary stimulus produced by the increase in public spending.

Further out, consumption increases. Again mechanisms which are different from those typical in the literature are at work here. The transmission mechanism noted earlier produced an appreciation in the nominal exchange rate. This lowers import prices, and this terms of trade effect lowers the NAIRU in the economy (see Nixon and Urga, 1997, for further discussion). Actual unemployment accordingly falls, by an appreciable amount (Figure 10.10). Hence, in these circumstances, monetary policy can be set to accommodate larger increases in employment without increasing inflation over the longer term. This increase in employment raises total incomes and hence consumption. By this indirect route, the Keynesian multiplier becomes positive for consumption also.[2]

CONCLUSIONS

In this chapter we have considered the case that the short-run Keynesian multiplier might be negative, as claimed in earlier work, owing to the effect of expected future tax cuts on present consumption. We find that, in the example provided by the United Kingdom, this case is difficult to sustain. The consumption ratio rose strongly in the middle part of the 1980s, as a result of the joint effects of optimistic expected income growth and financial liberalization. Once these are fully incorporated there appears to be little of a 'consumption puzzle' to explain, unlike the findings reported by GP for some other European countries. Finally, we are able to illustrate, using simulations based on different expectations assumptions, how governments committed to an anti-inflationary policy can have large effects on real variables such as consumption when government expenditure changes. As nominal (and then real) interest rates change, this has substantial effects on consumption, owing to enhanced interest rate elasticities in consumption functions following financial liberalization. In a world of inflation targeting, fiscal tightening will necessarily be offset by a loosening in monetary policy if the economy is not to be run permanently below trend. This reduction in interest rates can have a positive effect on consumption in the short run, especially in a country such as the United Kingdom which has such a high preponderance of mortgage debt. However, this effect is not sufficient to offset the reductions in overall aggregate demand and we find that cuts in government spending are associated with falls in output and increases in unemployment.

NOTES

1. We are grateful to Guglielmo Caporale and Geoffrey Williams for comments. We are also particularly indebted to Stephen Hall for his comments and guidance. Financial support from

ESRC grant No. L16251003, 'Macro Modelling and Policy Analysis in a Changing World', is gratefully acknowledged. The usual disclaimer applies.

2. Although using an entirely different methodology, based on VARs for the Danish economy, Bergman and Hutchison (1996) also argue that a terms of trade effect was probably instrumental in raising Danish consumption in the 1980s, not expected tax cuts.

REFERENCES

Allen, C. and Hall, S. (1997) *Macroeconomic Modelling in a Changing World*, Wiley, Chichester: *National Institute Economic Review*.

Allen, C., Hall, S.G. and Nixon, J. (1994) 'The New LBS model of the UK economy', London Business School, Centre for Economic Forecasting Discussion Paper, No. 18-94.

Allsop, C. and Vines, D. (1996) *Fiscal Policy and EMU*, London: NIER.

Bergman, M. and Hutchison, Y. (1996) 'The "German-View", Fiscal Consolidation and Consumption Boom: Empirical Evidence from Denmark', EPRU DP No. 1196-10, Copenhagen.

Blake, A. and Westerway, P. (1993) 'Why have UK Consumption Functions broken down?', NIESR DP No. 38, London.

Blanchard, O. (1985) 'Debts, Deficits and Finite Horizons', *Journal of Political Economy* **93**(2), 223–47.

Blanchard, O. (1990) 'Comment', *NBER Macroeconomic Annual*, 111–16.

Bryant, R.C. and Zhang, L. (1996) 'Intertemporal Fiscal Policy in Macroeconomic Models: Introduction and Major Alternatives', *Brookings Discussion Papers in Economics*, No. 123.

Caporale, G. and Williams, G. (1997) 'Revisiting Forward Looking Consumption and Financial Liberalisation in the UK', London Business School, Centre for Economic Forecasting, Discussion Paper; No. 22-97

Church, K.B., Mitchell Smith, P.N., and Wallis, K.B. (1995) 'Comparative properties of models of the UK economy', *National Institute Economic Review*, **153** (August).

Corry, B.A. (1959) 'Malthus and Keynes – A Reconsideration', *Economic Journal*, **LXIX**, 717–24.

Darby, J. and Ireland, J. (1994) 'Consumption, Forward Looking Behaviour and Financial Liberalisation', ICMM, DP No. 20, Strathclyde.

Garratt, A. and Hall, S.G. (1996) 'The Stability of Expectations Equilibria in the LBS Model', in C. Allen and S.G. Hall (eds), *Macroeconomic Modelling in a Changing World*, John Wiley.

Giavazzi, F. and Pagano, M. (1990) 'Can Severe Fiscal Contractions be Expansionary? Tales of Two Small European Countries', *NBER Macroeconomic Annual*, 75–116.

Giavazzi, F. and Pagano, M. (1995) 'Non-Keynesian Effects of Fiscal Policy Changes: International Evidence and the Swedish Experience', CEPR DP No. 1284, November.

Hall, S.G. (1997) 'Modelling Economic Policy Responses', London Business School, Centre for Economic Forecasting, Discussion Paper, No. 08-97.

Hall, S.G. and Nixon, J. (1997) 'Controlling inflation: modelling monetary policy in the 1990s', in C. Allen and S.G. Hall *Macroeconomic Modelling in a Changing World*, John Wiley.

Hall, S.G., O'Sullivan, J. and Sentance, A. (1996) 'UK Fiscal Policy over the Medium Term', London Business School, Centre for Economic Forecasting, Discussion Paper, No. 09-96.

Miles, D. (1994) *Housing, Financial Markets and the Wider Germany*, John Wiley.
Muellbauer, J. and Murphy, G. (1993) 'Income Expectations, Wealth and Demography in the Aggregate UK Consumption Function', mimeo, Nuffield College, Oxford.
Nixon, J. and Urga, G. (1997) 'Unemployment and the Capital Stock: Modelling the Supply Side of the UK Economy', London Business School Centre for Economic Forecasting Discussion Paper, No. 18-97.
Phillips, A.W. (1957) 'Stabilization policy and the time form of lagged responses', *The Economic Journal*, **67**, 265–77.
Sutherland, A. (1995), 'Fiscal Crises at Aggregate Demand: Can High Public Debt Reverse the Effects of Fiscal Policy?', mimeo, University of York.

PART IV

Macroeconomic Policy Beyond the OECD

11. Non-linear hyperinflationary exchange rate dynamics: the Polish zloty, 1988–90

David A. Peel and Alan E.H. Speight

INTRODUCTION

As long-standing editor of *Applied Economics* and its companion journals, *Applied Financial Economics* and *Applied Economics Letters*, Maurice Peston has for many years been a leading advocate of the application of quantitative applied economics to contemporary economic issues.[1] This is perhaps best exemplified in the 'aims and scope' of *Applied Economics*, whose primary purpose has been and remains 'to encourage the application of economic analysis to specific problems in both the private and public sector' and 'to foster quantitative studies, the results of which promise to be of use in the practical field and help to bring economic theory nearer the realities of life'.

The period of Maurice's editorship of *Applied Economics*, and recent years in particular, have witnessed substantive changes in the methodology and application of quantitative econometric techniques. Prominent amongst these developments has been the increasing attention paid to the potential for non-linearities in economic time series and the appropriate modelling of such non-linearities. A prominent real-world issue of recent times has been the rapid development of financial markets in the transforming Eastern European economies. Given that such development has frequently occurred from positions of extreme initial disequilibrium and during episodes of hyperinflation, these markets are ideally suited for the application of recently developed (and developing) econometric techniques in order to further understanding of the dynamics of market evolution and non-linear dynamic adjustment in particular.[2] The market for foreign exchange in Poland during the 1988–90 period is a prime example in this respect and the study of this chapter.

Prompted by the Sargent and Wallace (1973) theoretical analysis of hyperinflationary episodes, we test for the presence of non-linear stochastic dynamics in the free market zloty–dollar exchange rate using non-parametric methods and a specific non-linear form, the bilinear model, which has the capacity to approximate arbitrarily a wide class of non-linear models. Subsequently, we attempt to model the form of that non-linearity more explicitly using an exponential (threshold) autoregressive model which permits smooth transition between behavioural regimes and permits multiple equilibria, in keeping with the theoretical properties of the Sargent–Wallace model. We also take the opportunity to introduce a 'second-generation' non-linear model formed by conjunction of the bilinear and exponential autoregressive forms. While without theoretical precedent, this mixed model provides an interesting speculation that is successful in the context addressed here, and may prove useful in other applications. The resulting empirical models exhibit interesting dynamics, in keeping with certain features of the sample data. As a result, these non-linear models are able to account for between one-fifth and one-quarter of the observed variation in the zloty–dollar free market exchange rate over the period, and stand in stark contrast to linear models which indicate the absence of any conditional mean structure.

The remainder of the chapter is organized as follows. The next section describes the market for foreign exchange in Poland over the 1988–90 period, and notes our data source. The following section outlines the Sargent–Wallace model of hyperinflationary dynamics, and its implications for exchange rate dynamics in particular. Sample summary statistics and diagnostics are then reported. Further sections then outline the method and results of non-parametric kernel regression, and the general and estimated forms of the bilinear model of non-linearity in conditional mean. The penultimate section then reports the substantive empirical results of the chapter, initially employing the exponential smooth transition (threshold) autoregressive (ESTAR) model which in estimation reduces to a near exponential autoregressive (EAR) form, and in conjunction with the bilinear form, together with an analysis of implied dynamics, and deterministic and stochastic simulations. The final section summarizes our findings and offers some concluding remarks.

THE MARKET FOR FOREIGN EXCHANGE IN POLAND, 1988–90

The recent economic reforms in Eastern Europe marking the end of central planning, characterized by the extension of free markets and price liberalization, have generally been followed by periods of high inflation and foreign exchange market turbulence. Such events have been observed in Bulgaria, the former Czechoslovakia and Hungary, and most dramatically in Poland during 1989 following legalization of the free foreign exchange market and the introduction of economic reform. Figure 11.1 depicts the rate of change of the weekly free market exchange rate of the Polish zloty to the US dollar during the period October 1988 to January 1990, which includes the period of illegal black market trades prior to 15 March 1989 and legal trades thereafter. This period also spans the change in government regime in September 1989, at which time the Solidarity movement formed Poland's first non-communist government in the postwar period and initiated economic reform. The data are as compiled by Charemza (1996), computed from information published in the weekly *Gazeta Bankowa* (Warsaw), spot rates being the mean of bid and ask prices, those prices being population-weighted averages of data published for the five towns of Częstochowa, Katowice, Kraków, Poznań and Warsaw.[3]

The data in Figure 11.1 clearly exhibit periods of different dynamics. Between December 1988 and April 1989 the foreign exchange market was relatively stable. Following the introduction of legislation legalizing commercial trading in foreign currencies on 15 March 1989, the zloty price of the dollar started to rise substantially, from a low in Warsaw of 2750 zlotys per dollar in the third week of March to 12 400 zloty per dollar in the first week of September. This period also saw steadily rising inflation, at an annual rate of about 800 per cent, and the depreciation of the zloty has therefore been attributed to hyperinflationary expectations in anticipation of price liberalization, coupled with durable goods

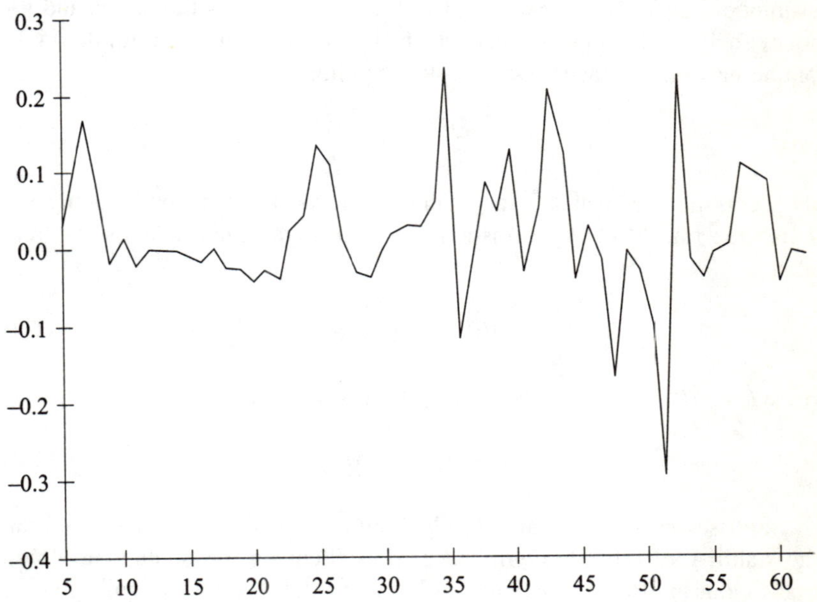

Figure 11.1 Rate of change of the zloty–dollar free market exchange rate (y_t) (Oct. 1988–Jan. 1990)

shortages and negative real interest rates, which raised the expected return on foreign currencies. Thereafter, the exchange rate increased sharply during the second half of June following substantial price increases in alcohol, sugar and tobacco, then fell sharply during the first half of July, subsequently stabilizing in response to a consumer price 'freeze' in July. Following the change of government and the appointment of a non-communist prime minister on 24 August, the exchange rate appreciated by around 50 per cent by early September, before a temporary market collapse saw the average price of the US dollar in Warsaw fall from 12 400 zloty to 8800 zloty in one week during mid-September 1989. The decline continued during October, the dollar falling to below 5000 zloty, before stabilizing at around 9000 zloty in January 1990 following the establishment of currency convertibility. The resulting foreign exchange market turbulence over this period is clearly evident in Figure 11.1.[4]

HYPERINFLATIONARY EXCHANGE RATE DYNAMICS

In their seminal paper on hyperinflation, Sargent and Wallace (1973) proposed a model to explain inflationary dynamics under circumstances where the government print money in order to finance a given real deficit. This behavioural assumption, under fixed real output and in conjunction with the demand for money function, implies that there can be up to two steady-state equilibria. In continuous time we have, in steady-state equilibrium:

$$\bar{G} = \dot{M}/P \tag{11.1}$$

where $\bar{G}$ is the fixed real deficit, P is the price level, M is the money supply and $\dot{M}$ its time rate of change. Assuming a semi-logarithmic demand for real balances:

$$M/P = A\exp(-\alpha\hat{P}) \tag{11.2}$$

where $\hat{P} = \dot{P}/P$. From (11.1) and (11.2), in steady state:

$$\bar{G} = A\hat{P}\exp(-\alpha\hat{P}) \tag{11.3}$$

which possesses a maximum at $\hat{P} = 1/\alpha$. For $\hat{P} \neq 1/\alpha$ there are two equilibria. The stability of the two equilibria is dependent on the manner in which expectations are formed. In continuous time models the higher equilibrium is stable and the lower equilibrium unstable if expectations are formed rationally. The converse is the case if expectations are formed adaptively (see, for example, Evans and Yarrow, 1981; Nobay and Peel, 1982; Bruno and Fischer, 1990). In discrete analysis the stability of the equilibria is less clear-cut. Marcet and Sargent (1989) found that a form of least squares learning leads to the lower equilibrium being stable, while Chappell (1996) demonstrates that complex dynamics, including 'chaotic' paths exhibiting sensitive dependence on initial conditions, can occur for some parameter values when expectations are formed adaptively.

The one clear prediction from this literature is that inflation will in general be described by a non-linear process that can exhibit multiple equilibria. Clearly, changes in the assumptions of the basic model, such as endogeneity of the deficit through, say, dependence on previous inflation, can increase the number of equilibria. Further, given that long-run purchasing power parity holds, exchange rate movements will predominantly reflect changes in domestic inflation under high inflationary conditions so that exchange rates will also follow a non-linear process. A parametric non-linear process that can exhibit multiple equilibria is the exponential autoregressive model of Haggan and Ozaki (1981), which arises as a special case of the exponential smooth transition autoregressive model introduced by Chan and Tong (1986), Luukkonen *et al.*, (1988), Teräsvirta and Anderson (1992) and Teräsvirta (1994), and recently promoted by Granger and Teräsvirta (1993). These models are described and applied below. First, however, we consider some basic properties of the data and non-parametric and parametric diagnostics for the presence of non-linearity in the free market zloty–dollar exchange rate return.

SUMMARY STATISTICS

We consider summary statistics for the rate of change of the zloty–dollar exchange rate, y_t, formally defined as the differenced logarithm of the free market exchange rate, including the mean, median, range, variance, skewness, kurtosis and Ljung–Box and Engle (1982) ARCH test statistics. Several issues arise. First, the mean rate of change over the sample is positive at 0.023, identifying the devaluation of the zloty relative to the dollar discussed above, at an average rate of 2.3 per cent, though this value is heavily influenced by extreme values associated with the events described above, as witnessed by maximum and minimum values of 0.251 and –0.299 and contrasting mean and median (0.003) values. Second, there is little evidence of skewness with a coefficient of –0.096, but strong evidence of excess kurtosis given a kurtosis coefficient of 5.499, implying non-normality. Third, there is no evidence of serial correlation in the data on the basis of fourth- and twelfth-order Ljung–Box statistics of LB(4) = 1.300 and LB(12) = 8.356. While not reported in full (but available on request), this finding is confirmed by Akaike and Schwarz model selection criteria in a consideration of the general class of autoregressive moving average ARMA models. It should also be noted, though again not reported in full, that

(Augmented) Dickey–Fuller and Phillips–Perron unit root test statistics confirm the non-stationarity of the zloty–dollar exchange rate and the stationarity of its logarithmic difference. Thus there is no linear structure in the data, the logarithm of the zloty–dollar exchange rate apparently evolving as a random walk with drift. Finally, while there is no evidence of fourth-order autoregressive conditional heteroscedasticity given a test statistic of A(4) = 6.609, there is evidence of significant first-order ARCH given A(1) = 4.343, indicative of non-linear dependence, to a closer examination of which we now turn.

NON-PARAMETRIC ANALYSIS

Our first non-linear diagnostic tool employs non-parametric kernel regression in order to construct plots of the conditional relationship between the differenced rate of change of the zloty–dollar exchange rate, Δy_t, and the lagged rate of change of the exchange rate, y_{t-1}. The rationale behind this diagnostic is that any tendency for mean-reversion from low (high) values for y_{t-1} will be manifest in positive (negative) values for Δy_t, with random walk behaviour for y_t in between giving rise to zero values for Δy_t. The non-parametric approach requires only that the conditional mean function is drawn from a dense family of continuously differentiable functional forms, and therefore provides a powerful and tractable means of identifying the presence and potential form of simple first-order non-linearities in conditional mean.[5]

More formally, for the amorphous univariate model $y_t = M(y_{t-1}) + e_t$ where M denotes the conditional expectation $M(y_{t-1}) = E(y_t \mid y_{t-1})$ and $E(e_t \mid y_{t-1}) = 0$, non-parametric kernel regression provides an estimated conditional expectation, $m(y_{t-1})$, as a weighted average of observed values of y_t, where the weight of any particular observation depends on the 'distance' between y_t and y_{t-1}, expressed here in terms of the Nadaraya–Watson (NW) estimator:

$$m(y_{t-1}) = \sum_{t=1}^{T} y_t r_t(y_{t-1}) = \left[\sum_{t=1}^{T} y_t k(w_t)\right] \Big/ \left[\sum_{t=1}^{T} k(w_t)\right] \qquad (11.4)$$

for $0 \leq r_t(y_{t-1}) \leq 1$, where $k(w_t)$ denotes the integral of $K(w_t)$, K denoting the kernel weighting function, and $w_t = (y_t - y_{t-1})/h$ with h defining a 'bandwidth' dependent on sample size ($h \rightarrow 0$ as $T \rightarrow \infty$) and relative to which 'distances' are assessed. Here we employ the Epanechnikov kernel:

$$K(w_t) = (3/4(\sqrt{5}))(1 - (w_t^2/2)) \text{ if } w_t^2 < 5.0;\ K(w_t) = 0 \text{ otherwise} \qquad (11.5)$$

and determine appropriate bandwidths by cross-validation. That the kernel estimator described is in general asymptotically unbiased and mean squares-consistent has been established for the case of independent observations (Rosenblatt, 1956, 1969; Prakasa Rao, 1983) and dependent observations (Robinson, 1983). More specifically, the kernel estimator is consistent under the following conditions regarding $K(z)$ and h (all integrals defined over the range $(\infty, -\infty)$):

$$\int K(z(dz)) = 1;\ \int ZK(z(dz)) = 0;\ \int z^2 K(z)dz < \infty;\ \lim_{T\to\infty} h \to 0;\ \lim_{t\to\infty} T\left(\prod_{j=1}^{P} h_j\right) \to \infty \tag{11.6}$$

That is, the kernel function $K(z)$ is a twice continuously differentiable Borel-measurable bounded real-valued function symmetric about the origin, the bandwidth vector h approaches zero as the sample size approaches infinity, and the product of the bandwidth h and the sample size approaches infinity as T approaches infinity. The specific kernel in (11.5) is the optimal kernel from a calculus of variations solution to minimizing the integrated mean square error of the kernel estimator.[6] The optimal bandwidth, H, which minimizes the integrated mean square error of $m(y_{t-1})$ is given by (Ullah, 1988):

$$H = \theta\sigma T^{-(1/5)} \tag{11.7}$$

where σ is the standard deviation of y_{t-1}, and θ, referred to as a 'scaling factor', is an unknown constant which depends on K and the underlying distribution of y_{t-1}: $\theta = \theta(K(.), f(.))$. A recommended approach to determining appropriate (θ, h), and that employed here, is through minimization of the leave-one-out cross-validation function:

$$CV(\theta, H) = \sum_{t=1}^{T}\left[y_t - m(y_{-t}, h(\theta))\right] \tag{11.8}$$

where $m(y_{-t})$ is the estimated conditional mean after excluding the tth observation, and $\theta(h)$ is a vector of bandwidths calculated according to (11.7) for various θ, and that (θ, H) which minimizes (11.8) also asymptotically minimizes the integrated mean square error of $m(y_{t-1})$ (Stone, 1974).

Using this procedure, the optimal scaling factor for the rate of change of the zloty–dollar free market exchange rate is determined as 1.62, and a plot of the resulting first-order difference–lag relationship is portrayed in Figure 11.2.

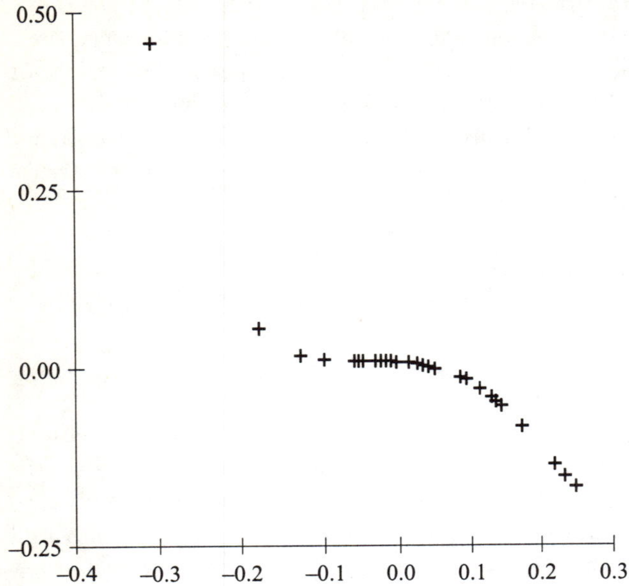

Figure 11.2 Non-parametric lag regression of the change in y_t against y_{t-1}

The resulting relationship is evidently non-linear in the dependence of Δy_t on y_{t-1}, of a smooth and symmetric functional nature, and clearly illustrates the phenomenon of mean-reversion in y_t at high and low values.

BILINEARITY

Our second diagnostic tool entails application of the bilinear (BL) model of non-linearity in conditional mean which provides a natural non-linear extension of the autoregressive moving average (ARMA) model which it nests as a special case, and has more generally been shown to be capable of providing an arbitrarily close second-order approximation to a wide class of underlying non-linear processes. Moreover, the BL form is capable of capturing complex time series trajectories under fairly simple parameterizations, and the significance of bilinear regression terms may be used as an indicator of the presence of non-linearities in conditional mean of specifically bilinear or generic form.

As is well known, in the context of any linear structural model, any stationary endogenous variable, say y_t, can be given a univariate time series representation. Specifically, the autoregressive moving average, ARMA(p,q) representation

$\alpha(L)y_t = \beta(L)\varepsilon_t$ where $\alpha(L)$ and $\beta(L)$ are polynomials of orders p and q in the lag operator L (that is, $L^d y_t = y_{t-d}$) respectively, more fully expressed as:

$$y_t = \alpha_0 + \sum_{i=1}^{P} \alpha_i y_{t-i} + \sum_{i=1}^{q} \beta_i \varepsilon_{t-i} + \varepsilon_t \qquad (11.9)$$

where $\{\varepsilon_t\}$ is a sequence of independently and identically distributed (*iid*) Gaussian random variables with zero mean and finite variance, $\varepsilon_t \sim IN(0,\sigma_\varepsilon^2)$, $\alpha_0, \alpha_i, \beta_i$ are real constants, and (11.9) is stationary provided that all roots of the AR(p) component are less than one in modulus.

However, models of the ARMA class are inappropriate in circumstances where the underlying structural process generating y_t is non-linear in either parameters or variables, and the requirement that $\{\varepsilon_t\}$ be *iid* therefore fails to hold (Priestley, 1981; Tong, 1990). In particular, such stationary Gaussian ARMA models are not well suited for data exhibiting time irreversibility or strong asymmetry (in view of their symmetric joint distributions) or data exhibiting sudden and irregular bursts of large amplitude (in view of their normality). These limitations are overcome in the bilinear extension of the Gaussian ARMA model, which has the general form:

$$y_t = \alpha_0 + \sum_{i=1}^{P} \alpha_i y_{t-i} + \sum_{i=1}^{q} \beta_i \varepsilon_{t-i} + \sum_{i=1}^{m} \sum_{j=1}^{n} \gamma_{ij} y_{t-i} \varepsilon_{t-j} + \varepsilon_t \qquad (11.10)$$

summarized as $BL(p,q,m,n)$, where $m \leq p$, $n \leq q$, the γ_{ij} are real constants and ε_t is *iid*. As noted above, the bilinear form has been shown to have the ability to approximate arbitrarily any non-linear model possessing a Volterra series expansion involving a 'reasonable' parameterization (Brockett, 1976; Sussmann, 1977),[7] and to be capable of capturing complex time series trajectories under fairly simple stationary parameterizations (Subba Rao and Gabr, 1984).

Formal conditions for the stationarity and invertibility of BL models have been established, but remain difficult to apply empirically in other than 'superdiagonal' ($m > n$) variants of (11.10) for $\beta_i = 0$. Moreover, the substitution of stationarity parameter restrictions into invertibility conditions, particularly where higher moment stationarity is considered, can lead to overall restrictions that are highly stringent. Indeed, where parameterizations of bilinear models border on the non-stationary, the trajectories of those models can exhibit pronounced amplitude volatility and complex behaviour similar to that more usually associated with chaotic systems, including sensitive dependence to perturbations in initial conditions and amplitude 'spiking' associated with market 'bubbles' and 'crashes'.

The parametric implications of BL stability conditions are therefore unclear in other than first-order systems, such as that which fortunately applies here. For example, for superdiagonal ($m > n$) and diagonal ($m = n$) variants of the single bilinear term BL(0,0,1,1) model $y_t = d_{mn}y_{t-m}\varepsilon_{t-n} + \varepsilon_t$ stability is ensured by $\lambda = d^2h^2 < 1$ where $E(\varepsilon_t^2) = h^2 < \infty$, and in the slightly more general case $y_t = \alpha_1 y_{t-1} + d_{11}y_{t-1}\varepsilon_{t-1} + \varepsilon_t$ by the condition that $\lambda = (\alpha_{11}^2 + d_{11}^2 h^2) < 1$.[8]

Applying the bilinear model to the log-differenced zloty–dollar free exchange rate under maximum likelihood yields the following estimates (t-ratios in parentheses):

$$\hat{y}_t = 0.011 + 1.309\ y_{t-1}e_{t-1}$$
$$(0.924)\ (1.702$$
$$\bar{R}^2 = 0.04;\ LB(4) = 2.08;\ \text{LB}(12) = 7.46;$$
$$\text{A}(1) = 0.81;\ \text{A}(4) = 1.94 \qquad (11.11)$$

where e_{t-1} denotes the lagged residual in estimation. Note that the diagonal first-order bilinear term is significantly different from zero at the 10 per cent level and the model is stationary by virtue of $\lambda = 0.01$. Also note that introduction of the bilinear term leads to a reduction in the intercept term which is now insignificantly different from zero. Residual diagnostics reported include the

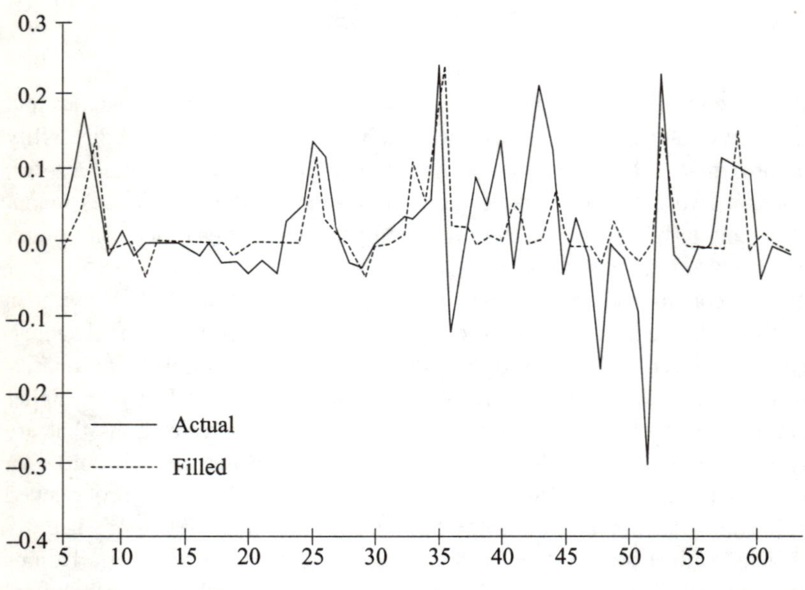

Figure 11.3 Actual y_t and fitted bilinear model values

adjusted coefficient of determination, fourth- and twelfth-order Ljung–Box test statistics, and first- and fourth-order ARCH test statistics, and confirm the adequacy of a bilinear specification in the sense of residual serial independence and autoregressive homoscedasticity. Plots of the fitted bilinear model and the actual data are provided in Figure 11.3, from which it is of note that the fitted model picks up the penultimate positive (depreciatory) 'spike' in the series associated with the temporary collapse of the zloty free foreign exchange market in September 1989, discussed above.

While the bilinear form serves to confirm the presence of non-linear dependence in the data owing to its approximation capabilities, it is not particularly well-founded theoretically in the current hyperinflationary context. However, an alternative non-linear specification premised on the notion of a process which switches between behavioural regimes and associated equilibria is naturally suggested by the theoretical model outlined earlier, and it is to the specification and properties of that model that we now turn.

EXPONENTIAL AUTOREGRESSION

Under the maintained assumption of purchasing power parity, the discrete-time analogue of the theoretical hyperinflation model of Sargent and Wallace (1973) outlined earlier implies that exchange rate changes will reflect movements in inflation, so that under a hyperinflationary money-financed government budget deficit the rate of change of the exchange rate will be non-linear, exhibiting up to two stationary equilibria. Usefully, the exponential smooth transition autoregressive (ESTAR) model has the ability to capture such dynamics, being non-linear, mean reverting and characterized by potentially multiple equilibria.

The class of STAR models introduced by Chan and Tong (1986) and developed by Luukkonen *et al.* (1988), Teräsvirta and Anderson (1992) and Teräsvirta (1994) belong to a more general class of 'regime-switching' regression models whereby the dependent variable exhibits different behaviour depending on the relationship of its own past values to certain 'threshold' values. More formally, the STAR model has the general form:

$$y_t = \alpha_0 + \sum_{i=1}^{p} \alpha_i y_{t-i} + \left[\pi_0 + \sum_{i=1}^{p} \pi_i y_{t-i} \right] F\left(y_{t-d}\right) + \varepsilon_t \qquad (11.12)$$

where π_0 and π_i are real constants, and F is a transition function defined over y with 'delay' d which allows the conditional expectation of the dependent variable to change between regimes. Various formulations for F have been proposed, including the cumulative distribution of the standard normal distribution, the 'heaviside' function, $F(y_{t-d}) = 0, y_{t-d} < c, F(y_{t-d}) = 1, y_{t-d} > c$, the logistic function $F(y_{t-d}) = \{1 + \exp[-\gamma(y_{t-d} - c)]\}^{-1}$, and the exponential transition function considered here:

$$F(y_{t-d}) = 1 - \exp[-\gamma(y_{t-d} - c)^2] \tag{11.13}$$

where c denotes a threshold value of y, about which the parameters of the state-dependent autoregressive model (11.12) change symmetrically. The resulting solution of the STAR form may involve a stable stationary point, a 'limit cycle' of repeated values independent of initial conditions, 'chaotic' sensitive dependence on initial conditions, or divergence (Teräsvirta and Anderson, 1992; Granger and Terasvirta, 1993; Teräsvirta, 1994).

Whilst the heaviside transition function may be more in keeping with microeconomic models of switching behaviour by individual agents, smooth transition models employing logistic or exponential transfer functions would seem to offer a more appropriate characterization of a macroeconomy consisting of many agents, each of whom switches behaviour abruptly but at different times. The exponential form employed also has the convenient property of nesting the linear AR case as either $\gamma \to \infty$ or $\gamma \to 0$. More generally, the 'scale' parameter γ indicates the speed of transition from one regime to another, where those regimes exhibit similar dynamics but the 'middle ground' may exhibit quite different dynamics. In the practical implementation of STAR models, estimation of the transition function adjustment parameter γ can prove problematic, for two reasons: first, simulation evidence suggests the potential for overestimation bias in small samples (Chan and Tong, 1986; Luukkonen, 1990); second, while the remaining model parameters achieve rapid convergence, estimates of γ do so only slowly, particularly where the true value is relatively large, such that there are a large number of γ-values and c-values yielding virtually identical F-values (Bates and Watts, 1988; Seber and Wild, 1989). It is therefore recommended that the γ parameter be rescaled in estimation (Granger and Teräsvirta, 1993). That is, by rescaling the argument of F by the variance of the dependent variable, yielding:

$$F(y_{t-d}) = 1 - \exp[(-\gamma/s_y^2)(y_{t-d} - c)^2] \tag{11.14}$$

where s_y^2 denotes the sample variance of y, following which an initial value of unity for γ is recommended.

Applying the ESTAR model to the rate of change of the free market zloty–dollar exchange rate using non-linear least squares and transition function adjustment parameter rescaling, after simplification to an appropriate parsimonious form (Teräsvirta, 1994), yields the following estimates (t-ratios in parentheses) and residual diagnostics:

$$\hat{y}_t = (-2.9547\, y_{t-1}) \{-\exp [(-23.6795 / (0.0889)^2)\, (y_{t-2} - 0.0238)^2]\}$$
$$(2.6371) \qquad (8.1260) \qquad (3.3240)$$
$$\bar{R}^2 = 0.191;\ LB(4) = 3.15;\ LB(12) = 15.71;\ A(1) = 5.58;\ A(4) = 7.61 \quad (11.15)$$

The transition function (11.13) implied by these estimates is portrayed in Figure 11.4. Note that the estimated model implies rapid and symmetric adjustment about a threshold value of approximately 2.4 per cent in the rate of change of the exchange rate with a delay of two periods. However, also note that these estimates confirm the absence of any linear structure in mean and therefore the exclusion of unity from the transition function. In the absence of such structure the estimated model implies smooth transition, not between linear autoregressive regimes, but between multiple equilibria. This is perhaps more clearly seen by noting that the estimated model in (11.15) may be alternatively expressed and interpreted in terms of the EAR form introduced by Ozaki (1978) and Haggan and Ozaki (1981):[9]

$$\begin{aligned} y_t &= \phi_1 y_{t-1} + \varepsilon_t \\ \phi_1 &= \pi_1 \exp[-\gamma\, (y_{t-2} - c)^2] \end{aligned} \qquad (11.16)$$

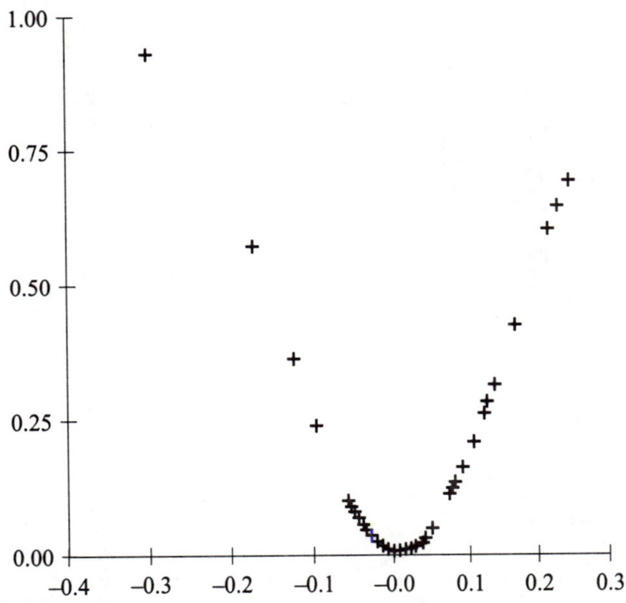

Figure 11.4 Plot of estimated E(ST)AR transition function: $F(y_{t-2})$ against y_{t-2}

This correspondence is of particular interest in view of the ability of EAR models to exhibit oscillatory behaviour where the amplitude of changes may take different values depending on whether past y_t is locally 'small' or 'large'. Thus, EAR models can give rise to 'amplitude-dependent frequency', 'jump phenomena' and 'limit cycles' involving multiple equilibria (Ozaki, 1978; Haggan and Ozaki, 1981; Priestley, 1988). Some illustrative simulations of STAR models under particular parameterizations which imply EAR forms are provided in Figures 11.5 and 11.6, and clearly illustrate the potential for such models to capture oscillatory dynamics and extreme realizations, respectively.

Expressed in terms of the EAR model (11.16), the STAR model estimated here implies that the autoregressive parameter ϕ_1 changes smoothly between values, depending in particular on the proximity of y_{t-2} to c. Thus, for $y_{t-2} = c$, we have $\phi_1 = \pi_1$, for large values $y_{t-2} \gg c$ we have $\phi_1 \simeq 0$, while for small $y_{t-2} \ll c$ we have $\phi_1 > \pi_1 > 0$. The amplitude of fluctuation is therefore a non-linear function, such that, as y_{t-2} passes through certain values, the switching nature of the relationship between y_t and y_{t-1} implies that y_t moves smoothly from one steady state to another.

Such dynamics in the estimated model are represented graphically in Figure 11.7 which depicts all possible equilibrium values of the estimated non-linear model. That is, all solutions of $y = (-2.9547x)\{-\exp\ [(-23.6795/(0.0889)^2)$

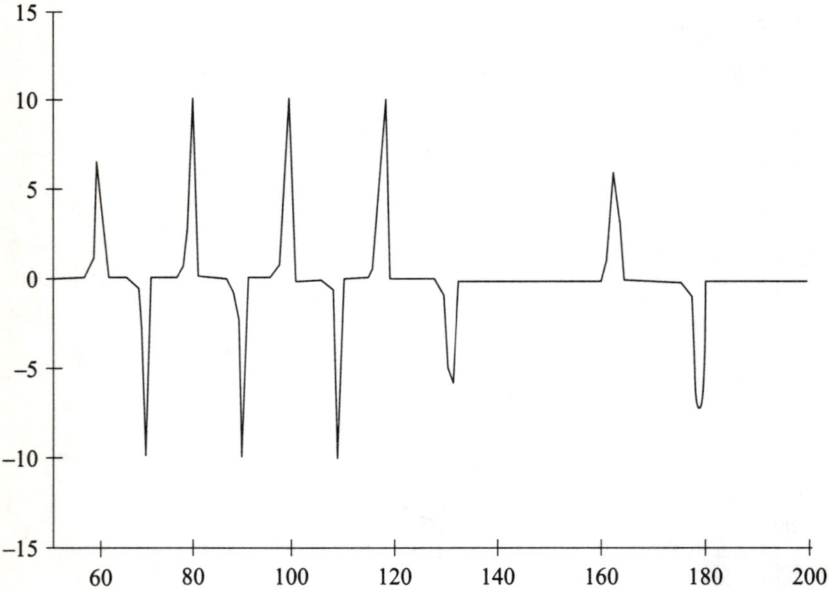

Figure 11.5 Illustrative E(ST)AR model simulation (I):
$y_t = exp(-2y^2_{t-1})(6.1y_{t-1}-1.2y_{t-2})$

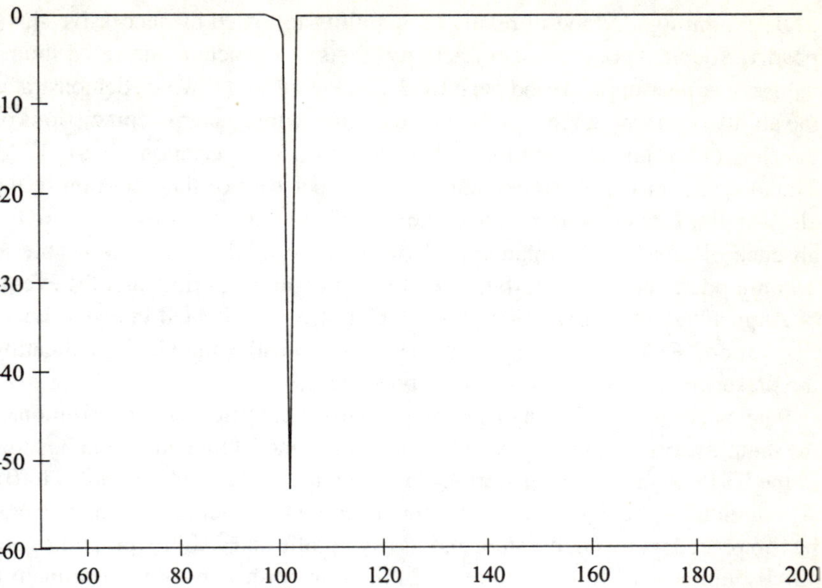

Figure 11.6 Illustrative E(ST)AR model simulation (II):
$y_t = exp(-2y^2_{t-3})(6.1y_{t-1}-1.2y_{t-2})$

$(x - 0.0238)^2]\}$ where x spans 1000 points of the (0,1) interval, being constructed as $x = z/999$, $z = 0,1,2, ...,999$. Also depicted is the equilibrium condition $y = x$. The intersections of these schedules then determines the steady states of the estimated model, confirmed numerically but not reported in full, as the three values 0.0000, 0.0043, and 0.0443. Closer inspection of the dynamics implied by Figure 11.7 reveal that the steady state at $y = 0.0043$ is unstable from both above and below, the steady state at $y = 0.0443$ is unstable from below with possible oscillation about that value ultimately returning the system to a value near the origin, and the steady state at the origin is stable from above for $x < 0.0043$. These dynamics are partially illustrated in Figure 11.8. Thus, for values of x slightly in excess of the intermediate steady state, the model generates a burst of activity, as illustrated for a value of $x = 0.01$ in Figure 11.9, where the modelled rate of change of the zloty–dollar exchange rate rises to nearly 20 per cent over three periods (weeks) before reverting to zero by the fifth period. The model is therefore deterministically globally stable, but when subject to stochastic shocks may exhibit successive bursts of activity as the intermediate steady state is disturbed. Simulation of the model subject to random shocks with the same variance as obtains in the estimated model over 120 periods (after discarding the first 40 simulated data points) is portrayed in Figure 11.10, and closely matches the properties of the actual zloty–dollar exchange rate in Figure

11.1, exhibiting a period of relative tranquillity followed by successive sharp positive (depreciatory) bursts of activity. Plots of the actual and fitted model values over the sample period are provided in Figure 11.11, which demonstrates the ability of the model to successfully capture the three sharp depreciations of the zloty up to and including June 1989 and the final depreciation in early 1990. Thus the model is able to explain almost 20 per cent of the variation in the zloty–dollar free market exchange rate over the period, in stark contrast to the absence of any linear explanation. However, the model is less well able to accommodate the market turbulence of the intervening period, and the events of August and September 1989 in particular. This is reflected in a significant first-order ARCH test amongst the residual diagnostics in (11.15), indicating the presence of residual non-linear dependence.

In an attempt to provide a more comprehensive empirical characterization of the sample period, we implement a final non-linear model formed by combination of the ESTAR and BL specifications in equations (11.12), (11.13) and (11.10). Although this 'second-generation' model (in the terminology of Tong, 1990) has no precedent in the literature and its asymptotic and stability properties are strictly unknown, we conjecture that this joint form may prove useful in a variety of applications owing to the approximation capabilities of the bilinear component, and particularly where smooth transition between symmetric

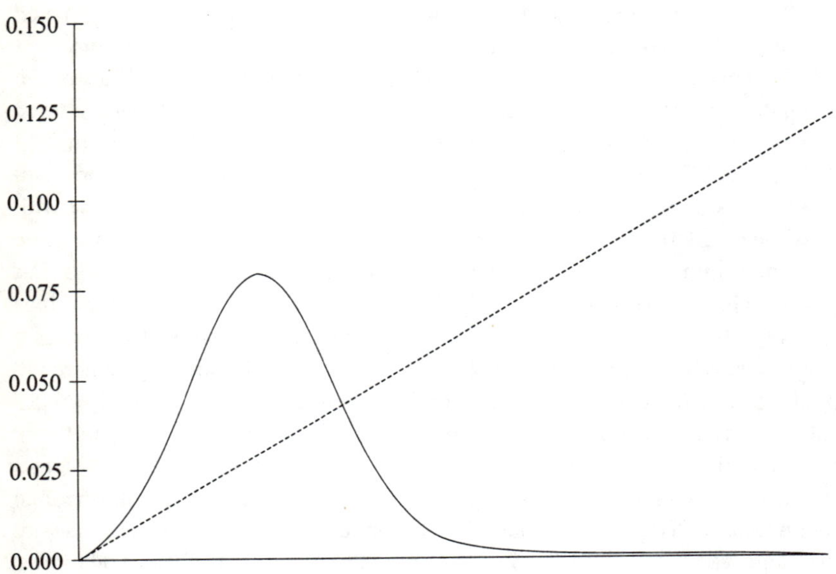

Figure 11.7 Illustration of estimated E(ST)AR model steady states

dynamics of adjustment are accompanied by intermittent sharp bursts in activity. Estimating this model over the sample period by recursive non-linear least squares yields the following estimates, *t*-ratios and residual diagnostics:

$$\text{(Zzz)}\ \hat{y}_t = \underset{(3.3470}{(-3.0270y_{t-1})}\{-\exp[\underset{(2.5960)}{(-29.4711}\,/\,(0.0889)^2)\,y_{t-2}$$

$$\underset{(8.3605)}{-\,0.0236)^2]\}} + \underset{(2.4200)}{1.6640y_{t-1}e_{t-1}}$$

$$\bar{R}^2 = 0.257;\ LB(4) = 3.18;\ LB(12) = 15.90;\ A(1) = 0.01;\ A(4) = 0.53 \quad (11.17)$$

These estimates confirm the significance of the first-order bilinear component, the coefficient and the *t*-ratio being increased relative to the values obtained under bilinear estimation alone, with E(ST)AR coefficients relatively unchanged and still highly significant. Residual diagnostics suggest that there is no remaining linear or non-linear dependence in the data, the joint model accounting for some 25 per cent of the variation in the zloty–dollar free market exchange rate over the period. As revealed in Figure 11.12, the dynamic properties of the estimated model are very similar to those of the E(ST)AR model alone, but now with steady

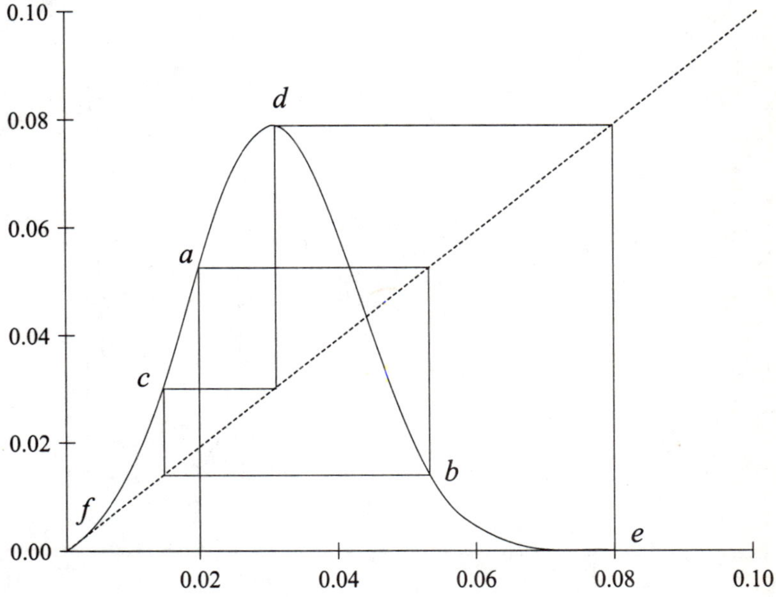

Figure 11.8 Illustrative dynamics of estimated E(ST)AR model

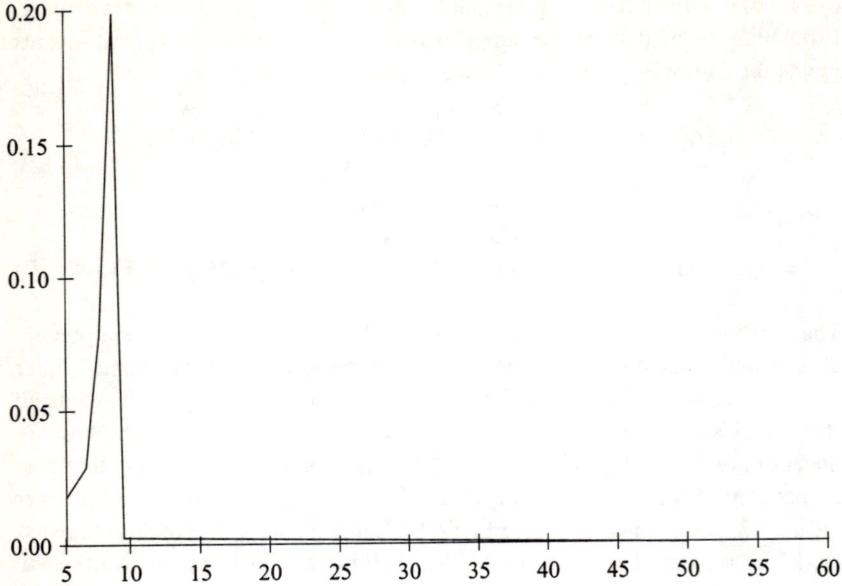

Figure 11.9 Deterministic simulation of estimated E(ST)AR model

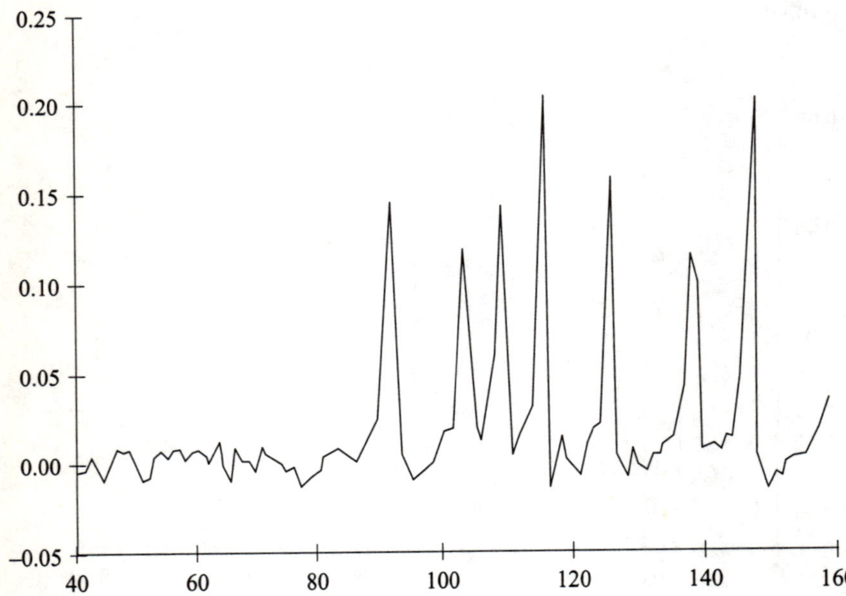

Figure 11.10 Stochastic simulation of estimated E(ST)AR model

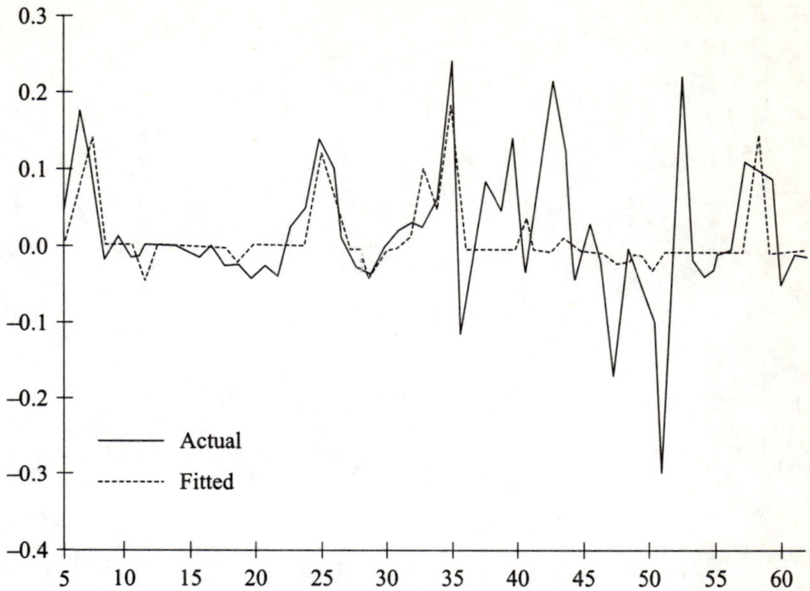

Figure 11.11 Actual y_t and fitted E(ST)AR model values

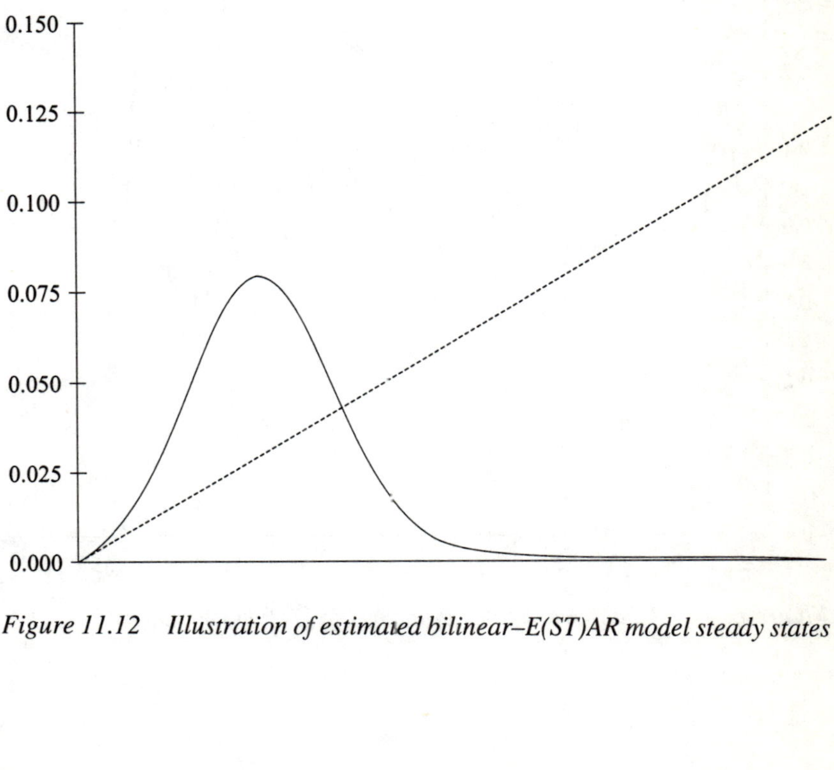

Figure 11.12 Illustration of estimated bilinear–E(ST)AR model steady states

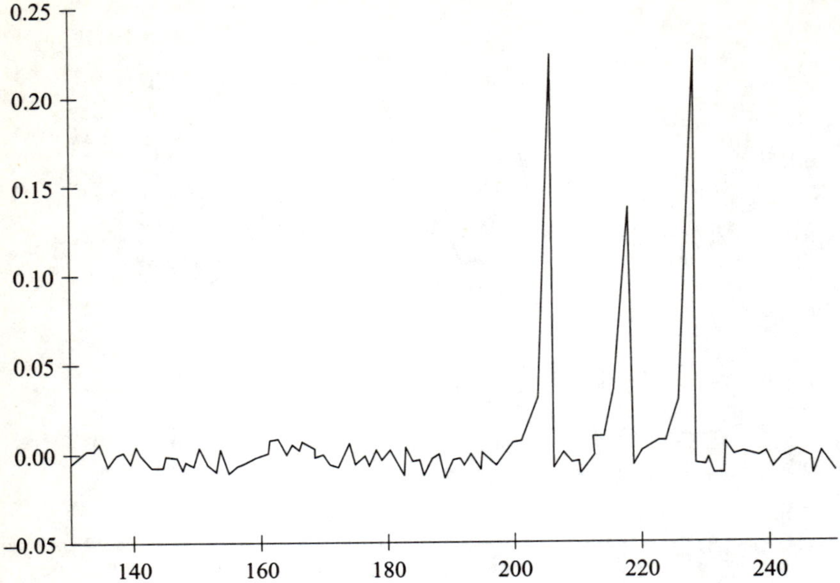

Figure 11.13 Stochastic simulation of estimated bilinear–E(ST)AR model

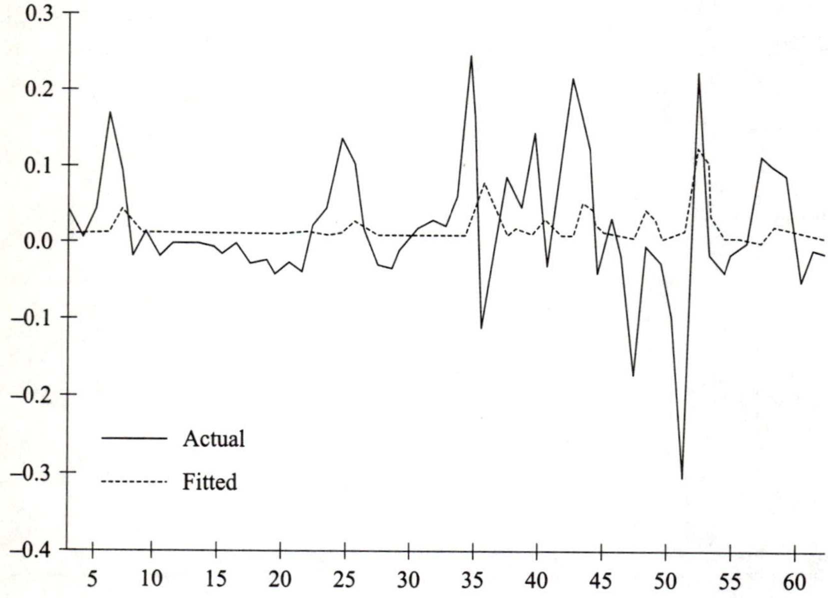

Figure 11.14 Actual y_t and fitted bilinear–E(ST)AR model values

state values of 0.0000, 0.0061 and 0.0440. Simulation of the joint model under shocks with variance equivalent to that holding in the estimated model gives rise to the behaviour depicted in Figure 11.13, which demonstrates the capacity of the model to capture pronounced spikes in activity. Indeed, as noted earlier and as revealed in Figure 11.14, this property allows the joint specification to model successfully the sharp increase in the dollar price of the zloty associated with market recovery following the collapse of September 1989. This again illustrates a particular property of the bilinear model noted elsewhere (Peel and Speight, 1998): that is, the capacity of the bilinear form to describe the response of economic and financial systems to exceptionally large shocks.

CONCLUSION

This chapter provides an empirical examination of exchange rate dynamics under hyperinflation for the case of the Polish zloty over the period from late 1988 to early 1990, a period not only of hyperinflation but also of substantial economic and political reform. On the basis of the Sargent–Wallace model of hyperinflationary dynamics, we were led to examine the potential for non-linearities and multiple equilibria in the rate of change of the free market zloty–dollar exchange rate over this period. Preliminary diagnostics indicated the absence of any linear conditional mean structure over the sample period, but the presence of identifiable and significant first-order conditional mean non-linearities on the basis of non-parametric and bilinear estimation results respectively. We therefore proceeded to estimation of an exponential autoregressive form with the capacity to exhibit the properties implied by the theoretical hyperinflationary model. Resulting estimates further confirmed the presence of significant non-linearity and indicated the presence of three equilibria and interesting dynamics. That is, while the model is globally stable at zero and small shocks to the system lead to rapid monotonic re-establishment of that equilibrium, slightly larger shocks which raise the rate of change of the exchange rate above the near-zero intermediate steady state result in a burst of large and potentially oscillatory values before returning to the globally stable equilibrium. The model is therefore able to generate several of the features of the sample data in simulation, and in estimation accounts for around one-fifth of the variation in the data over the sample period, and prior to July 1989 in particular. However, remaining non-linear dependence in the residuals of the model led us to consider a 'second-generation' hybrid model, not previously considered in the literature, formed by conjunction of exponential autoregressive and bilinear forms. This conjectured model may be motivated by the fact that the former component has the capacity to accommodate cyclical dynamics and is mean-reverting for large deviations from equilibrium, while the latter has the ability to capture abrupt changes and extreme values. In estimation here, this joint model raises the explained variation in the data to around one-quarter, largely as the result of successfully modelling the recovery of the exchange market following its collapse in September 1989. However, by way of closing caveat, neither model is able to explain fully the exchange market turbulence during August and September 1989, which might therefore be attributed to the political events of the period rather than a hyperinflationary policy regime. Nevertheless, the methods and models described and applied here may prove useful in the analysis of other hyperinflationary episodes, and in the analysis of non-linear dynamics more generally.

NOTES

1. Also see, for example, Peston (1974).
2. For previous investigations of the Polish zloty exchange rate data considered here, see Charemza (1990, 1996) and Funke *et al.* (1994). The former investigates the possible existence of rational expectations speculative bubbles in the free market exchange rate, while the latter authors examine the potential presence of non-linear dynamics using the BDS test of Brock *et al.* (1987), GARCH-M modelling (Bollerslev, 1986; Engle *et al.* 1987) and the Hamilton (1989) model of discrete Markov regime switching.
3. We are grateful to Wojciech W. Charemza of Leicester University for kindly making the data available to us. For further details and discussion of the data, see Charemza (1990, 1996).
4. For further discussion of the period and ensuing developments, see Lipton and Sachs (1990), Crane (1991) and Blanchard (1994).
5. For a general introduction to non-parametric methods, see Silverman (1986) and Härdle (1990). For more analytical surveys with reviews of previous and potential applications in economics, see Ullah (1988) and Delgado and Robinson (1992).
6. See Ullah (1988) and Delgado and Robinson (1992) for relaxations of these assumptions and requirements for weak consistency, and on the optimality of (11.5).
7. More specifically, any non-linear model that may be 'reasonably expressed' in terms of the Volterra series expansion of the vector of ARMA regressors.
8. Such conditions become more complex in the presence of higher-order ARMA components. For further details, see Bhaskara Rao *et al.* (1993).
9. It should be noted that the strict EAR form imposes $c = 0$ but permits a non-zero mean for ϕ_1. The re-expression in (11.16) can therefore be seen as a generalization of a second-order EAR form by permission of an intercept for ϕ_1 that is time-varying owing to dependence on y_{t-2}: that is, $\phi_1 = \phi + \pi_1 \exp[-\gamma(y_{t-2})^2]$ where $\phi = \pi_1 \exp[-\gamma(c^2 - 2cy_{t-2})]$.

REFERENCES

Bates, D.M. and Watts, D.G. (1988) *Nonlinear Regression Analysis and its Applications*, New York: Wiley.

Blanchard, O.J. (1994) 'Transition in Poland', *Economic Journal*, **104**, 1169–77.

Bollerslev, T. (1986), 'Generalized autoregressive conditional heteroscedasticity', *Journal of Econometrics*, **31**, 307–27.

Brock, W. Dechert, W.D. and Scheinkman, J. (1987), 'A test for independence based on the correlation dimension', University of Wisconsin, Economics Working Paper SSRI-8702.

Brockett, R.W. (1976), 'Volterra series and geometric control theory', *Automatica*, **12**, 167–72.

Bruno, M. and Fischer, S. (1990) 'Seignorage, operating rules and the high inflation trap'. *Quarterly Journal of Economics*, **105**, 353–74.

Chan, K.S. and Tong, H. (1986), 'On estimating thresholds in autoregressive models'. *Journal of Time Series Analysis*, **7**, 179–94.

Chappell, D. (1977) 'Chaotic behaviour in a simple model of inflation', *Manchester School of Economic and Social Studies*, **65**, 235–43.

Charemza, W.W. (1990), 'The free market for foreign exchange in Poland: cointegration, speculative bubbles and error-corrections', University of Leicester, Department of Economics, Discussion Paper No. 133.

Charemza, W.W. (1996) 'Detecting stochastic bubbles on an East European foreign exchange market: an estimation/simulation approach', *Structural Change and Economic Dynamics*, **7**, 35–53.

Crane, K. (1991) 'Institutional legacies and the economic, social and political environment for transition in Hungary and Poland', *American Economic Review*, **81**, 318–22.

Delgado, M.A. and Robinson, P.M. (1992) 'Nonparametric and semiparametric methods for economic research', *Journal of Economic Surveys*, **6**, 201–49.

Engle, R.F. Lilien, D.M. and Robins, R.P. (1987) 'Estimating time varying risk premia in the term structure: the ARCH-M model', *Econometrica*, **55**, 391–407.

Evans, J.L. and Yarrow, G.K. (1981) 'Some implications of alternative expectations hypotheses in the monetary analysis of hyperinflation', *Oxford Economic Papers*, **33**, 61–80.

Funke, M. Hall, S. and Sola, M. (1994) 'Empirical properties of the black market zloty/dollar exchange rate 1988–1990', London Business School, Centre for Economic Forecasting, Discussion Paper 8-94.

Granger, C.W.J. and Teräsvirta, T. (1993) *Modelling Nonlinear Economic Relationships*, Oxford: Oxford University Press.

Haggan, V. and Ozaki, T. (1981) 'Modelling nonlinear random vibrations using an amplitude-dependent autoregressive time series model', *Biometrika*, **68**, 189–96.

Hamilton, J.D. (1989), 'A new approach to the economic analysis of nonstationary time series and the business cycle', *Econometrica*, **57**, 357–84.

Härdle, W. (1990), *Applied Non-parametric Regression*, Econometric Society Monograms, Cambridge: Cambridge University Press.

Lipton, D. and Sachs, J. (1990) 'Creating a market economy in eastern Europe: the case of Poland', *Brookings Papers on Economic Activity*, 75–147.

Luukkonen, R. (1990) 'Estimating smooth transition autoregressive models by conditional least squares', in R. Luukkonen (ed.), *On Linearity Testing and Model Estimation in Nonlinear Time Series Analysis*, Helsinki: Finnish Statistical Society.

Luukkonen, R., Saikkonen, P. and Teräsvirta, T. (1988) 'Testing linearity against smooth transition autoregressive models', *Biometrika*, **75**, 491–9.

Marcet, A. and Sargent, T.J. (1989) 'Least-squares learning and the dynamics of hyperinflation', in W.A. Barnett, J. Geweke and K. Shell (eds), *Economic Complexity*, Cambridge: Cambridge University Press.

Nobay, A.R. and, Peel, D.A. (1982) 'The government behavioural constraint in rational expectations models', *Economics Letters*, **9**, 221–7.

Ozaki, T. (1978), 'Nonlinear models for nonlinear random vibrations', University of Manchester Institute of Science and Technology, Department of Mathematics, Technical Report No. 92.

Peel, D.A. and Speight, A.E.H. (1997) 'Modelling business cycle nonlinearity in conditional mean and conditional variance: some international and sectoral evidence', *Economica*.

Peston, M.H. (1974) 'Economics and Quantitative Economics: A Defence', *Omega*, **2**, 147–56.

Prakasa Rao, B.L.S. (1983) *Nonparametric Functional Estimation*, New York: Academic Press.

Priestley, M. (1981) *Spectral Analysis and Time Series*, New York: Academic Press.

Priestley, M.B. (1988) *Nonlinear and Non-stationary Time Series* Analysis, London: Academic Press.

Robinson, P.M. (1983) 'Nonparametric estimators for time series', *Journal of Time Series Analysis*, **4**, 185–207.

Rosenblatt, M. (1956) 'Remarks on some nonparametric estimates of a density function', *Annals of Mathematical Statistics*, **27**, 832–7.

Rosenblatt, M. (1969) 'Conditional probability density and regression estimators', in P.R. Krishnaiah (ed.), *Multivariate Analysis II*, New York: Academic Press.

Sargent, T.J. and Wallace, N. (1973) 'Rational expectations and the dynamics of hyperinflation', *International Economic Review*, **62**, 328–50.

Seber, G.A.F. and Wild, C.J. (1989) *Nonlinear Regression*, New York: Wiley.

Silverman, B.W. (1986) *Density Estimation for Statistics and Data Analysis*, London: Chapman & Hall.

Stone, M. (1974) 'Cross-validatory choice and assessment of statistical predictions', *Journal of the Royal Statistical Society*, Series B, **36**, 111–33.

Subba Rao, T. and Gabr, M. (1984) *An Introduction to Bispectral Analysis and Bilinear Time Series Models*, Lecture Notes in Statistics, Vol. 24, Berlin: Springer-Verlag.

Sussmann, H.J. (1977) 'Existence and uniqueness of minimal realisations of nonlinear systems I: initialised systems', *Journal of Mathematical Systems Theory*, **10**, 263–84.

Teräsvirta, T. (1994), 'Specification, estimation and evaluation of smooth transition autoregressive models', *Journal of the American Statistical Association*, **89**, 208–18.

Teräsvirta, T. and Anderson, H. (1992) 'Characterising Nonlinearities in Business Cycles Using Smooth Transition Autoregressive Models', *Journal of Applied Econometrics*, **7**, S119–S 136.

Tong, H. (1990) *Non-linear Time Series: A Dynamical System Approach*, Oxford: Clarendon Press.

Ullah, A. (1988) 'Non-parametric estimation of econometric functionals', *Canadian Journal of Economics*, **21**, 625–58.

12. Islands of tranquillity in a turbulent world? Macroeconomic adjustment processes in the micro states of the Eastern Caribbean

Michael Anyadike-Danes

CONTEXT

Providing a relatively predictable framework for the conduct of its trading and financial relationships with the rest of the world is difficult for any small state. And it is even more so the case for the micro states of the Eastern Caribbean much of whose economic life is almost physically integrated with nearby industrial economies. But there is an uneasy tension between the minimal restrictions on international transactions needed to maintain the credibility of the monetary framework and the control over those transactions needed to preserve some scope for the exercise of discretionary policy.

The national income of these Eastern Caribbean islands, like that of all small open economies, is largely driven by external developments. So in order to understand how national income is determined, and the role of policy in that process, we need to focus on the balance of payments: on the country's foreign trade performance and on inflows and outflows of foreign funds. Many of the most important factors shaping these international relationships are, to a very large extent, beyond the control of local decision makers or, even more particularly, beyond the control of macroeconomic policy makers. Let us look, for example, at banana exports, an important source of foreign exchange for some of them. Although farmers can, of course, affect the amount and quality of this key crop, the links between their activities and the value of banana sales abroad is quite loose. Aside from the effects that weather conditions have on supply, there are critical factors on the demand side (ranging from the rules of the European banana regime to the actions of UK supermarkets) over which they have no influence. And even more significantly, since our main concern here is with macroeconomic policy, there are no obvious *macroeconomic* levers which the government might use to manage banana export values.

Similarly, although for different reasons, inflows of foreign funds are largely outside local control too. A government's success in raising money abroad is often critically affected by factors which are, from its point of view, entirely irrelevant (like whether any major developing country borrower looks likely to default, or the state of relations between the US president and the Congress). Indeed, neither the government's record of economic management, nor its creditworthiness, may even enter the picture. Equally, flows of foreign capital to the private sector or local banks are unlikely to respond much to changes in the state of these economies, they will likely depend much more on changes in conditions elsewhere.

Eight of the islands have sought to contain some of their macroeconomic difficulties by participating in a collective monetary arrangement, the Eastern Caribbean Central Bank (ECCB).[1] This institution is responsible for issuing a common currency and maintaining its external convertibility (currently pegged at a fixed rate to the US dollar). The ECCB's principal policy instrument is the requirement that the currency issue be backed by holdings of foreign assets. Moreover, both the convertibility objective and the foreign asset-backing requirement are constitutionally entrenched and can only be altered with the unanimous agreement of the member governments.

Needless to say, one immediate implication of the foreign-asset backing requirement is that the extent to which the ECCB is able to accommodate its member governments' needs for finance is quite strictly circumscribed (in addition, it is even more specifically limited by a further, entrenched, constitutional provision). This restriction aside, though, a member government has an entirely independent choice of fiscal policy. It can choose its own level of spending, its own tax rates, and is free to run whatever deficit it can finance by borrowing at home or abroad. Of course, in practice the domestic sources of funds are confined pretty much to the commercial banks since, as was noted above, overseas borrowing is tightly constrained.

This chapter explores the consequences of this set of constraints for the process of macroeconomic adjustment at the national level, focusing in particular on its implications for national economic management. The discussion is organized around a simple model of the process of national income determination. Despite its simplicity, however, the model is founded on an accounting framework which is sufficiently rich to provide a comprehensive description of the financing implications of alternative assumptions about the externally determined variables and policy choices. It should be noted right at the outset, however, that having been constructed to serve a particular purpose, there are important questions on which the model is silent. For example, it offers no insight into longer-run processes of growth and development.

The following discussion is arranged in four sections. The first summarizes the structure of the model. It is followed by a section which describes the process of national income determination, while the third section outlines some of the properties of the model, in particular the responses to changes in external developments and to alternative policy choices. The final section draws out some implications.

THE STRUCTURE OF THE MODEL

The simplest way to introduce the structure of the model is by setting out the accounting framework. The economy has been divided into five sectors: two financial, the monetary authority (the ECCB) and the commercial banks; and three non-financial, the government, the private sector (including both individuals and businesses) and the rest of the world or foreign sector. Each of these sectors is represented in the accounting framework by either a balance sheet (in the case of the financial sectors) or a sources and uses of funds statement (in the case of the non-financial sectors) and these accounting relationships are set out in part A of Table 12.1. In part B of the table we have a list of 'behavioural' relationships where an endogenous variable is represented as the product of parameters and variables. All the parameters are assumed to be exogenous. Table 12.2 lists the variables of the model, their names and definitions.

The ECCB

Let us start with the balance sheet of the ECCB, equation 1. The ECCB issues domestic currency which is held by banks (*NCB*) and by the private sector (*NCP*), while its assets are its loans to the government (*MLG*) and its holdings of foreign assets (*FRM*).

Of these variables, two are determined by the choice of policy parameters, the commercial banks' cash by a required reserve ratio δ, as set out in equation 8, and holdings of foreign assets by a parameter λ which represents the foreign asset backing required by the domestic currency issue,[2] as recorded in equation 9. The private sector is assumed to choose the amount of its cash holdings as a proportion γ_1 of its financial asset holdings (*FA*), according to equation 10. The funds available for lending to the government are then determined as the difference between the ECCB's total liabilities and its foreign asset holdings.

The Commercial Banks

The commercial banks' balance sheet is set out in equation 2. They accept deposits from the private sector (*BD*), and lend to the government (*BLG*) and the private sector (*BLP*). They also hold cash (*NCB*) and foreign assets (*FRB*).

Table 12.1 The model

A Accounting relationships

1. ECCB balance sheet
$NCB + NCP \equiv MLG + FRM$

2. Commercial banks' balance sheet
$BD \equiv NCB + BLG + BLP + FRB$

3. Government sources and uses of funds
$T + \Delta MLG + \Delta BLG + \Delta PLG + \Delta FLG \equiv G$

4. Private sector sources and uses of funds
$YP + \Delta BLP + \Delta FLP \equiv PE + \Delta FA$

5. Rest of the world sources and uses of funds
$X + \Delta FLG + \Delta FLP \equiv M + \Delta FRM + \Delta FRB$

6. Definition of private disposable income
$YP \equiv Y - T$

7. Definition of private sector stock of financial assets
$FA \equiv NCP + BD + PLG$

B Behavioural relationships

8. Commercial banks' holdings of domestic currency
$NCB = \delta^* BD$

9. ECCB holdings of foreign assets
$FRM = \lambda^*(NCP + NCB)$

10. Private sector holdings of domestic currency
$NCP = \gamma_1{}^* FA$

11. Private sector holdings of commercial bank deposits
$BD = \gamma_2{}^* FA$

12. Taxes
$T = \tau^* Y$

13. Imports
$M = \mu^* Y$

14. Private expenditure function
$PE = \alpha^* YP + \Delta FLP + \Delta BLP + \beta^* FA_{-1}$

Table 12.2 Listing of variables

1 Endogenous	
BD, private sector holdings of commercial bank deposits	(11)
BLG, commercial bank lending to the government	(3)
BLP, commercial bank lending to the private sector	(2)
FA, private sector holdings of financial assets	(4)
FRM, ECCB holdings of foreign assets	(9)
M, imports of goods	(13)
MLG, ECCB lending to the government	(1)
NCB, commercial bank holdings of domestic currency	(8)
NCP, private sector holdings of domestic currency	(10)
PE, private sector spending	(14)
PLG, private sector lending to the government	(7)
T, tax collections	(12)
Y, national income	(5)
YP, private disposable income	(6)

2 Exogenous

Policy

G, government spending

δ, commercial banks' cash reserve ratio

γ_1, private sector cash to financial assets ratio

γ_2, private sector bank deposits to financial assets ratio

λ, foreign asset backing of domestic currency ratio

τ, average tax ratio

Behaviour

μ, imports to national income ratio

α, β, parameters of the private expenditure function

Other

FLG, foreign lending to the government

FLP, foreign lending to the private sector

FRB, commercial banks' foreign asset holdings

X, exports of goods and net exports of services, factor incomes and transfers

Note: Number in parentheses indicates the equation used to solve for the variable.

One of these variables, foreign asset holdings, is treated as exogenous, while some others are determined by the policy authorities, like cash (by the required reserve ratio) and, more importantly, bank lending to the government (a matter to which we will return). Bank deposits are assumed to be chosen by the private sector; like cash holdings they are determined as a proportion, in this case γ_2, of the private sector's financial asset holdings, as we see in equation 11. Finally, bank lending to the private sector is residually determined: it is the amount remaining after other claims on the banks' funds have been satisfied.

The Government

Equation 3 in Table 12.1 records the government's sources and uses of funds statement. On the left-hand side we have the sources: tax collections (*T*), and government borrowing from the ECCB (*MLG*), the commercial banks (*BLG*), foreigners (*FLG*) and the private sector (*PLG*). The government uses these funds to pay for its spending (*G*).[3]

Now the government can choose some of these variables. Specifically, it sets the level of spending, and chooses a tax rate τ, which when combined with the level of national income generates a flow of tax revenues, as set out in equation 12. Most of the sources of funds, though, are assumed to be beyond the government's control, since the ECCB, foreigners and the private sector each choose the amount they will lend to the government. The final source of funds is government borrowing from the commercial banks, and this borrowing is treated as the residual source of finance for the government's budget. While this means, in principle, that the government could rely to a very considerable extent on the banks to cover spending in excess of its tax collections, this does not happen in practice. Rather, the government generally undertakes only those capital projects for which funding has been identified and, as a consequence, the residual financing role has typically required the banks only to fund unexpected overruns of current spending and relatively minor capital items.

The Private Sector

The private sector's sources and uses of funds are set out in equation 4 of Table 12.1. We have on the left-hand side the sources of funds: the disposable income of the private sector (*YP*); and its borrowing, both from the banks (*BLP*) and foreigners (*FLP*). These funds are used, as the right-hand side records, either to finance private spending (*PE*) or to add to its holdings of financial assets (*FA*).

It is assumed here that the private sector takes the sources of funds as given. As we can see from equation 6, its disposable income depends on the economy-wide forces which determine national income and the government's choice of tax rate, while its borrowing is assumed to depend on decisions by lenders. In respect of borrowing, then, we are assuming that the private sector is prepared to borrow whatever funds the commercial banks, and foreigners, make available to it. What the private sector can choose is the use made of the funds, whether they are spent or accumulated as holdings of financial assets. The spending decision is represented in equation 14 and the formulation is a very simple one. The private sector is assumed to spend differing proportions of its different sources of funds, including both its income and borrowing,[4] and also of the stock of financial assets which it has carried over from the previous period. Given the value of private spending then, by virtue of the sources and uses equation, any remaining funds are simply added to the private sector's overall holdings of financial assets. Mention has already been made of two of the assets held by the private sector, cash and bank deposits, but as we can see from equation 7, the private sector also has an asset: its lending to the government. Since cash and bank deposits are, as we saw, mixed proportions of private sector financial asset holdings, equation 7 serves to determine private sector holdings of government debt.

The Rest of the World

Finally, we come to equation 5. Now this relationship could have been written down in either of two ways. It could be written as a sources and uses of funds statement for foreigners or, looked at from the other side, as the country's balance of payments account, a statement of its sources and uses of foreign funds. Let us take it in this second sense. So on the left-hand side we have the country's sources of foreign currency: exports of goods and services (including net transfers) (*X*) and foreign borrowing by the government (*FLG*) and the private sector (*FLP*). The uses of foreign currency are recorded on the right-hand side: imports of goods (*M*); and the holdings of foreign assets by the ECCB (*FRM*) and the commercial banks (*FRB*).

As we have already seen, foreign borrowing is assumed to be determined elsewhere, and this is assumed to be true of exports as well. It should not, however, be inferred that exporters have no control over the value of their sales, but rather that their sales are largely independent of either national income or of the authorities' macroeconomic policy choices.[5] The determination of most of the uses of foreign exchange has also already been discussed. As will be recalled, the monetary authority's holdings of foreign assets are tied to the currency issue, while the commercial banks choose the amount of foreign assets that they wish to hold. The remaining use, imports, depends on the level of national income. More specifically, as set down in equation 13, it is assumed that the relationship is one of simple proportionality, with μ representing the average ratio of imports to national income. So, as national income changes, so too do imports.

Although the detail is, of course, important, the model's basic structure can be summarized pretty simply. Each sector takes the most significant items on the liability side of its balance sheet (for the financial sectors), or of its sources of funds (for the non-financial sectors), as largely outside its control, while it generally has more influence over the allocation amongst assets (for the financial sectors) and the uses to which it puts its funds (for the non-financial sectors).

THE DETERMINATION OF NATIONAL INCOME

Given the dependence of the economy on external economic conditions, it should not be surprising that the process of national income determination should be closely bound up with the balance of payments. Indeed, the solution for national income is derived from equation 5 of Table 12.1, the relationship which describes the sources and uses of foreign currency.[6] As we saw earlier, the sources of foreign funds (export receipts and borrowing) are determined elsewhere in the world and one use of foreign currency is exogenous too (banks' holdings of foreign assets). However, the other two uses, the purchase of imports and the ECCB's foreign asset holdings, do not just depend on local decision making but are, more specifically, linked to national income. So the level of national income is that which equates the sources and uses of foreign currency.

National Income and the Sources and Uses of Foreign Currency

Solving the model for the level of national income involves expressing the two endogenous elements in the relationship between sources and uses (imports and the ECCB's holdings of foreign currency) in terms of national income and the exogenous variables of the model. For imports, this is of course quite straightforward, since the value of imports is just a parameter, the import ratio μ, multiplied by national income. Solving for the determinants of the ECCB's foreign asset holdings is a little more involved because, as we know, this depends on the amount of domestic currency in the economy and, therefore, on the relationship governing the private sector's accumulation of financial assets.

Ultimately, the process of solution leads us to an expression which can be written down with the sources of foreign currency on one side and the uses on the other,

$$X + \Delta FLG + \Delta FLP + \beta * \varphi * FA_{-1} = \Delta FRB + \{[\varphi * (1 - \alpha) * (1 - \tau)] + \mu\} * Y$$

where $\varphi \equiv \lambda * (\gamma_1 + \delta * \gamma_2)$.

This appears to be a slightly complicated expression, but its basic structure is really quite simple. On the left hand side we have first the values of the exogenously given sources of foreign currency. The inclusion of the final term on the left, involving the inherited stock of financial assets, as a source of foreign currency may appear a little anomalous. So let us examine it more closely, taking first the components of the compound parameter φ. The terms in parentheses $(\gamma_1 + \delta^*\gamma_2)$, when multiplied by the private sector's asset stock, determine the domestic currency associated with that stock: γ_1, that held by the private sector, and $\delta^*\gamma_2$, the holdings of the commercial banks. When multiplied by λ, the ECCB's asset-backing parameter, we then have a term which represents the amount of foreign currency which the ECCB holds to back the domestic currency associated with the private sector's inherited stock of assets. Notice that these ECCB holdings are multiplied by β. As we saw earlier, this is the parameter from the private expenditure function which determines the proportion of the inherited asset stock which is spent each period. Now putting these linkages together we have a relationship between private spending and the use of foreign currency. Clearly, if a proportion of the inherited asset stock is being spent, the ECCB will not be required to hold foreign currency to back the domestic currency associated with that part of the stock: so the ECCB will be adding that amount to the sources of foreign currency .

On the right-hand side we have first the exogenously determined use of foreign currency, the amount absorbed by changes in the banks' holdings of foreign currency. Then we have the national income-related uses. Again, as might be inferred from the appearance of the parameter φ, the first of the terms which multiply national income, $[\varphi^*(1 - \alpha)^*(1 - \tau)]$, is also connected with private sector behaviour. As will be appreciated, multiplying national income by $(1 - \tau)$ yields private disposable income, and, since $(1 - \alpha)$ is the proportion of private disposable income which is not spent, the combined effect of these two is to determine the amount of private disposable income which the private sector adds to its holdings of financial assets. Evidently, then, the further multiplication of this term by φ will determine the amount that the ECCB will have to add to its holdings of foreign currency. Finally, we have the last uses term, the import ratio, μ, multiplied by national income: this represents, of course, the country's import bill.

Having understood the logic of the expression, we can now rewrite it in a more conventional way, as an equation which relates national income to its determinants. In the numerator we have the exogenous sources and uses, and in the denominator the parameters which relate uses of foreign currency to the level of national income. It resembles a conventional multiplier formulation.

$$Y = \frac{[X + \Delta FLG + \Delta FLP - \Delta FRB + \varphi * \beta * FA_{-1}]}{[\mu + \varphi * (1-\alpha) * (1-\tau)]}$$

where $\varphi \equiv \lambda^*(\gamma_1 + \delta^*\gamma_2)$. Very roughly, the numerator tells us the amount of foreign currency available, and the denominator records the amount of it used up either by imports or by the ECCB's holdings of foreign currency expressed as a ratio to national income. So, for example, if roughly 50 cents out of every dollar in foreign currency was spent on imports or was added to the ECCB's holdings, then an extra $1m of foreign currency would support a $2m increase in national income.

However, as will be appreciated, such a calculation only captures the first period or 'impact' effect of such a change. As national income rises, so too does the private sector's holdings of financial assets. Consequently, even a temporary, say one-year, shock to sources of foreign currency will have repercussions in succeeding years. These repercussions are, in fact, carried forward by the inherited asset term in the numerator of the expression and this solution for the level of national income is referred to here as the *period-by-period solution*.

Private Sector Financial Asset Accumulation and The Process of Adjustment to Change

As we have seen, the inherited stock of financial assets plays a critical role in determining how national income responds to changes in sources of foreign currency. Indeed, if it were not for the inherited stock term, national income would adjust, *fully and immediately*, to any change either in the exogenously determined amount of foreign currency or in the multiplier. Clearly, then, since the properties of the adjustment process turn on the dynamics of the private sector's accumulation of financial assets, we need to examine private sector behaviour a little more closely.

The most straightforward way to proceed is to write down an expression for financial asset accumulation by the private sector. We can do this by substituting the determinants of private spending from the private expenditure function (equation 14 of Table 12.1) into the private sector's sources and uses statement (equation 4) and then rearrange it to put asset accumulation on the left-hand side. This yields

$$\Delta FA = (1 - \alpha)^*YP - \beta^*FA_{-1}.$$

What now becomes clear is that the accumulation of financial assets represents a balance between two terms: the unspent proportion of disposable income and a term which subtracts from it the proportion of the inherited stock which is spent. So it is the difference between these two terms which drives the adjustment process.

To see how, let us consider an example. We will start from an initial situation where there is no asset accumulation going on, so the asset stock is constant, and assume then that there is a permanent \$1m increase in private disposable income. As we can see from the above equation, there will be an immediate impact on asset accumulation: $\$(1 - \alpha)$m is added to the private sector's holdings of financial assets. Since the asset stock is now higher, we know that in the next period a proportion β of that increase in the asset stock is added to spending, and so will be subtracted from asset holdings. So in the second period, the increase in assets will be less than in the first: $\$[(1 - \alpha) - \beta(1 - \alpha)]$m. Now this process will continue, and the asset stock will rise, but as it does the amount added each period will shrink. Eventually, the term being subtracted will rise sufficiently (being $(1 - \alpha)$ multiplied by the sum of higher and higher powers of β), for asset accumulation to cease all together.[7] Thenceforth the rate at which the stock of assets is being drained by expenditure is exactly equal to the rate at which it is being replenished out of income. It must therefore be the case that

$$\beta * FA_{-1} = (1 - \alpha) * YP.$$

Since we can write private disposable income (using equations 6 and 12) as

$$YP = (1 - \tau) * Y$$

the condition linking assets, income and foreign lending to the private sector becomes

$$\beta * FA_{-1} = (1 - \alpha) * (1 - \tau) * Y.$$

Now let us return to the economy-wide relationship between the sources and uses of foreign currency, and focus on that part of the expression which is connected with the private sector's accumulation of financial assets. So we are interested in those terms which determine the changes in the holdings of domestic currency (directly the private sector's holdings and indirectly the commercial banks' holdings, through the private sector's holdings of bank deposits and the required reserve ratio). On the left-hand side we have $\varphi * \beta * FA_{-1}$, and on the right-hand side $[\varphi(1 - \alpha) *)(1 - \tau)] * Y$. Obviously, these are simply φ times the terms from the private sector's asset accumulation relationship. Moreover, as we have just seen, when the asset stock is fully adjusted they are equal to one another. Necessarily, then, they will therefore be cancelled out of the expression for the sources and uses of foreign currency. So what this implies is that, when asset accumulation ceases, the rate at which foreign currency is being released by private sector spending from its inherited stock of financial assets exactly matches the rate at which the ECCB is acquiring foreign currency to support the domestic currency issue.

The equality between these two terms has, however, a further important implication. If the private sector's stock of financial assets is constant, we can eliminate these terms from the expression for the sources and uses of foreign currency which can be rewritten in a much simpler form:

$$X + \Delta FLG + \Delta FLP = \Delta FRB + \mu * Y.$$

Evidently then, when the private sector's accounts are in balance, national income will be at a level where the sum of exogenous sources of foreign currency is completely absorbed by the country's import bill In 'multiplier' form,

$$Y = [(X + \Delta FLG + \Delta FLP - \Delta FRB) / \mu].$$

The Sustainable Level of National Income

So we can see that, when the asset stock is not changing, national income is simply equal to the exogenous flows of foreign currency divided by the import ratio. Now, of course, this is a special case of the general period-by-period solution for national income. But it is a special case of considerable significance, because it can tell us what level of national income will be associated with a given value of foreign currency inflows. It tells us the level of national income that can be *sustained* by a given value of foreign currency inflows.

At this stage, however, it is important to distinguish between the different types of inflows. Although there is a generic similarity between exports and the other exogenously determined sources and uses of foreign exchange, there is also an important difference. Notice that exports are inherently a flow, whereas the other sources (except capital grants) represent changes in stocks. It is, for example, the *change* in the stock of the government's foreign debt which appears in the expression. Therefore, in order for foreign borrowing to produce the same effect on national income as a permanent increase in the value of exports, it would require a permanent increase in the annual rate of government borrowing from abroad. And this, of course, would imply continuous growth in the government's stock of foreign debt. In other words, although an increase in the level of national income could be produced by foreign borrowing, it would seem a little misleading to describe such a level as sustainable, since it could only, in fact, be sustained by a permanently rising stock of foreign debt. Moreover, such borrowing would ultimately have to be repaid and, even before that, its servicing would also absorb foreign currency. Perhaps, even more importantly, rising debt service and indebtedness might well deter the potential lenders whose funds are needed just to maintain national income unchanged.

As a consequence, we will define the *sustainable* level of national income as equal to the value of export receipts divided by the import ratio. The description of this solution as sustainable is intended to convey the fact that if exports and the import ratio remain unchanged, then the level of income could remain at the same level, year after year. So we can write the solution for the sustainable level of national income as

$$Y^S = X / \mu.$$

Now the sustainable level of national income provides us with an important conceptual benchmark against which to judge the impact on national income of changes in the model's exogenous variables. We can infer straight away, for example, that, since none of the policy instruments under the direct control of either the government or the ECCB enter the solution, none of them can affect the sustainable level of national income. Of course, that does not mean that the economy cannot be affected by policy, but it does imply that there might be significant limitations on the extent to which policy can influence macroeconomic performance. Moreover, this expression tells us nothing about the path that national income will take, after a change in exports say, as it moves from one sustainable level to another. In order to address both of these questions, the role of policy and the shape of the adjustment process, we need to look a little more closely at the workings of the model.

EXPLORING THE PROPERTIES OF THE MODEL

Rather than undertake a comprehensive examination of the period-by-period response of national income to each one of its exogenous determinants in turn, we are going to be a little selective here and consider just one example, a fall in exports. Needless to say, the effects of such a change are broadly representative of changes in any of the foreign currency flows. Following on from that discussion we will consider the ways in which the instruments of fiscal policy interact with, and affect, the process of national income determination.[8]

A Fall in Exports

We know, of course, what the end result of a fall in exports will be: a decline in the sustainable level of national income. But here we will examine the process of adjustment as well as the implications of the fall in national income for the different sectors of the economy. To keep matters simple, we assume that there is no change in any of the other exogenously determined sources or uses of foreign currency. We will assume too that instruments of fiscal policy (government spending and the tax rate) and monetary policy (the asset-backing parameter and the cash reserve ratio) remain unchanged.

The adjustment path followed by national income depends, as we know, on what is required to balance sources and uses of foreign currency. On the sources side, export receipts have, of course, fallen. But the other source, the *inherited* stock of assets has, by definition, yet to be affected. So it is just the fall in export receipts which has to be balanced by a decline in income-related uses. Clearly, then, national income must fall sufficiently to match the import bill plus the change in the ECCB's holdings to the available foreign currency. As we know, though, the initial fall in imports will only take them part of the way to their new sustainable level, because the income-induced decline in domestic currency holdings means that the ECCB will be reducing its foreign currency holdings. Indeed, the slope of the downward path of income, and therefore imports, will depend, in turn, on how quickly the ECCB's holdings are reduced – or, what amounts to the same thing, how quickly the private sector's asset holdings approach the level appropriate to the new sustainable level of national income.

This part of the adjustment story is all pretty familiar from the earlier discussion of private sector behaviour, so let us turn to a topic which is not: the implications of the adjustment process for the fiscal accounts. We have assumed that in the initial situation, before exports fell, the government's budget was in balance. With fiscal policy unchanged (that is, government spending and the tax rate at their initial values), the contraction in national income will reduce tax collections and the budget will move into deficit. Now the finance for this deficit comes, of course, from the banking system. Therefore there will be a diversion of funds from bank lending to the private sector towards bank lending to the government. Indeed, the contraction in bank lending to the private sector will be larger than just the amount needed to finance the budget deficit. With the decline in the domestic currency issue, the ECCB's lending to the government will shrink as well. So commercial bank lending will have to replace, not just the reduction in tax collections, but government's loan repayments to the ECCB as well. Moreover, since bank deposits will have declined with the overall stock of assets, the government will be borrowing a large amount from the smaller amount of funds that the banks have available for lending. Of course, the contraction in lending to the private sector will put some additional downward pressure on private spending too, further increasing the government's share of the lower overall spending total.

This process of diversion of commercial bank loans away from the private sector towards the government will continue throughout the process of adjustment. But, as national income approaches its new sustainable level, the private sector's asset stock will stabilize and, as that happens, the government's repayments to the ECCB will shrink to zero. The size of the deficit will stabilize too, but of course the unchanged level of spending will exceed the tax collections associated with the sustainable level of national income. So, at the new level of income, the fiscal accounts will be in permanent deficit, with a constant amount of additional financing being provided each year by the commercial banks. Moreover, since the private sector's asset stock is constant, and with it the size of the banking system's balance sheet, these additional loans to the government are, indirectly, being provided by a matching annual contractions in lending to the private sector. Evidently, then, private disposable income will be exceeding private spending by the amount of the government's deficit. The private sector is, in effect, paying for the excess of government spending over taxes through the banking system.

More significantly, though, the government's indebtedness to the commercial banks will be steadily mounting (balanced by a steady contraction in bank loans outstanding to the private sector). Needless to say, such a state of affairs cannot be regarded as sustainable. Eventually, the commercial banks will refuse further requests to accommodate the government. At which time, of course, a fiscal adjustment will become necessary, taking the form of either a reduction in spending or an increase in tax rates. The critical conclusion here, though, is that there is no built-in mechanism which triggers an automatic fiscal adjustment to a change in the availability of foreign currency. National income adjusts automatically to a deterioration in external conditions in a way which ensures that no balance of payments 'crisis' emerges, but the consequent worsening of the fiscal accounts, the fiscal 'crisis', requires purposive action if it is to be corrected.

A Decrease in Government Spending

Although, as we have just seen, changes in national income may ultimately prompt fiscal action through their effects on the budgetary position, we know that the converse is not true. Changes in the setting of fiscal policy instruments will not affect national income or, at least, will not affect sustainable national income. Nevertheless, it is worth examining the implications of changing fiscal policy to see how the changes work themselves out.

Let us start by considering the effects of a decrease in the level of government spending, again starting from a sustainable level of national income with the budget in balance and holding all else constant. The implications of lowering government spending are pretty transparent. Since government spending does not appear in the period-by-period solution for national income, we know that national income will not be affected. What will change, however, is the budgetary position; with national income unchanged, tax collections will remain the same and so, with government spending lower, the budget will move into surplus. The financing consequences of this surplus will be that the government's indebtedness to the commercial banks will be reduced. There will, of course, be a matching increase in bank lending to the private sector and private spending will, in fact, rise by exactly the amount that government spending has fallen. Needless to say, this shift in the composition of total spending will take place straight away, and will become permanent. Each year tax collections will exceed government spending by the same amount and, to exactly the same extent, private spending will exceed private disposable income. Of course, this outcome carries with it the seeds of unsustainability. It can only persist as long as the banks are prepared to allow the private sector's indebtedness to continue expanding. What might seem more likely, in practice, is that the government would adjust the tax rate. Then the private sector could continue to spend at the same rate, but its spending could be financed without borrowing, out of its now larger disposable income.

An Increase in the Tax Rate

The economy reacts rather differently to changes in the tax rate than it does to a change in spending, most particularly because the tax rate affects the period-by-period solution for national income. Its impact is, as will be appreciated, bound up with the effects it has on the private sector's accumulation of financial assets. A rise in the tax rate will cause the private sector to run down its holdings of financial assets, and the consequent contraction in holdings of domestic currency will lead the ECCB to release some of its holdings of foreign currency. As a result, national income will rise and with it the import bill, which will drain the additional foreign currency out of the economy. Of course, since sustainable national income is independent of the tax rate, we know that this rise can only be temporary. Indeed, the decline in private sector asset holdings will only continue until its normal relationship with the new, lower, level of private disposable income is re-established.

Needless to say, the temporary rise in national income has an impact on the fiscal accounts. Tax collections will rise under the combined influence of the higher tax rate and increased national income. The budget will therefore move into surplus, and the government's indebtedness to the banking system will decline. Matching that decline will, of course, be an increase in bank lending to the private sector which will finance a level of private spending in excess of private disposable income, cushioning somewhat the immediate impact on private spending of the fall in disposable income. Indeed, with government spending constant, it is the private sector's spending which is the source of the demand for the extra imports. Notice, though, that not all the government's surplus will be flowing to the commercial banks; as currency holdings contract, so will

ECCB lending to the government, and the government will use some of its surplus to repay its borrowing from the ECCB.

As national income returns to its sustainable level, private spending will eventually decline too. However, we know that the government's surplus will prove permanent, and so bank lending to the private sector will continue and, as a result, private spending will permanently exceed private disposable income. Ultimately, then, we have the same configuration of intersectoral financial relations after an increase in taxes as we did after the decrease in government spending: the private sector will be spending more than its income, and be becoming increasingly indebted to the banks. There are differences, though. Since national income is the same in both cases, the private sector will be spending a relatively smaller share of national income after an increase in tax rates. And, of course, with private disposable income lower, the private sector's stock of assets will be smaller too, which means in turn that the balance sheets of both the banks and the ECCB will have shrunk.

IMPLICATIONS

There are some important practical implications which follow from our discussion of the model's properties and these relate to the connection between the balance of payments and fiscal policy. An adverse permanent shock to one of the sources of foreign currency (exports or borrowing) implies more or less automatic adjustment towards a new lower level of national income. But the properties of the monetary arrangement are such that the process of adjustment will guarantee that there will be no dramatic decline in the country's foreign exchange reserves. In other words, there will be no balance of payments 'crisis' of the familiar kind typically associated with a deterioration in a country's external circumstances. However the process of adjustment will be accompanied, unless there is some change in fiscal policy, by a widening budget deficit and an emerging fiscal 'crisis'. And this conclusion is symmetric: a fiscal 'crisis' which is triggered by a discretionary loosening of fiscal policy will not show itself in a balance of payments 'crisis'. By virtue of the ECCB's rules of the game, the level of national income is pretty directly, and immediately, determined by external circumstances and so fiscal policy operates more or less as a mechanism for sharing the burden of adjustment between the government and private sectors.

While the systemic properties of the ECCB arrangement can ensure that there is never a foreign currency 'shortage', that does not imply that the monetary regime is 'crisis-proof'. The problems that emerge, though, will typically do so when the government finds the commercial banks unwilling to extend any further credit and the government starts to slow the payment of its obligations and arrears begin to build up. Now amongst the bills which go unpaid there will likely be some foreign obligations, but notice that these payments difficulties do not reflect a shortage of *foreign* currency: the government is short of domestic currency too. Such a state of affairs might appear, from a broader international perspective, somewhat anomalous. But it is a straightforward implication of membership of the ECCB arrangement where, because of the foreign asset backing of the currency issue, for most practical purposes units of domestic and foreign currency are, in fact, interchangeable.

Evidently, a rule-bound central bank like the ECCB protects the member country's foreign reserves against adverse external shocks and ill judged fiscal policy, which has the effect of pushing relations between the government and the commercial banks to the centre of the stage. These banks become, in effect, the guarantors of fiscal discipline. Now, as a matter of practical political economy, this might have something to recommend it, as long as the management of the commercial banks act in the interests of their shareholders and display prudence in their lending. Until quite recently, the commercial banking sector in the ECCB region was dominated by quite tightly controlled subsidiaries of foreign banks (mainly Canadian and British) which rendered them relatively immune from local political pressure. However, the decade or so since political independence has seen the emergence of an indigenous banking industry. In each member country there is at least one large local commercial bank typically owned by the government.[9] As a consequence, the effectiveness of the control imposed on governments by the commercial banking system has become somewhat more questionable. It follows, then, that the limit to fiscal indiscipline which would elsewhere be imposed by a balance of payments crisis may, in the ECCB region, show itself instead in a 'banking crisis' in an individual member. At that stage the ECCB would have to choose. It could allow the 'crisis' to run its course or it could intervene to 'bail out' the banking system (and by extension the government). Needless to say, this latter course might undermine the integrity of the monetary arrangement as a whole.

Certainly, the ECCB arrangement has, thus far, provided its member countries with a greater degree of monetary stability than have arrangements elsewhere in the Caribbean where governments have privileged access to central bank funds. What our analysis has revealed, though, is that, while this monetary framework, relying on a constitutionally independent central bank, may provide a more immediate guarantee of fiscal discipline than other arrangements, it too has limits.

NOTES

1. The ECCB members are Anguilla; Antigua and Barbuda; Dominica; Grenada; Montserrat; St. Kitts-Nevis; St. Lucia; and St. Vincent and the Grenadines. Using population as an indicator

of size, the smallest of these has a population of less than 10 000, the largest a population around 150 000; their combined population is about 500 000.

2. The ratio between foreign assets and domestic currency is set, statutorily, at 60 per cent, but this is a minimum, and in practice the ratio has generally been much higher, around 80 per cent. It should be noted that the operations of the ECCB referred to here relate only to a single member. So, for example, the ECCB's foreign assets represent the single member's 'share' of the ECCB's total holdings of foreign assets.
3. Although not explicitly represented here, the government's budget deficit can be defined as the difference between its spending and its revenue from taxes and grants, and is financed by transactions in financial claims.
4. You will notice that foreign and commercial bank lending to the private sector have coefficients of unity, which means we are assuming that the private sector borrows to spend. Assuming that some of this borrowing is not spent immediately and so adds to asset holdings complicates the algebra but does not have an important effect on the characteristics of the national income determination process of interest here.
5. It is perhaps worth recalling at this stage that the one policy weapon with potential to have a direct impact on export prospects, the exchange rate, is not one over which the government has any immediate influence. By the rules of the ECCB arrangement, the exchange rate can only change if there is unanimous agreement amongst the member governments.
6. The term 'foreign currency' is used here as shorthand to refer to any financial claim denominated in a foreign currency.
7. By a process of repeated substitution it can be shown that the asset accumulation relationship can be written as $\Delta FA = (1 - \alpha)*YP*\{(1 - \beta) - \beta*(1 - \beta)*[1 + (1 - \beta) + (1 - \beta)^2 + (1 - \beta)^3 + ...]\}$. Formally, the β terms in the square brackets form a geometric progression whose sum to infinity is $(1 / \beta)$. Ultimately, then, the term in braces will go to zero, and when this happens asset accumulation will stop.
8. We focus on fiscal policy instruments because only these are under the control of an individual member government.
9. The rationale for the foundation of these banks was to provide competition for the existing foreign-owned institutions. However, much of their growth has been bound up with their role as banker to government and government-owned entities, most notably the social security system.

Index